SOCIOLOGY OF POSTMODERNISM

Written by a noted scholar in the field, this book considers the differences between modernism and postmodernism, describes the historical and social contexts which gave rise to both, and provides the clearest explanation of why postmodernism is important. Lash shows the relevance of the concept for studying problems of identity, collectivity, and class. The book offers the readers one of the most helpful guides to a key concept of modern times.

INTERNATIONAL LIBRARY OF SOCIOLOGY

Founded by Karl Mannheim

Editor: John Urry
University of Lancaster

SOCIOLOGY OF POSTMODERNISM

SCOTT LASH

London and New York

First published 1990
by Routledge
11 New Fetter Lane, London EC4P 4EE

Simultaneously published in the USA and Canada
by Routledge
a division of Routledge, Chapman and Hall, Inc.
29 West 35th Street, New York, NY 10001

Typeset by Witwell Limited, Southport
Printed and bound in Great Britain by Mackays of Chatham PLC

British Library Cataloguing in Publication Data
Lash, Scott
The sociology of postmodernism
1. Culture. Postmodernism
I. Title
306

Library of Congress Cataloging in Publication Data
Lash, Scott
The sociology of postmodernism/Scott Lash
p. cm. - (International library of sociology)
Includes bibliographical references.
1. Sociology. 2. Postmodernism–Social aspects.
I. Title.
II. Series.
HM73.L35 1990
301–dc20   89-24184
CIP

ISBN 0-415-04784-6
0-415-04785-4 (pbk)

FOR MY FATHER AND MOTHER

CONTENTS

CONTENTS

INTRODUCTION

Postmodernism is, patently, no longer trendy. It is, however, a cultural paradigm which is arguably worthy of serious study. Marxian and Weberian social science have classically been devoted, among other things, to the exploration of linkages between social and cultural realms. This book thus consists of a coherent and unified set of serious sociological analyses of postmodernism. It addresses postmodernism in terms of social theory, the sociological investigation of culture, and the social-stratificational bases of postmodernism.

I was rather early to publish substantial scholarly articles on postmodernism that were sociological in the strict sense of the word. This book republishes some of those earlier essays, a few of which are available only in journals which are not always easily accessible for students. But the substantially greater part of what is written here is new material. And the book should function, not so much as a collection of essays, but as a reasonably unified whole.

Sociology of Postmodernism is not in any sense a sort of overview of the literature. It is instead unified by three coherent and interrelated theses. These are as follows.

(1) A thesis of cultural change. This is that modernization is a process of cultural differentiation while *post*modernization is a process of cultural '*de*-differentiation'.
(2) A thesis of cultural type. This is that modernism is a 'discursive' cultural formation while postmodernism is a 'figural' cultural formation.
(3) A thesis of social stratification. This is that the producers and

relevant audience of modernist and postmodernist culture are
found in particular declining and emergent social classes and
class fractions.

This said, Chapter 1 spells out in some detail all three of these
theses. It is the book's chapter which is most fully addressed to
those new to the study of postmodernism. Here I (i) outline what
is meant by the difference between 'discursive' (modernist) and
'figural' (postmodernist) signification; (ii) trace schematically
the cultural processes of modernist differentiation and autonomization, and of postmodernist de-differentiation; (iii) examine how modernism/postmodernism relate to the structuring
and de-structuring of collective identities of various social
classes; (iv) look at how the processes of modernization and
postmodernization are played out in the context of urban space;
and finally (v) consider the political economy of postmodernism
in regard to production, consumption, and commodification.

Chapters 2 through 5 address postmodernism through analysis
of social theory. Chapters 2, 3, and 4 are preliminary explorations
into the nature of figural – and postmodern – culture in contrast
to discursive, modernist forms. Thus Chapter 2 contrasts
modernist abstraction with postmodern signification that is
concretely particularized in 'the body', drawing on the work of
Nietzsche, Foucault, and Deleuze. And Chapters 3 and 4 contrast
an again abstracted modernist focus on language and structure
with the poststructuralist and postmodernist problematics of
'desire'. Here the main theorists drawn on are Foucault, Lyotard,
and Habermas. If modernization is a long historical process of
cultural differentiation, spanning Renaissance and Enlightenment, then *full* differentiation and autonomization only comes
with the advent of turn-of-the-nineteenth-century aesthetic
modern*ism* itself. Chapter 5 argues that the birth of sociology
itself is part and parcel of this process of full autonomization, via
consideration of the work of Max Weber.

Chapters 6 and 7 follow this model of differentiation and de-
differentiation into the sociology of culture. Chapter 6 looks at
postmodern de-differentiation via the implosion of the cultural
into the social, with the eclipse of modernist 'aura'. And Chapter
7 treats postmodernism as a 'regime', not of (modernist) 'discursive signification', but of 'figural' signification, in which the

signifier is collapsed both into signified and referent. Chapter 7 is my fullest treatment of the 'discursive' and the 'figural' to date; it and Chapter 1 provide, perhaps, cornerstones for the rest of the volume. Chapters 6 and 7 illustrate de-differentiation in post-modern culture through evidence drawn from cinema, theatre, painting, and architecture.

Chapters 8 and 9, each of which is quite lengthy, link modernist and postmodernist culture, as regimes of signification, with changes in economy and society. And this linkage is carried out first and foremost through the mediation of social class. Hence Chapter 8 analyses comparatively the various cultural modernisms of turn-of-the-century Paris, Vienna, and Berlin. Here the assumption is that modernism disrupts bourgeois identity. And modernisms can be comparatively understood in terms of different constellations of bourgeois identity. The key to this latter, this chapter shows, is the analysis of the hegemonic power bloc of these three cities. Chapter 9 looks at modernization and postmodernization through the prism of Pierre Bourdieu's work. For Bourdieu, we will see, modernization is a process of the differentiation and autonomization of social structures. Each of these (e.g. political, legal, aesthetic, and intellectual) structures is the arena of struggle between contending collectivities. Some of these social groups are locked in struggle for the modernist autonomization of a given stucture, while other classes and class fractions have ideal and material interests in structural de-differentiation.

Chapter One

POSTMODERNISM: TOWARDS A SOCIOLOGICAL ACCOUNT

'Postmodernism' has become a household word. Major news-papers in more than one country have run series of articles on it. There have been countless TV shows addressing the problems it poses. Hair stylists and employees in boutiques where young people buy clothes or records from Los Angeles to Berlin will have heard of postmodernism and may well have an opinion of it. Better-spoken taxi drivers in the world's major metropolises will be able to drive the visitor to their city's district where the new postmodern architecture is to be found.

In becoming a household word, it has at the same time become something of a resounding cliché. Just about all the topical academic periodicals with any sort of connection to things cultural have published a special issue on postmodernism. New series of books coming out of various publishing houses have featured, embarrassingly, the word postmodernism, sometimes in a majority of their titles. One American publisher is bringing out an entire series entitled 'Women and Postmodernism'. The word has come indeed to make a number of serious academics and intellectuals of a left political persuasion cringe. Periodical editors proclaim proudly that *we*'ve never had an issue on postmodernity. At an historic gathering in Frankfurt in December 1987 of German Socialist intellectuals brought together by SPD political-culture guru Peter Glotz, the utterance 'postmodern' figured frequently, but solely as a term of derision when not of abuse.

Yet, at the time of writing in summer 1989, some half decade after the term has left the ghetto of debates on architecture to pervade the mainstream of intellectual and public life, especially younger intellectuals are still highly attracted to postmodernism. Roundtables and conferences on postmodernism will still turn up higher numbers, especially among the young, than on just about any other subject. This is partly because *every*body has something to say about postmodernity. Everybody has an opinion on the subject. Everybody is *already* an expert on it. Even as the term 'postmodernism' loses entirely its cult value, and becomes almost an embarrassment for even avowed post-modernists, the questions and issues it raises shall remain centre stage for quite some time – the opponents of the new cultural paradigm, for example German philosopher Jürgen Habermas, calling as much or more attention to it than its enthusiasts. Its continuing centrality will be due, among other things, to a question of intellectual generations. To a generation whose formative years were in the late 1970s and early 1980s, post-modernism in some form is arguably as central as Marxism was to a generation which reached intellectual maturity at the end of the 1960s. Among this younger, 'post-punk' cohort will also be found a much greater sympathy towards Marxism than is gener-ally found among their mainstream academic counterparts. Yet their older, 'Sixty-eighter' teachers can be just as intolerant towards their seemingly 'culturalist' ideas as the 'end of ideology' generation of the 1950s were intolerant to the Sixty-eighters.

Given this continued, and likely to continue, interest in the problem, if not in the term, postmodernism, what is the state of play at the current juncture? On the one hand there is uncritical and even irresponsible celebration by, for example, French social theorist and commentator, Jean Baudrillard. On the other there is dismissal by much of the Marxist left, or attacks and the moral-philosophical denunciations of, for example, Habermas. Post-modernism has been the object of, above all, aesthetic discourse, of moral discourse, of political discourse. What it hasn't often been is the object of serious systematic *analysis*. It in particular has not been the object of serious *sociological* analysis.

Such sober sociological analysis is the aim of this book. My aim is to rescue postmodernism as a social (or cultural)-scientific concept from both those whose visions are of panacea and of carnival, and those who have dismissed it or relegated it to cliché. My aim is to convince both those in the *wissenschaftlich* community and on the political left to take postmodernism

2

seriously. I want to do this through first giving to post-modernism, so to speak, an 'operationalization'. That is I shall offer a systematic and sociological description of postmodernism. Then, I shall outline a very straightforward sociological explanation of this cultural 'paradigm'. Simplicity, claimed philosophers of science such as Pierre Maurice Marie Duhem and Jules Henri Poincaré, is a virtue in a scientific theory. Simplicity also means the necessity of constructing models or types, which greatly abstract from the complexity of concrete phenomena. But I shall draw on a great variety of concrete phenomena as illustrations in order to convince the reader of the validity of my schematic descriptive and explanatory models.

I am not a postmodernist. I am, in some significant ways, 'populist' and even 'commercial' in my tastes. I like football games and still play basketball. I have been known to tape *Miami Vice* to watch episodes when I get home at night. I like drinking in Irish bars in New York City. I think Steve Martin is a superb comic. Yet it seems to me axiomatic that Klee and Kandinsky are of a significance in the visual arts that Warhol and Lichtenstein and now Baselitz plainly are not. I take Marxism and the legality and 'natural rights' of the liberal and socialist traditions very seriously indeed. My own mode of procedure in the present study is quite rationalist indeed with no excuses made. Its *modus operandi* deals with, and through, eminently modernist distinctions between 'the cultural', on the one hand, and the economic and the social on the other. And especially between (social) scientific explanation and artistic exposition. I also think that postmodernist culture has not on balance produced a favourable terrain for the political left. Modernism has offered a much more favourable arena in which to wage the left's cultural struggles. Yet, I hope to show in the course of this book that the cultural terrain on which we now all live, work, love, and struggle is pervaded by postmodernism. And if this is true, it would be unwise for the left to ignore it.

There are a (very) few theses which structure this book. The first set of theses has to do with what postmodernism is, and the second has to do with how we can sociologically account for it. Postmodernism is, for me, not a condition, nor, as part of a fabric with post-industrialism, a type of society, in the sense that people speak of industrial society, or capitalist society, or modern

society. Postmodernism is instead, I think, confined to the realm
of *culture*. Post-industrialism is one important property of
contemporary capitalist economies. But it is a strictly economic,
not cultural, property. Post-industrialism thus is not part of
postmodernism, as for example it seems that Jean-François
Lyotard, author of the influential *Postmodern Condition*,
believes. It stands instead in a relationship of *compatibility*, and
in specific relations of compatibility with an importantly post-
industrial capitalist economy.

DESCRIBING POSTMODERNISM

A regime of signification

Postmodernism is then, for me, strictly cultural. It is indeed a sort
of cultural 'paradigm'. Cultural paradigms, like scientific paradigms, are spatio-temporal configurations. 'Spatially' they comprise a more or less flexible symbolic structure which, when bent
too much out of shape, begins to constitute another distinct
cultural paradigm. Temporally, they – like Kuhn's scientific
paradigms, or Michel Foucault's discourses – take shape, persist
for a duration, and then disintegrate. When Talcott Parsons in
The Structure of Social Action characterizes religions in terms of
whether their cosmology assumes the sacred to be either immanent or transcendent, he is beginning to describe cultural paradigms.[1] Or when Max Weber traces the history of the four
elements – rationalism, universalism, transcendence, and ethics –
of *Ancient Judaism*, he is more substantially delineating a
cultural paradigm. These four elements are the conditions of
existence of Judaism.[2] Other cultural paradigms which one
might speak of include, for instance, modernism, realism, the
baroque, and the Gothic.

More specifically, postmodernism and other cultural paradigms are what I want to call *'regimes of signification'*. The idea
for this comes from the political economists of the 'Regulation
School' and their notion of 'regime of accumulation'.[3] Regime of
accumulation is a particularly attractive concept because, unlike
the notion of, say, 'mode of production', it clearly connotes a
temporal dimension. Further, unlike mode of production,
regimes of accumulation are as importantly determined by how

4

people consume as by how they produce. Regimes of accumulation thus attribute as much importance to the market as they do to the point of production. In 'regimes of *signification*', however, only *cultural* objects are produced. All regimes of signification comprise two main components. The first is a specific 'cultural economy'. A given cultural economy will include (1) specific relations of production of cultural objects, (2) specific conditions of reception, (3) a particular institutional framework that mediates between production and reception, and (4) a particular way in which cultural objects circulate. The second component of any regime of signification is its specific *mode* of signification, by which I mean that its cultural objects depend on a particular relationship between signifier, signified, and referent. Here the signifier is a sound, image, word, or statement; the signified is a concept or meaning; and the referent is an object in the real world to which signifier and signified connect. The notion of mode of signification is explicated below in Chapter 7 and is wholly straightforward. Those with little or no knowledge of linguistics or semiotics will have no difficulty in grasping the discussion.

Modernization and differentiation

Postmodernism is a very idiosyncratic regime of signification. It is a regime of signification whose fundamental structuring trait is 'de-differentiation'. What I mean by de-differentiation has a certain amount in common with Baudrillard's concept of 'implosion'.[4] My starting point, however, is not Baudrillard, but conventional sociology. It is the standard structural–functionalist idea of social modernization by means of differentiation. But, following Weber's famous methodological essays on the sociology of religion[5] and Habermas in *The Theory of Communicative Action*,[6] I want to confine this differentiation and modernization to the realm of culture alone. What I want to claim is that if modernization is a process of cultural differentiation, or what German analysts call *Ausdifferenzierung*, then '*post*modernization' is a process of de-differentiation, or *Entidifferenzierung*.

On these lines it is convenient to conceive modernization as roughly consisting of three phases: the 'primitive', the 'religio-metaphysical', and the 'modern'. This periodization stems from Piaget, and parallels his developmental psychology. An initial major and systematic treatment of cultural modernization in terms of a differentiation model is Hegel's mature writing on aesthetics.[7] Please accept the following paragraphs, not as evidence of the validity of this model, but as illustrations which clarify the model's parameters.

In broadest outline here, in primitive societies, culture and the social are as yet undifferentiated. Indeed religion and its rituals are part and parcel of the social. The sacred is immanent in the profane. Further, nature and the spiritual remain undifferentiated in animism and totemism. The magician's role underscores the ambiguity of distinction between this-worldly and other-worldly, and the priests' functions have not yet become separate and specialized.

In the second, 'religio-metaphysical phase', modernization brings about the differentiation of the cultural from the social, the sacred from the profane, in the world religions. Here the modernization process seems to be at work in the more radical differentiation of the spiritual from the social in Christianity than in Eastern religions, in Protestantism than in Catholicism. Further modernization takes place, in this trajectory, in the Renaissance autonomization of secular culture from religious culture, and in the eighteenth-century tripartite and Kantian differentiation of theoretical, ethical, and aesthetic realms. This differentiation and autonomization opens up the possibility for the development of 'realism' both in art and in epistemology.

Aesthetic realism is only possible on the basis of three prior types of differentiation, as follows.

(1) The cultural must constitute a separate realm from the social. Aesthetic realism is premised on the possibility of 'representation', in which one type of entity must represent another type of entity. 'Symbolism', unlike representation, does not presuppose two separate realms. Symbolism exists in primitive societies in a sense and on a scale that representation does not. Thus the anthropologists' conception of culture as undifferentiated from the social is tied to symbolism in a sense that the idea of culture dominant in today's culture and media studies is tied to notions of representation. One of the important contributions of the Birmingham Centre for Contemporary Cultural

6

Studies has been to bring symbols, alongside representations, into the study of contemporary culture.[8] Representations, like symbols, do signify. However, symbols signify, so to speak, immanently, while representations signify transcendentally and presuppose a pre-existing differentiation of the cultural and the social.

(2) Aesthetic realism presupposes the separation of the aesthetic from the theoretical. That is, it must be clear in an important sense that representations in painting and literature are not 'true' in the same way that propositions or concepts in the sciences are.

(3) Aesthetic realism presupposes the separation of secular from religious culture, and assumes the conventions of the former for art forms. Hence pictorial realism is rooted in the break with religious assumptions of Quattrocento perspective. Alberti's literally 'window on the world' conception was based on the tracing of a three-dimensional object in a two-dimensional space. So that the space intervened between the object and the eye. Its geometrical perspective and proportion assumed lines drawn from the object, through the two-dimensional space and converging on the eye. The two-dimensional space was literally to be conceived as a 'window', onto which reality was to be transcribed.[9] Pictorial realism was thus conceived as a break with the religious world view of mediaeval painting, in which scientific principles displaced the latter's flattened perspective and distorted proportion, which did not on the religious world view matter, because is was symbols and not reality which was to be rendered.

'Narrative realism' also is dependent on the differentiation of scientific from religious world view. Narrative realism, perhaps best exemplified in the nineteenth-century novel, presumes that a narrative has beginning, middle, and end, and that events follow one another as cause and effect. It is almost always based on a sort of psychological causation, in which actions are effects whose causes are either the character traits or the goals of individuals. In narrative realism, events cannot be a matter of coincidence, as in melodrama, but they must, on Aristotle's conception, have minimal levels of plausibility and predictability in terms of preceding events.[10] Neither can causation be teleological, from an outside cause, or a 'final cause', as in Greek myth or Christian

~~theology. Causes must either temporally precede or be simulta-~~
neous with effects.

Epistemological realism, which assumes that concepts or ideas can give a more or less true picture of reality, is also dependent on differentiation in the modernization process.[11] It presupposes again the differentiation of secular culture from religious culture and hence a departure from theologically informed conceptions of reality. And it presupposes a differentiation of ideas from nature (and the social) so that the former can represent nature. Much the same is true in the area of ethics and morality. The 'natural law' ethical thought of Hobbes, Locke, Rousseau, and Kant assumes a break with theologically grounded ethics (as found in, for example, Thomist thought), and the grounding of morality in nature and/or reason. But natural law also importantly presupposes a systematic differentiation of the cultural from the social and reproduces itself in the separate realms of 'the ought' and 'the is'. The sacred of 'the ought' in such moralities is either rendered as the realm of nature or of reason, quite distinct from the profane social realm of existing every-day life.

Modernist autonomy

Further differentiation and autonomization brings us to a fully-fledged cultural modernity. In 'the modern', each of the cultural spheres attains the fullest possible autonomy. Each sphere attains what Weber called *Eigengesetzlichkeit*. This means that each sphere becomes self-legislating. It is fashionable to say that modernist (or even more erroneously, postmodernist) cultural forms are 'self-referential'. I find that this is misleading. The idea of self-referentiality here probably comes from the Saussurean notion of signification through difference. What many analysts take this for is that signifier–signified relations are in fact a matter of the differences among a plurality of signifiers in a langue. Saussure himself is rather inexplicit on this matter, though latter-day Saussureans have made this oversimplification. This is indeed an oversimplification because in any langue, signification depends as much on the relationship among signifieds as among signifiers and on set of rules that connect signifiers and signifieds.[12] And even if meaning were fully determined by the differences among signifiers, that would not mean that the signifiers were *self*-referential. It would mean that their ability to refer outside of themselves, i.e. to signifieds, was determined by the differences among themselves. The other model for the 'self-referentiality' argument is the 'flatness' of the modernist picture surface. Granted, this entails that the aesthetic validity of a modernist painting is not in its ability to refer to a referent in the outside world. But it does not at all entail that its aesthetic value lies in its ability to refer to itself.

Weberian 'self-legislation' seems to me to be much more telling as a criterion of modernism than self-referentiality. To say a sphere is self-legislating is to say that it develops its own conventions and mode of valuation. This means that value within a sphere is dependent on how well a cultural object in the sphere measures up to the norms proper to that sphere itself. Hence the value of a proposition in the theoretical sphere becomes less dependent on the extent to which it reproduces reality, and more dependent on the argument and evidence adduced in 'theoretical discourse' to back up that proposition. The same would be true for arguments proper to ethics in debates about practical reason. Value in the aesthetic sphere would be a matter, not of reproducing the real, but of the systematic working through, as Clement Greenberg has proposed, of the potential in a given aesthetic material.[13]

Fully-fledged modernism in aesthetic, moral-practical, and theoretical spheres – I borrow this trichotomy from Habermas – means thus a break with 'foundationalism'. Foundationalism is the opposite of self or autonomous legislation. It is *heteronomous* legislation from another, universalist 'instance' such as nature, or reason, or the real, or God. Thus in modernity, in the theoretical and aesthetic spheres there is no longer heteronomous legislation from 'the real'. In ethics, natural law theories and categorical imperatives are broken with. Rational argument supports ethical propositions rather than the Kantian grounding in a hypostatized vision of reason.

Before proceeding to 'post-modernization', I must make two brief further introductory points about modernity. The first is about the origins of classical sociology. Classical sociology is born roughly contemporaneously with the changes in ethics, aesthetics, and epistemology that I've just touched on. Classical sociologists such as Weber and Durkheim break with realist

9

epistemology and rationalist ethics, to opt (like Marx and Nietzsche) for 'sociologistic' epistemologies and ethics. This means the determination of ethics and knowledge by social factors and/or social interests. Note first in this context that – unlike in art and the more philosophical discussion of modernist ethics or epistemology above – what is at issue is, not the validity of a theoretical or normative propostion, but its source. Such sources are not the self-legislation of a given sphere, but another social entity such as a social class or nation. These are however not universalist entities, such as 'nature' or 'the real', so this is not a fully-fledged foundationalism. Indeed in these, Weberian and Durkheimian, sociologistic accounts of culture, the ethical or theoretical is part of the same 'form of life' as a nation or social class, and so has its own 'internalist' conventions.

The second point is the issue of rationality. Some analysts such as Carl Schorske, Daniel Bell, and David Frisby understand modernism as a largely anti-rationalist phenomenon. Others such as Habermas, Adorno, and Greenberg argue that it is basically rational in character.[14] I think that the autonomization of culture spheres leaves space either for irrationalist *or* rationalist developments. That is, the departure from heteronomous legislation opens up paths in either direction. Hence the discovery of an unconscious level of the instincts under the rational ego leaves space open for, either the Freudian colonization of the ego by reason itself, or the Nietzschean irrationalist celebration of the will to power of the instincts. In painting, the shift from heteronomous legislation by the real leaves open the irrationalist and subjectivist developments of expressionism and the pre-eminently rationalist productions of cubism or constructivism. Classical sociology itself is mainly, it seems to me, part of the rationalist departure in modernism. Sociology is made possible by the reaction of particularist romanticism against Enlightenment Reason. But once the particularisms of class, *conscience collective*, and nation are come to terms with, sociology exemplifies their reconquest by reason. This sociological, modernist rationality is visible in the new science's characteristically nomothetic propositions. Moreover, only rational argument is allowed in support of these propositions. Further, the concern with social order of the Classics Simmel, Durkheim, and Weber was tantamount to a search for a set of regularities, even of rationality in the social itself. Finally, there was a moral concern with a rational set of social prescriptions among these theorists.

Postmodernist de-differentiation

If cultural modernization was a process of differentiation, then postmodernization is one of de-differentiation. If the paradigmatic theorist for the modern (and modernization as differentiation) was Weber, for the postmodern it is, again not Baudrillard, but Walter Benjamin. There are four main components to a given cultural paradigm. They are: (1) the relationship among types of cultural object produced – i.e. aesthetic, theoretical, ethical, etc.; (2) the relationship between the cultural as a whole and the social; (3) its 'cultural economy', whose elements in turn are conditions of production and consumption, the institutions of culture, mode of circulation, and the cultural product or good itself; and (4) the mode of signification: i.e. relations among signifier, signified, and referent. If modernization presupposed differentiation on all of these counts, then postmodernization witnesses de-differentiation on each of these four components.

First of all, the three main cultural spheres lose their autonomy, in a process in which, for example, the aesthetic realm begins to colonize both theoretical and moral-political spheres. Second, the cultural realm is no longer 'auratic', in Benjamin's sense; that is, it is no longer systematically separated from the social. This has to do with the partial breakdown of the boundaries between high and popular culture and the concomitant development of a mass audience for high culture. But it is also a matter of a new immanence in the social of culture, in which representations also take on the function of symbols. Third, the 'cultural economy' becomes de-differentiated. On the production side is the famous disintegration of the author celebrated by poststructuralists, or alternatively the merging of author into the cultural product as in the late 1980s biographical novels or performance art from Laurie Anderson to Bruce MacLean. On the consumption side, de-differentiation takes place in, for example, the tendency of some types of theatre since the mid 1960s to include the audience itself as part of the cultural product. One of the most important 'institutions' of culture is criticism, which mediates between cultural product and consumer. And a number of critics have come to dispute the distinction between literature and criticism, which is the same as the distinction between institutions and cultural objects. Other 'institutions' include those which commercially circulate cultural objects, and use of advertisements in doing so. With the advent of the pop video and adverts which themselves masquerade as pop songs (in the late 1980s as soul music from the early 1960s) one is hard put to say where the commercial institution stops and where the cultural product starts.

Most important perhaps is the *mode* of representation itself. Modernism, as noted above, had clearly differentiated and autonomized the roles of signifier, signified, and referent. Postmodernization on the contrary *problematizes* these distinctions, and especially the status and relationship of signifier and referent, or put another way, representation and reality.[15] In this, first an increasing proportion of signification takes place through images and not words. This is de-differentiation in that images resemble referents to a greater degree than words. Equally, a far greater proportion of referents themselves are in fact signifiers. That is, our everyday life becomes pervaded with a reality – in TV, adverts, video, computerization, the Walkman, cassette decks in automobiles, and now, increasingly, CDs, CDV, and DAT – which increasingly comprises representations. This invasion of the space of the signifier by the referent, and invasion of the place of the referent by that of the signifier, is the conscious subject of Andy Warhol's silk-screens which seem to be a return to realism, but in which the real object depicted is itself an image. It is underscored in David Cronenberg's film *Videodrome*, in which the body of protagonist James Woods increasingly takes on the functions of a video recorder, while the video cassettes themselves become squishy and somehow organic.

There are a number of advantages to this model of postmodernism that I have proposed. One is that the idea of regime of signification is aimed at covering the whole range of postmodern cultural objects, not just in, say, architecture but right across the spectrum. It is equally a model that attempts to account for both the 'textual' aspects of cultural objects as well as conditions of production and reception. A third advantage lies in the periodization by differentiation/de-differentiation. A number of writers have been unclear as to whether they were speaking of postmodernism in contradistinction to, on the one hand, realism or, on the other, modernism. This model views realism as part of cultural modernization. Realism is simply a point here at which differentiation had not proceeded as far as in modernism

Let me make plain at this point that I do not think that the whole, or even necessarily most of contemporary culture is postmodern. There are instead all sorts of cultural objects in circulation at the same time – including modernist, realist, and pre-realist types such as Gothic and Christian cultural objects. Second, many empirically existing cultural objects have combinations of realist, modernist, and postmodernist traits. Hence I am using 'postmodernism' and 'modernism' as ideal-types. In actual history as well there is no strict chronology of succeeding cultural paradigms. I shall argue, for instance, that surrealism is in part postmodern, yet it surfaced in the heyday of modernism. Given this, however, the schema in this book assumes that modernist cultural objects became pervasive from the late nineteenth century and postmodernism begins to make significant inroads in the past two to three decades.

All this said, there is a specific distinction between modernism and postmodernism that seems to me to be more significant, somehow more basic, than the others. It is that *modernism conceives of representations as being problematic whereas postmodernism problematizes reality*. Let me explain this. According to the ideal type of 'realism', cultural forms are, unproblematically, signifiers which are supposed, again unproblematically, to represent reality. Thus realism takes neither representation nor reality as problematic. Modernist autonomization, as I mentioned above, is also the autonomization of cultural forms from the real, hence representations take on a certain opacity at the same time as they become self-legislating. What this does is draw the viewer's attention to the 'picture surface', that is, to the representation itself; or, on the lines of Greenberg's aesthetic, to the author's use of the aesthetic materials or to the 'signifying practice'. What Greenberg could thus see in Picasso is not all that much different than what analysts of the next generation, such as Baudry, could see in the films of Godard – i.e. the call of attention to the signifying practice or the 'laying bare of the device'.[16]

To say that modernism *problematizes* the representation is to see cultural production in modernism as a sort of pursuit in 'problem solving' (or even as a learning process), in which the working out of the possibilities in the aesthetic material is the problem to be solved. Adorno spoke of modernism in terms of 'aesthetic rationality', a term whose meaning he was never very clear about. Perhaps to think of it as problem solving is one way towards inroads on what aesthetic rationality might be. What postmodernism, in contraposition, sees as problematic is not the signifying process, not the picture's surface – that is, not the representation, but reality itself. Thus surrealism seems to be a departure from 'high modernism', to use a term whose ubiquity stems from Jameson,[17] in the direction of realism. But its juxtaposition of two or more objects, clearly out of place with one another – and both figures often out of context with their ground – problematizes reality. It does so from the standpoint of the Freudian primary process which, surrealism suggests, is somehow more real than the phenomena of every-day life. A half century later, the problematization of the real comes not from the depths of the id but from a society whose very surface, whose very empirical reality, is largely made up of images or representations. What Magritte said about surrealism, that is that it was 'philosophical' rather than painterly,[18] could be used to distinguish postmodernism from modernism as entire cultural paradigms. Postmodernism thus can be seen also as a problem-solving pursuit – that is, as a search for a working out of the permutations and implications of how our reality is transformed and indeed made flimsy by its penetration by invading images. Postmodern culture itself, at its best, could in this way be seen as a problem-solving enterprise and in no way inherently 'irrationalist'. If our contemporary reality has indeed become destabilized through a number of social and cultural processes, then, though it may seem irrationalist to celebrate this new flimsiness of reality, it would surely be a highly rationalist pursuit, either aesthetically or theoretically, to try to make some sense of it.

If this analysis is correct, then postmodernism can pose a greater threat to social and cultural order than modernism has done. This is, first, because postmodernism pervades both high and popular culture, while modernism has been confined to the realm of high culture. A further threat concerns stabilization in cultural paradigms. If realism promises stability and order in both representation and reality, then modernist autonomization and self-legislation effectively destabilizes the *representation*. Postmodernist de-differentiation on the other hand puts chaos, flimsiness, and instability in our experience of *reality* itself.

EXPLAINING POSTMODERNISM - COLLECTIVE IDENTITY

To see cultural change and the development of realism, modernism, and postmodernism in terms of differentiation and de-differentiation is to present what is mainly a descriptive model of cultural change. This descriptive model has perhaps within it the basis of an explanatory framework. But such explanation is admittedly thin and unsatisfactory to the sociologist and remains one which is internalist - that is, confined to the cultural level. Equally, the transition from the process of modernization and differentiation to that of postmodernization and de-differentiation would remain unaccounted for. This latter might be speculatively understood in terms of a chronology of the increase in the pervasion of representations in society. If all the objects of significance in the social world were divided up into those which were real and those which were representations, in which the two categories are seen as mutually exclusive and exhaustive, history could be seen in terms of an increase of the proportion of those objects which are representations. On this account, to a certain point in historical time, representations came to constitute a sufficient proportion of all objects, so that they came to be taken seriously in all their opacity and complexity. This point would be the advent of modernism. If at a later historical point in time the pervasion of representations increased to a point at which real objects began to be challenged for their hegemony as objects of social significance, what might come to be problematized would be, no longer the representations, but the status of the real itself. This would be the point at which postmodernization would begin to set in.

But such an explanation is again strictly internal to the realm of culture and badly in need of sociological grounding. I believe that four properly sociological explanations go some way in accounting for the phenomena of modernism and post-

modernism. Put simply as possible, the first is that modernist
culture effectively destabilizes bourgeois identity, while postmodernist culture in large part is associated with the restabilization of bourgeois identity. Second, the rise of the working class as a collective actor is a condition of modernist culture,
while postmodernist culture is a catalyst of working-class
fragmentation. The third links modernism and postmodernism
to the changing material and cultural structure of the built
environment. And the fourth lies in the consideration of the
political economy of postmodern culture.

Modernist destabilization of bourgeois identity

I can best clarify what I mean by these explanatory hypotheses by
returning to the periodization schematized above. Realist culture,
on this account, has in Weber's sense an 'elective affinity' with
the naissant bourgeoisie. The causal arrows point both ways
here. First, in order for realist cultural forms to persist on any
extensive scale, an appropriate audience must exist as a reception
class. This reception class must subscribe to an ontology compat-
ible with the realist paradigm. For realism this was importantly a
secular ontology, with a mechanistic world view, and correspondingly a sense of a linear temporality in which history was
seen as progress. Realist cultural forms in their turn were
constitutive of identity, i.e. important in identity formation, for
bourgeois individuals. That is, realist cultural forms reinforced
and deepened a set of beliefs fundamental to the identity and
developing habitus of the new bourgeois grouping.[19] Realism, as
Critical Theorists have argued, thus contributed to the development of a bourgeois public sphere.

A number of, often catalogued, developments towards the end
of the nineteenth century serve to destabilize this bourgeois
identity, and to threaten to shatter the bourgeois public sphere.
(1) Collective actors, monopoly corporations, and, most significantly, an organized working class made their appearance on
the historical stage, challenging the individualism central to the
bourgeois world view, not to mention the individualistic and
psychological causation central to narrative realism.[20] (2) A now
largely literate working class – themselves influenced by realist
cultural forms – comes to adopt the assumptions of secularism, of

16

natural rights, and of historical progress which had been so central to the bourgeois world view. Only the ideology of working-class organizations wanted to subordinate these discourses to a whole different set of goals. Ideas of natural rights and historical progress, now put to the service - in Marxism and other left doctrines - of working-class organizations, no longer seemed to correspond to the ideal interests of the bourgeois and hence came under fire.[21] Thus, Lukács argues in *Die Zerstorung der Vernuft* that the destabilization of the Enlightenment world view, whose vehicles are in part aesthetic modernism and philosophers such as Nietzsche, explains the pervasion of fascist ideologies among the European middle classes in the interwar years. I do not think that Lukács's views should be, as is fashionable today, dismissed. His explanation is not so much wrong, as it is partial. Surely, the bourgeois world view is destabilized, but that does not entail that the middle classes will opt for fascism. Though there is some overlap, the audience among the middle classes in the early decades of modernist culture is vastly different from that which was attracted politically to fascism. Moreover, aesthetic modernism, as I argued above, can take an irrationalist colouration, or it can represent a deepening of Enlightenment rationality. What is true is that the destabilization of the bourgeois world view creates a situation in which (at least) two solutions are possible: the reconstruction of identity around fascist political culture or a receptivity to aesthetic modernism. (3) Urbanization: the rapid growth of large cities accompanied by the revolution in transportation in the second half of the nineteenth and early twentieth centuries contributed to a de-centred perception of time and space.[22] Thus an audience was sensitized to the disordering and re-ordering of time, space, and harmonic structures that characterize aesthetic modernism. The early producers of modernist art came largely among urban bohemians. Its early audience and the institutions which made its representation possible were found in close proximity with this bohemia. It is arguably changes in the nature of urban space and the usage of social space in the city, in Haussmann's Paris, in Ringstrasse Vienna, in Berlin of the early decades of the twentieth century that made possible the initial existence of this bohemia.

Two points here are essential to note. The first is that, as in the case of realism, the pattern of causation is dialectical. That is, a set of conditions, the rise of new collective actors and urbanization, makes an audience receptive to modernist cultural forms, which themselves serve further to destabilize bourgeois identity. The second is that these social changes are of course concomitant with the accumulation of capital. All of these changes – the growth of monopolies, the establishment of the working class as a collective actor, forced-paced urbanization, the growth of use of the railways, and the beginnings of urban rapid transport – accompany the transition in Western countries from liberal capitalism to *organized* capitalism. All were conditions of renewed growth in capitalist economies in the Kondratieff wave originating in the 1890s which signalled this transition to an organized capitalist economy.[23]

Aesthetic modernism thus stands in sort of elective affinity – sometimes of compatibility, sometimes incompatibility – with organized capitalist structures. Postmodernism stands, we shall see, in a rather similar relationship with the *dis*organization of capitalist economy and society.

Postmodernist restabilization

There are several ways in which postmodernist culture no longer poses a challenge to the bourgeois habitus as did modernism. One is the decline in experimentation with the aesthetic material, illustrated, for example, in the return to figuration in the visual arts, both in pop art and among the, for instance, *neue Wilden*, Baselitz, Kiefer, and others in Germany. A second is the postmodernist rejection of the avant-garde. Thus the huge new audience for jazz is radically other than that which witnessed the experimentation of Charlie Parker, John Coltrane, and Ornette Coleman.[24] Its jazz is largely a comfortable, easy-listening music, bought on compact discs and listened to on expense accounts footing the $25 cover charges which effectively exclude musicians themselves from the audiences in New York and London. The postmodernist de-differentiation which assumes the dissolution of aesthetic avant-gardes assumes equally the rejection of political avant-gardes. The problematic, yet unmistakably anti-bourgeois alliance of aesthetic and political avant-gardes of modernism is scarcely to be seen in the late twentieth century.

18

Further, modernism was, as I mentioned above, critical of commodification in a way postmodernism surely is not.

A large part of the literature in Culture Studies looks at how various cultural forms 'position the subject'. It is often argued in this context that, for instance, realist cinema creates fixed positions for the subject (in the audience), while modernist films would leave space open for a more flexible and active subjectivity.[25] Postmodernist culture would on this account, I am arguing, tend once again to create fixed subject positions. This is largely what I mean by postmodernist restabilization or bourgeois identity.

If we note an elective affinity between postmodernist culture and bourgeois identity, we must really be more specific and say what is meant by bourgeois and what is meant by identity or subjectivity. In this I want to draw on Pierre Bourdieu's notion of the 'habitus'. I want to understand the habitus and thus identity along the lines of Durkheim's *conscience collective*, which itself has two components: (1) a component of 'group', which defines identity in terms of in-group and out-group, in terms of the boundaries between the individual or collective actor and those different from, and often standing in opposition to, the individual or collective actor; (2) a component of classification. Part of our identity is determined by how we classify.[26] We cannot make sense out of the world of objects or of the social world without somehow putting some sort of classificatory schema on these worlds. We classify individuals into genders, age groups, ethnicities, social classes, and status groups. We classify objects of consumption, from cars to TV shows to holidays. To classify is necessarily at the same time to valuate, i.e. to make invidious distinctions. This is true for social classifications and for the classifications of objects. Different social classes and class fractions, observes Bourdieu, have different systems of classifications.[27]

The older dominant bourgeois groupings do not put a very positive valuation on postmodernist cultural objects. But the new bourgeoisie does. When I say old bourgeoisie here, I include much of the so-called 'new middle classes'. The 'new middle classes' expanded on an enormous scale during the era of 'organized', or classical industrial capitalism. The qualitative process of 'tertiarization', to take a term from the architectural historians,[28] of our cities took off and expanded exponentially from the end of the nineteenth century. This created the new middle classes. What I am talking about, however, are the middle classes created by the more recent wave of tertiarization of the past two to three decades and especially of the 1980s. The original new middle classes were created on the wave of tertiarization whose rhythm was set by principles of accumulation along norms set by industrial capitalism. The more recent grouping was created in an era in which the industrial principle no longer is unambiguously dominant in regulating accumulation.

It is these newer, post-industrial middle classes, with their bases in the media, higher education, finance, advertising, merchandising, and international exchanges, that provide an audience for postmodern culture. Their cultural credentials are doubly dubious to the more established bourgeois groupings. They are often upwardly mobile, and not from families of the old established groupings. They often have not gone to the elite universities, but to institutions of other levels, which themselves have been partly successful in establishing and legitimating their own cultural capital *vis-à-vis* the established institutions. The post-industrial middle classes, further, are often based in different jobs and are from a different and younger generation than the older established bourgeoisie. That is, they have a whole range of different sources of identity than the older groupings and are likely to perceive their own 'ideal interests' in terms of a whole different range of symbolisms and a whole different range of cultural objects than do the older groupings. Hence the populism and image-centredness of postmodernism is more appealing to the new groupings than to the old elite. The old elite's adherence to modernist 'aura' is of less relevance to the new elite. And this is because the new 'elite' has effectively become no elite at all, but a 'mass', i.e. part of the masses. This massification of what was an elite has created a very large audience for putatively high cultural objects such as art films or the 'New Hollywood cinema' of Woody Allen, Francis Coppola, David Lynch, and others.[29] This massification of elite culture, largely through means of electronic communication, in an age of electronic reproduction, has helped pose the very question of problematizing the distinction between elite and mass culture, and the notion of aura. Bourdieu speaks of battles for hegemony in terms of 'classificatory struggles'. This new post-industrial middle class thus could be entering into this sort of struggle with older dominant groupings in order to impose their own classificatory schema, which is comfortable with and valuates postmodern cultural objects, as hegemonic for the whole of society.

'Distinction' or 'difference'?

Postmodern culture thus can be seen in terms of a set of symbols and legitimations which promote the ideal interests of this new, 'Yuppified' post-industrial bourgeoisie. It is partly constitutive of identity for this grouping. The sort of habitus, identity, and classificatory schemata that it constructs is rigid and fixed. It is of a piece with the new intensive phase of the deepening of commodification in late twentieth-century capitalism. And it serves as a set of status symbols establishing invidious distinctions between this new bourgeoisie and groups which are different from and 'below' them.

But there is another possibility. The postmodernist rejection of avant-gardes and of aura is of a piece with the cultural paradigm's unhappiness with elites and hierarchy. Warhol himself may have been a partisan of the commodity form, but Warhol's pictures have attracted large numbers on the left for decades, who have read them as a send-up of the consumer society. Perhaps most significant, the postmodernist return to figuration, its refusal to lay bare the device and instead encourage the immediate investment of the spectator's desire in the image, seems to return to the 'closed text' and fixed subjectivity of realism.[30] But the reality which is once again foregrounded turns out itself to comprise images or representations; turns out itself to be artificial and/or flimsy, turns out to be anything *but* stable. The postmodernist *text* itself is indeed 'closed'; it will not distantiate; it will not provoke an activist spectator *vis-à-vis* the text. But the *referents* of these stable postmodernist signifiers are indeed another matter. The postmodernist film – think for example of cult films of 1980s mass art cinema such as *Diva, Videodrome, Subway,* or *Blue Velvet* – for all its arguable political implications won't call attention to filmic conventions, refuses to 'show the author's hand' à la Godard or Brecht. Instead it draws the viewer, with a force greater than straightforward realist narrative cinema, right into the referent, right into the reality that the film is creating. But this absent challenge to stylistic norms leaves open to us a reality whose own regulative, but also constitutive, norms are indeed subject to challenge. Fixed, harmonic, even 'smooth' and 'slick' stylistic conventions bring us immediately into a reality whose conventions are anything but fixed and harmonic. The closed text reveals an open reality. The 'play of the signifier' may have ceased, but the referent – think of the paintings of Francis Bacon or Lucian Freud's very biological portraits and nudes – seems to have slipped more or less totally out of control.

The side of postmodernism can result in a positioning of the subject that is anything but fixed. In terms of the conscience collectives, it can lead to a 'group', whose boundaries between the 'same' and the 'other', between 'us' and 'them', are not rigid, but flexible and permeable; to a more flexible set of classificatory categories. Indeed, if to classify is to valuate, the valuational component of classifications can surely be more or less prominent. This other side of postmodernism can promote a subjectivity, thus, whose classificatory schemata have more in common with 'difference' than they do with the hierarchy of 'distinction'.

In fact Bourdieu himself, in books such as *Ce que parler veut dire*[31] and elsewhere, acknowledges his indebtedness to Saussure. For Saussure, knowledge and meaning was at bottom linguistic, and determined by 'difference', that is the relationship not of sign to referent, but between the signs in a langue. For Bourdieu as sociologist, knowledge, taste, and meaning are fundamentally social, and at the bottom line determined by the relationships of classes and class fractions in a 'social field'. The 'terms' (or elements) whose relationships determine meaning are in Saussure linguistic and in Bourdieu social. But whereas in Saussure these terms are very equal in weight, in Bourdieu they are hierarchical. Thus Saussurean 'difference' is vastly other than Bourdieuan 'distinction'.

This brings us back full circle to the new middle classes. Their identities or habituses can be fixed, rigid, status-conscious on the caricatured model of the Yuppie – that is, on the model of 'distinction'. On the other hand these same social groupings also

22

form in large part a constituency for the new social movements. Their habituses or identities can thus also be constructed importantly along lines of gender, minority ethnicities, minority sexual practices, environmentalism, in opposition to nuclear war. That is, along lines of difference rather than of invidious distinction.[32] And a habitus established along lines of difference, with looser group, looser grid, and classifications whose valuative component is minor, is also a habitus which is based on principles of toleration of difference in others. Hence the, to some, bewildering appeal of a number of postmodern cultural objects, not just to Yuppiedom, but to those whose sympathies lie much more with the left. Or, better put, the appeal of the second side of postmodernism, or another reading of postmodernism, as well as its possibilities for a now pluralized left political culture.

This second, disruptive side of postmodernism can perhaps better be understood when seen through a sort of Kantian prism. In *The Critique of Pure Reason*, Kant made a fundamental distinction within subjectivity between a 'transcendental logic', which contained *inter alia* the categories of the understanding, and the 'transcendental aesthetic' which contained the categories of time and space. *Perception* of phenomena, Kant claimed, took place through the transcendental aesthetic's categories of time and space, while cognition or knowledge was also conditional upon the operation of the logical categories.[33] Both the sciences, in the broadest sense, and the arts are dependent on some admixture of cognition and perception, in which, in the sciences, cognition plays the greater role, while, in the arts, Kant's transcendental aesthetic, or perception, has a relatively more important part. One might hypothesize then that changes in perception in every-day life would sensitize an audience to the reception of a particular cultural paradigm in the arts. For modernism, this change in perception was that associated with the rise of the great city, and its concomitant disordering/ reordering of our perception of time and space, which then in turn were problematized in modernist cultural forms.[34] In post-modernism the change is not so much in the way we perceive time and space as in terms of *what* we are perceiving. What we are perceiving, in TV, in video, in the spread of information technology, on the Walkman, on the audio cassettes we listen to in our cars, in advertisements, in the huge increase in popular magazines we look at, are representations, are mostly images. We are living in a society in which our *perception* is directed almost as often to representations as it is to 'reality'. These representations come to constitute a very great proportion of our perceived reality. And/or our perception of reality comes to be increasingly by *means* of these representations. Even much of our *perception* of representations comes via representations, as we search our newspapers for the cultural sections, or we look at Max Headroom, who is only willing to appear on television on television. Thus we are sensitized as an audience to cultural forms which experiment, not so much with the subjective disordering/reordering of time and space, but with the problematic nature of reality and the relationship of reality to representation.

One point here needs to be highlighted in terms of this Kantian dualism of cognition and perception. In principle, perception – though it operates through the categories of time and space – is immediate. Cognition on the other hand is mediated by representation, be they concepts or propositions. Perception is concrete, cognition is abstract. Perception is variously seen as operating via sensation, or as in Kant, a matter of 'intuition'. Cognition is contingent upon abstract categories or logic, on abstract classification.

To represent, either in science or in art, is to operate in the realm of the subject. Surely the amount of mediation in art is less substantial for Hegel or for Kant than in science, but both science and art operate through representations in not the realm of the object, but that of subjectivity. In modernism, then, though both perception and representation are made problematic, there persists the Kantian dualism of subject and object. In modernism, changes in perception in every-day life and hence a disordering of our notions of time and space are reproduced in art in the realm of representation. In postmodernism it is the status of the two separate realms which are rendered problematic. What is key here is that it is *representations themselves which become objects of perception*. That is, already abstract entities which previously were integral to subjectivity come to enter into the wholly unreflexive realm of the object itself.[35] In Kant's and Hegel's dualism, culture (and representations) in the sciences and arts are somehow reflexive, somehow rational. They, for one thing, are able to operate reflexively versus the world of sensation and the object. In this rational world of culture, representations take sensations in the realm of perception as their object. In postmodernism all this is inverted, as unreflexive sensation takes representations themselves as its own object.

Working-class identity

Now let us consider identity and class identity. Modernism, I just claimed – and shall argue at length in Chapter 8 – has had primarily a destabilizing effect on bourgeois identity. This is partly because modernist 'texts' are much less accessible to the middle classes than realist texts are, so they cannot play the same pervasive role in identity formation. It is partly also intention; that is, the disordering/reordering of time and space is often explicitly intended to *épater le bourgeois*. Now modernism was confined to an audience of elites. But what about the working classes? From 1890 the working class came to be exposed instead to a variety of realist cultural forms, which were important in their own identity formation. Postmodernism, in contrast to modernism, is not at all confined to elites. The effects of postmodernism may, then, be rather differential. Postmodern culture, partly displacing modernism among elites, could serve to *re*stabilize bourgeois identity. But as a successor to realist culture among the popular classes, postmodernism may tend to *de*-centre working-class identity.

The rise of modernism takes place at about the same point in time as the formation of the working class as a collective actor. Class formation for the proletariat has often been cited as a key reason for the destabilization of bourgeois identity in the decades spanning the turn of the twentieth century. And the latter is seen as a condition of the rise of cultural modernism. The working class is not of course a central reception class for cultural modernism but, as Jameson observed, shifts towards a secular, realist culture at about the same point in time that modernism makes a significant impact among elites.[36] Now stable (and often) oppositional working-class individual and collective identities were importantly constituted by this realistic culture. Its content was very often 'social' in comparison with its individualistic bourgeois counterpart.

The spread of a new non-realist departure in popular culture from the mid to late 1950s has arguably contributed to the fragmentation of working-class identity. What I am referring to is the rise of rock music, teenage spending power, and the birth of adolescence as a major source of identity itself. This pop culture was, especially not initially, 'postmodernist' *per se*. Yet it did share key characteristics with the latter. Its foregrounding of 'spectacle', similarly to postmodernism, threw down the gauntlet to realist narrative. It was bound to image and sound rather than to language, and its language – for example in rock music – functioned as much as incantation as semantic value. It began importantly to blur the distinction between what was commercial and what was properly cultural, and, as importantly, between cultural representation and advertisement. The latter is inseparable from the process from the late 1950s of representations becoming symbols. This takes place for example in the use of pop star images on T-shirts, in hair styles, in the shaping of whole subcultures.[37] The representation, as noted above, must be separated from the social in order that it be able to carry out its function, i.e. to represent. The symbol is no longer differentiated from the social. It *refers*, but it does not represent. The symbol has meaning, and connects thus to a signified. Symbols do not and cannot however refer to referents. Only representations can.

Bernice Martin in her important *Sociology of Contemporary Popular Culture* argued that cultural change had a destabilizing effect on working-class identity from the late 1950s. This was a question of the loosening of both 'grid' (the way people classify) and of 'group' (distinction between in-group and out-group) in the proletarian habitus. Popular culture, and more particularly rock music culture (with its much more flagrant transgression of conventional norms than earlier popular culture), she observes, became widespread with the growth of teenage spending power from the late 1950s. This economic variable together with the incursion of rock culture and the weakening of the working-class family contributed to what some have described as the birth of adolesence as a socially constructed category. Traditionally a working-class male lived with his family, then entered into a half-adult realm during his apprenticeship, during which time his behaviour was regulated by a set of more or less strictly circumscribed traditional norms. Then he entered into his trade and into establishing a family of his own. Adolescence, its rock culture, and its new subcultures created a period in life, a temporal span, in which this rigid normativity was challenged and de-centred.[38]

This process was complex and only a few general points can be made here. What was going on was *two* processes of de-centring of identity – that is, of both (1) individual and (2) collective identity. This is made even more complex by the 'external' forces which were coming into being at about the same point in time, in particular the fragmentation of working-class communities and attendant 'embourgeoisement', and the numerical 'shrinkage' of the working class itself as a proportion of the population. It has been commonplace for visitors from other Western countries to remark on the pervasion of a specific working-class culture in Britain. I do not think that this is unconnected to the fact that the historical numerical predominance of working-class population in this country has been not even nearly matched by other Western nations. During the interwar years, some 70 per cent of Britain's 'economically active' population comprised employed manual workers in manufacturing, mining, or construction. In no other major Western country did that proportion ever reach even 50 per cent. In the USA it never even reached 40 per cent. I think that the decline in the importance and general pervasion among other social classes of working-class norms and values in Thatcherite Britain at the very end of the 1980s is partly conditioned by the very numerical decimation of the working class. Britain has gone in the space of a few decades from one of the most overwhelmingly working-class societies to one of those with the lowest proportion of proletarians, well below the level now in Sweden, Germany, France, and Japan.

In any event it makes sense to speak of a distinction in the de-centring of individual identity from that of collective identity in the working class, although the two surely are intertwined. The shake up of individual identity is a matter, for instance, of the rejection of parental control and the lessening of restrictions on sexuality. The decline of collective identity is registered in, say, identification with the Labour Party, with the trade unions, with an 'us' versus 'them' mentality. Both are portrayed in some of the

'British realist' films whose subject matter was working-class life
in the north of England. Films like *Room at the Top* and
Saturday Night, Sunday Morning not only showed young working-class males flouting the authority of their parents and
engaging in a freer sexuality than local conventions were
comfortable with. They also portrayed a striving for upward
mobility, and a desolidarization with collectivist values
altogether.[39]

In any event, this cluster of factors was understood by commentators as explicable of the period of working-class
quiescence, experienced in most Western nations in the 1950s and
first half of the 1960s. But what of the broad wave of industrial
struggles that broke throughout Europe, in the late 1960s and
early 1970s? One thing these strike waves had in common – in
Britain, France, Germany, Sweden, and Italy – was their *decen*-
tralized form. They were not strikes centrally directed or called
but, in the main, grassroots and shopfloor affairs. This new
decentralized worker action, several analysts have observed, was
infected by the militancy of the students' movement of the late
1960s, and shared an ethos of resistance to authority, challenge to
hierarchy, and grassroots democracy with the latter.[40] This great,
decentralized worker mobilization generated a series of debates
that as yet remain open and unresolved. Initially there were two
types of interpretation. In Britain, both neo-Weberian conflict
theorists and Marxists saw it in terms of traditionalist working-
class struggles. They argued that the resurgence of militancy
proved that the theorists of embourgeoisement, who had argued
that some sort of fundamental change was happening inside of
the working class, were themselves fundamentally wrong. In
France, writers such as Serge Mallet, Alain Touraine, and Andre
Gorz put forth another argument. They agreed a fundamental
change had been going on inside of the working class. But they
maintained that this would not lead to quiescence or necessarily
to a sort of possessive individualism. They argued that a new
working class instead was forming, who rejected the values of
hierarchy, statism, and corporatism which marked the old working class. This new working class was part and parcel of the
revolution of 1968, and it would take its place – it was Touraine
who formulated this with the utmost clarity – in the later
twentieth century as one of several social movements, all sharing

the values of radical democracy, decentralization, opposition to bureaucracy, and local control.[41]

Samuel Beer, Harvard University political scientist, pushed this argument in effect a bit further. Beer made the link between popular culture and radical democratic values within the working class in Britain. He argued that the anti-authoritarian ethos of pop culture moved workers not only to dispute the authority of employers and the bureaucratic state, but to oppose hierarchy within trade unions, the Labour Party, and the working-class community themselves. Such grassroots opposition, claimed Beer, upset the 'corporatist bias', in which union and Labour Party leadership exercised social control over their constituent members. This 'corporatist bias', as Keith Middlemas underscored, had kept the social peace in Britain from the early 1920s through the mid 1960s, during historical decades when violent and ideological class struggles were the *mot de jour* on the Continent.[42]

Samuel Beer is, at least in some important respects, a neo-conservative. Like Samuel Huntington, his Harvard colleague and like a number of German neo-conservatives, his greatest fear has been of a crisis of 'ungovernability'. According to the ungovernability thesis Western states and economies are 'overloaded' by a surplus of demands. People and organized groupings want to consume more than they want to produce, thus a group of 'instrumentalist' demands is put on state and economy. This is accompanied by what Huntington suggests is a surplus of democracy, as a number of radical-democratic demands are also put on state and economy.[43] The result, it is prophesied, is ungovernability along the lines of the model of Germany in the Weimar Republic. Other neo-conservatives like Daniel Bell and Bernice Martin have brought, implicitly or explicitly, the effects of postmodernist popular culture into this. Postmodernist culture, or those qualities of postmodernism that are at present in popular culture, tends to undermine the work ethic and promote consumerist values. Throw in Beer's claims about underpinning values of radical democracy, and the outcome is ungovernability. If these advocates of consensus are pessimistic about the effects of postmodernist culture, analysts of the left are pessimistic from their own characteristic point of view. Here the argument is that the earliest secular and realist narratives of working-class culture were essential in the formation of oppositional identity. Among these working-class narratives were the 'metanarratives' of Marxism and also of social democracy. If Lyotard is correct about the eclipse of the meta-narratives inherent in postmodern culture, [44] then the destruction of working-class identity must be imminent. As postmodernist spectacle replaces realist, narrative, mass culture would come to displace class culture. The upshot is not, as the neo-conservatives would have it, radical democracy, but instrumentalist individualism and mindless consumerism.

My own view is, much as I argued with respect to the new middle classes above, that postmodernist culture can cut either way in the working class. As analysts on the left have claimed, the old overarching and 'meta' collective identity has been in fact undermined. The result however has not always been 'possessive individualism', but the formation of more localized collective identities, based on the shopfloor or the community. As neo-conservatives claim, it is true that postmodernism has undermined authority. But social control can be effected either through coercion or ideology. If authority is undermined, and workers come to accept much the same values (consumerism, individualism, instrumentalism) as their employers and managers, then hierarchical authority is perhaps not needed for social control.

The postmodern cultural objects which have found the working class as an audience are, like all postmodernist objects, characterized by de-differentiation. Which way such objects are likely to cut, *ceteris paribus*, is perhaps primarily conditioned by what type of de-differentiation they foreground. If the differentiation between the cultural and the commercial is primarily transgressed, in for example most pop videos, then the effect is likely to be a politically conservative one. If on the other hand distinctions between superordinates and subordinates or between gender roles are challenged, the effect is likely to be rather an opposite one. In any event, if the 'grid' and 'group' of working-class identity is somehow destructured and loosened, then tolerance for other racial, ethnic, gender, and sexual identities on the part of working-class individuals is more likely, as well as perhaps willingness to work within an inevitably pluralist – if it is to prosper – left political culture.

THE CITY

There are several ways in which the city stands in relation to modernism/postmodernism. First, in writers such as Berman and Bell, the city or urbanization is taken as a cause of modernism; that is, the forced-pace development of the great metropolises from the end of the nineteenth century is something which makes modernism, as it were, happen. Second, in, for example, looking at differential modernisms in Paris, Vienna, and Berlin, the city is a space in which modernism happens. Third, change in the city is, so to speak, an effect of modernism, or modernism is something that happens to the city. It is in this last sense that it is possible to speak of modern and postmodern cities, or modernist and postmodernist characteristics of the city. In such discussion, modernism and postmodernism are not just qualities that characterize works of art and what clearly are cultural objects, but are qualities of cities too.

Is architecture, are cities, however, 'cultural objects'? They are in the sense that they can function as symbols. Architecture and cities cannot function as representations in the sense as do other cultural objects, in literature, the fine arts, film and music, or even TV series. That is, it makes little sense to speak of architecture or urban forms in terms of mimesis; they cannot be 'realist' in any meaningful sense of the word. Symbols, as distinct from representational cultural objects, do not partake of the famous semiotic triangle of signifier, signified, and referent, but only of signifier and signified. Symbols thus have meaning, but do not connect to referents. They have, so to speak, a purchase on meaning but not on reality. Thus the way which I treat postmodernist signification in other areas – that is, in which referents turn out to be signifiers (problematization of reality), or in which referents take the place of signifiers (problematization of the signifier) – do not seem to be applicable to architecture and the city.

Further, buildings and cities have a *material* side that is much more prominent than that of other cultural objects. That is, individuals stand in relation to a house or a city in a way as similar as they stand to a desk, a machine, a kitchen utensil, as that in which they stand to a painting, a film, or a pop song. The content of some objects such as films, paintings, books, magazines, and lectures and seminars in university, is primarily cultural. The content of other objects such as machines, barricades, kitchen utensils, is primarily material. In each type of these objects either the cultural or material is, so to speak, the 'regulating principle' of the object. In, say, films and paintings the cultural content is the regulating principle of its material form; while in machines and refrigerators the material content is the regulating principle of its cultural form. Architecture and cities stand right in the middle here at a point of remarkable ambiguity. That is, no writer on design, no matter how anti-Marxist, would argue that suitcases and machines are primarily cultural objects. And no writer on television and film, no matter how Marxist, and no matter how much he/she held claims for the economic determination of such objects, would argue that such objects were not somehow most prominently cultural. For analysts of architecture and cities, whether determination is either material or cultural, what primarily *qualifies* buildings and cities themselves is, and must be, left ambiguous.

Finally the built environment is different from other cultural objects in (1) not just the way it signifies and (2) its pronounced materiality, but in (3) where it stands in the 'cultural economy'. Buildings and cities do not circulate as do other cultural and material goods, but cultural and material goods circulate in cities and buildings. Note here that cultural objects enter into the 'cultural economy' by way of markets. And once they enter into this economy and market networks they take on new quality, i.e. they now also are 'goods'. But cities and buildings provide a space in which cultural and material goods circulate. They also of course provide a space in which people circulate. Cities and buildings are thus in fact neither cultural nor material objects. This is well reflected in the literature in urbanism, which is pretty much split right down the middle in terms of materialist and culturalist treatment.[45]

All this said, if we are to speak of the built environment as somehow modernist or postmodernist, then we are privileging *eo ipso* its cultural dimension, or the dimension in which it functions as symbol. We are also saying that the mode of spatial regulation in a city (or building complex) is structured by culture and mode of signification, rather than by the economy, and regime of accumulation. Now this is not at all necessarily my belief. I think it makes as much sense to speak of a 'post-Fordist' or 'disorganized capitalist' or late capitalist city as to speak of a modernist or postmodernist city. But in, for example, Chapter 8 what I shall be discussing is how regime of signification shapes spatial configurations. Hence I shall be operating from a model that is much more culturalist rather than from a materialist model, as seen in the work of David Harvey and Manuel Castells.[46] My own view is that cultural paradigms are themselves dependent on material factors, especially capital accumulation and class formation and fragmentation, but that these cultural factors, once established, play an important role in imparting structure to urban space.

It may well be, in this context, that there are two, and not one, contemporary challenges to modernist spatial configurations, both of which are arguably postmodernist. One of these focuses on the ornamental, on a sense of play, and uses historical quotations in its building styles. It is supremely individualistic and cares not for any concept of the city, but focuses on isolated works of architecture.[47] This first sort of spatial paradigm is conventionally called postmodern. The second type is not so conventionally labelled. Its model is not market regulation, but community regulation. One of its themes is the non-separation of work and leisure. Its urban vision is based on the Gothic labyrinth of the mediaeval city. It foregrounds a strong sense of locality. It has connections with the community-type architecture prescribed by Mumford and also Rossi, by Jane Jacobs, and by 'critical regionalism'.[48] Such an urban vision has at times been supported by the new social movements. It includes a heightened sense of the mix of ethnicity and diverse cultural groupings. It foregrounds also a sort of metaphysics of 'the street'.

To the extent that spatial paradigms are structured by culture or regimes of signification, we can speak of postmodern and modern spatial arrangements in not a far different sense than one speaks of Gothic or baroque or Ancient Greek urban space. In this sense the Gothic city is structured by a symbolism of a mystical Christianity. Its metaphor is the 'labyrinth'. It is composed of narrow winding streets, each, if we can ideal-typify, containing the living places and working places of masters, journeymen, and apprentices of a different craft guild; the guilds themselves held together materially through a network of mutual funds, and symbolically through patron saint, rituals, and the 'mysteries of the crafts'. On holidays the guilds would line up in a procession that would wind through these mediaeval streets, in which there never was a straight line of sight on the cathedral, until all of a sudden one would be in the cathedral square and the eye would be from close range overwhelmed by the very size, and then by the abstruseness and mysteries locked into its Gothic structure.[49]

In 'early modernity', first Renaissance and then baroque ideas began to spell the beginning of the end for the *Gemeinschaft* of the mediaeval labyrinth. What is striking is that a theory of spatial arrangement very similar to the vision of pictorial realism develops at the very outset of early modernity. Not only are the theories similar, but the theorist, Alberti, is the same. Leon Battista Alberti's architectural treatise *De re aedificatoria* followed his 1436 *On Painting* by about a decade and a half. In both treatises, Alberti, one of the great early humanists, advocated a secular and rationalistic world view. In painting, the painter was no longer to work from the Classical Greek or Christian principle of 'the ideal image in the painter's soul' but from the 'optical image in his eye'.[50]

In the built environment, Alberti wanted to put great modern boulevards right through the old cities. He endorsed the geometric arrangement of streets, of straight streets at right angles to one another to replace the mediaeval labyrinth. The idea for the modern to replace the labyrinth was taken up much later on a large scale by the baroque architects. The latter were active at the high point of the absolutist state. And their aim was to highlight kingly power. Hence long, wide, tree-lined streets (the lead up to St Peter's in Rome is the most oft-mentioned case) were laid out, leading up to huge, open squares, or piazzas, in the middle of which would be great cathedrals or palaces or later other public buildings (e.g. the ideas, only partly implemented by Christopher Wren in London, in St Paul's cathedral, though the typical absolutist vistas were impeded by the continued existence of the mediaeval street plan until about 1960).

This process of the extension of the geometrical principle on the ideas of the baroque, and bit-by-bit destruction of the mediaeval and later working-class labyrinth has proceeded through the centuries. Its final victory was the flurry of construction of boulevards which transmogrified western cities from the last decades of the nineteenth century, most famously along the Haussmann model in Paris, but also notably in Vienna, Berlin, New York (and its avenues). There were important differences, though, in this recent extension of this both baroque and rationalist principle: (1) the profit motive now was essential; (2) the aim was no longer to highlight monumental public buildings, but partly to improve the movement and circulation of traffic and pedestrians; focus was not on the building but on the street, or on the circulation in the streets; (3) streets and new boulevards became places to stroll on, on which different classes would see one another.[51]

But this entailed further destruction of the labyrinth, as Walter Benjamin noted. Benjamin observed that the old working-class, revolutionary districts of 1789, 1830, 1848, and the 1871 Commune, were being torn down, and workers were evicted who then had to move to suburbs.[52] The new boulevards – he and their designer Baron Haussmann observed – unlike the old winding streets, made it very difficult to block the movement of police and soldiers through the erection of barricades. Further, the boulevards facilitated the movement of the troops into the working-class districts in the case or urban insurrection. The boulevards led directly from the main railway stations, where troops would come into Paris from the provinces, to the working-class districts.

In fully-fledged architectural modernism, which does have links with and arises at about the same time as modernism in the novel, painting, and so on, this principle of rationality is extended from the city streets to the buildings themselves. Like modernist painting (and unlike realism), architectural modernism broke with historical styles, for principles of function and a sort of geometric rationality in building. It also used the latest materials – steel, concrete, glass. It began in department stores and factories and railway stations (bridges) in the first decade of the twentieth century, and was extended to most all types of buildings by the much more self-conscious modernist Bauhaus architects and their counterparts such as Corbusier. In its fully developed form it built council houses in Germany and the IIT complex in Chicago. It further helped speed the decline of the street and characteristic public spatial proportions of the mediaeval city. It, in its socialist or social-reformist refusal of urban working-class congestion, adopted the model of the English country house. It built thus on vast isolated green spaces with little or no connection to the urban fabric. The resultant alienating vast spaces were rarely used by the buildings' inhabitants.[53]

The aforementioned postmodernist critique throws down the gauntlet to all this. The cultural model which structured change both in early modernity and modernism was grounded in a process of *differentiation*. First, in the break with the mediaeval labyrinth in the differentiation of secular culture from religious culture. Not symbolism, but secular, rational principles governed the new street plans. Yet the symbolism remained in the historical reference of the buildings. Full modernism would only come here with the International Style, in which partly in the name of a greater universality, the break with history was made and architectural signifiers detached from any signifieds whatsoever, in the name of function and rationality itself. Architecture became a separate and 'auratic' realm with its creative 'author' and consistent structuring principle, along the lines of Adornian or Greenberg's aesthetic rationality. And architectural practice took on a Weberian *Eigengesetzlichkeit*. Postmodern architecture exemplifies de-differentiation in that (1) an 'auratic' style is replaced by a populist and playful one, (2) the consistent working through of the possibilities of a building material, such as glass, or concrete, or a principle is abandoned in favour of pastiche, (3) it is once again historical. But its historical references are as flimsy as the realism in Warhol's silk-screens. The referents that Warhol's silk-screens had purchase on are elusive and dissolve in a world of hype. The signified or meaning that postmodern architecture signifiers latch onto is similarly substanceless and dissolves into a vacuum of kitsch.

Let us call the first, conventional postmodernism 'mainstream' and the second, critique of the modern, 'oppositional'. The oppositional postmodern conception of space, mentioned above, works off another set of de-differentiations. It favours the challenge versus the 'auratic' conception of the architect in its much more craftsmanlike vision of buildings. It wants to supersede separation of work and leisure, of cultural and economic functions. It wants to overcome the separation of architecture from the community.

TOWARDS A POLITICAL ECONOMY

Thus it makes sense to speak of two types, one 'mainstream', the other 'oppositional', of postmodernism. Allow me for simplicity's sake grossly to schematize and ideal-typify. Each of the two foregrounds different types of de-differentiation. Mainstream postmodernism, or postmodernism No. 1, privileges, for instance, the implosion of the cultural and the commercial and the eclipse of the avant-garde. Postmodernism No. 2 will instead privilege the problematization of the real as image, in, for example, 'gender bending'. They have a divergent effect on identity. Postmodernism No. 1 (PM1) positions subjects in fixed places and fosters social hierarchies based on cultural objects functioning as status symbols and the principles of 'distinction'. Postmodernism No. 2 (PM2) fosters an open subject positioning and *eo ipso* the tolerance of a variety of other subject positions; cultural objects here function not to create invidious distinctions, but to construct collective identity on the non-hierarchical principle of 'difference'. Each connects with different outcomes concerning social class identity. PM1 furthers the hegemonic project of the new middle classes, while PM2 tends to foster different types of collective identity for the same members of these new middle classes around collective symbols and struggles in the new social movements. PM1 tends to promote the values of consumer capitalism inside the working class, while PM2 would tend to foster radical-democratic and decentralized worker resistance. Finally each fosters a different vision of the urban: PM1 along the lines of the individualist, ornamentalist, and historicist architecture of the new financial districts; PM2 for the reconstruction of community, street, and 'the labyrinth'.

As foreshadowed above, both PM1 and PM2 are opposite sides of a 'regime of signification' which articulate with a regime of capital accumulation. The new restructured regime of capital accumulation has been known variously as 'post-Fordism' or as 'disorganized capitalism'. Let me, in what is a culture studies book after all, use these terms interchangeably. The shift to post-Fordism (or the end of 'organized capitalism') entails a departure from mass production and mass consumption, the shift towards a service and information economy, working-class shrinkage and fragmentation; the fragmentation of opposition into decentralized social movements; the resurgence of individualism, albeit in Thatcherite/Reaganite form, and so on.[54]

Following the 'new institutional economics' of Oliver Williamson, Philippe Schmitter and Wolfgang Streeck have spoken of various 'modes of governance' of economic sectors. They have in specific spoken of 'state', 'corporatist', 'market', and 'community' modes of governance.[55] In part I would see the shift from the old regime of organized capitalism as a transition from statist and corporatist to market and community modes of governance. In terms of a mode of governance of urban space, mainstream postmodernism, or PM1, corresponds to market governance, and oppositional postmodernism to community governance. To speak of a transition from organized to 'disorganized' capitalism is to speak of processes (1) of restructuration and (2) of literal social disorganization. By the latter I mean that organized interests are now less coherently structured; that organization and what previously were more or less unified are now fragmented; that unifying ideologies on the left and ideological modes by which power legitimates itself have gone into crisis; and I mean the literal social disorganization of urban blight and violent rebellion by minority and marginal groups whether in Detroit, Liverpool's Toxteth, or Berlin's Kreuzberg.

This literal disorganization is the unacceptable face of the market mode of governance in the new regime of accumulation. It is no accident that the postmodernist urban landscape features, on the one side, the individualistic and ornamentalist and playful architecture of the new financial districts and, on the other, the urban blight and dystopia of *Blade Runner*, *Robocop*, and *Terminator*.

How then, in specific, does culture, and in particular postmodern culture, articulate with the economy in the new post-Fordist, or disorganized capitalist, era? I think it is less useful in this context to speak in terms of the base–superstructure notion of 'articulation' and instead consider culture as part and parcel *of* the economy. And here I am not speaking of the economy as some sort of model, or heuristic, as in Freud's 'libidinal economy' or the notions of 'cultural economy' that Bourdieu has used, and I have used above. I am instead speaking of the concrete and empirical economy. In this context a very general observation must be made to begin with. This is that the new regime of accumulation is becoming itself progressively more and more a regime of signification. That is, a greater and greater proportion of all goods produced comprises cultural goods. It is that the means of production are becoming increasingly cultural and that relations of production are becoming increasingly cultural. That is, relations of production are thus, not so often now mediated by material means of production, but are questions of discourse, of communications between management and employees, the latter illustrated in the large-scale use of 'quality circles' and 'team briefings' by managers in recent times.

This said, I want to limit myself in this introduction to a brief outline of items for which a political economy of postmodern culture must be able to account. In this it is convenient notionally to divide the economy into (1) a demand side, (2) a supply side, and (3) the goods which are the object of demand and supply.

Demand side

On the *demand* side, any political economy of postmodernism must be able to account for the following.

(a) *'Specialized consumption'* The shift to the post-Fordist regime of accumulation is one from mass production to flexible production and from mass consumption to specialized consumption.[56] The connections between economy and culture here can be understood notionally in, say, architecture – in which there is a sort of 'mass-ness', abstraction, and generality characteristic of modernist architecture, while postmodernist architecture breaks with this mass-ness for various sorts of particularisms – or in clothing styles. Consider for example a photo of British (soccer) football supporters in the interwar period. The similarity and 'mass-ness' of their dress is striking to the contemporary observer. Compare this, then, with the very diversity of clothing styles and associated subcultures among British working-class youth in more recent times. In both the cases of architecture and clothing the shift has not just been of one from mass-ness to specialization but also from a focus on function to a concern with style. In clothing, these characteristics in conjunction with the newer aesthetics of the shocking (and even the ugly) have justified the label of postmodern.

Specialized consumption is not only a matter of the psychic investment of consumers with style, or the symbolic. It is more than just a shift in concern towards 'sign-value'. It is also a question of the development of demand for more specialized use-values. Hence, for instance, certain developments in microcomputing allow employees to be able to work from home. This is also true in terms of shifting demands for welfare services. Part and parcel of the post-Fordist shift from mass to specialized consumption takes the form of the challenges posed to the welfare state. Here challenges from both right and left to the generality, and mass-ness of welfare bureaucracies are challenges that proffer a model of specialized consumption.[57] In parallel to the above discussion of mainstream versus oppositional postmodernism, what are posed here are on the one hand individualist and on the other community forms of consumption. Both of these forms of specialized welfare consumption operate more or less via markets. That is, both challenge centralized and bureaucratic planning of the production of welfare services. The difference is that the individualist form operates from commodified markets while the community form of governance is based on what may be 'decommodified' markets. The individualist critique does not imply a reduction in the quantity of supply of welfare service, but it does entail a redistribution in the ability to consume such services to the upper economic strata. The community governance model assumes that supply will not be determined by ability to pay but by socially defined need. This may still mean the shift from a bureaucratic to a market model, but it does not assume the extension of capitalist relations or commodification. Socially defined need in the community mode of governance could be determined by decentralized groups of welfare recipients (pensioners, single mothers, minorities), themselves with specialized needs.[58]

(b) *Demand overloads* Postmodernist culture, we have just noted, encourages the consumption of goods as 'sign-values' rather than use-values. If the consumption of use-values implies that there is at some point coherent limits to the level of consumer demands, the consumption of sign-values does not.[59] If goods function primarily as symbols, and individuals use them to establish invidious distinctions between themselves and other

40

individuals, then there are in principle no limits to consumer demand. This is partly what Fred Hirsch was referring to when he spoke of 'positional consumption'. Traditionally, Hirsch notes, only a small elite engaged in positional consumption, while the mass of individuals in a society consumed use-values on a more or less subsistence level. In the past, then, positional consumption would have had little or no effect on macroeconomic indicators. More recently, however, he argued, the masses themselves have come to engage in positional consumption, creating an overload of demands, which themselves lead to high budget deficits, balance of trade problems, and inflation, followed by bouts of unemployment.[60] Others such as Daniel Bell and Samuel Beer have suggested that what we have referred to here as postmodern culture encourages consumerism as a general set of values, hence leading to an economy and state overloaded by demands. There is an initial implausibility about this demand overload thesis. The neo-conservative analysts, including Bell, Beer, and above all Samuel Huntington, who have formulated it, have primarily been concerned by the putative overloads imposed by welfare recipients on the state budget, and by trade union wage demands. It is probably, especially in the late 1980s, with the decimation of trade unions and cuts that individual recipients have received in welfare benefits, that it is the middle and upper income groups who are most responsible for such demand overloads. But the connection between reception of postmodern culture and overheated consumer values can only be demonstrated by empirical research, taking the individual as the unit of analysis.

(c) *Consumption and collective identity*   For Charles Sabel and Michael Piore, the 'motor' of transition to the new regime of accumulation is specialized consumption. That is, for them it is shifts in taste and thus consumption that lead to the spread of flexible production methods, which itself leads to qualitative changes in labour relations, and so on. If all follows then from the advent of specialized consumption, the question is then what is the cause of specialized consumption? The cause as in Weber's spirit of capitalism is in all likelihood cultural, and has to do with the individual and collective identities of emergent and receding social groupings. The new 'disorganized' capitalist conditions of accumulation bring with them a largely modified class structure with a largely modified set of collective and individual identities. And this will produce new demand patterns, for both material and cultural goods.

Supply side

Now shifting over to the *'supply* side', any political economy of postmodernism must be able to account for the following.

(a) *Problematization of the work ethic* Neo-conservative ana-lysts such as Bell and Christopher Lasch[61] have suggested that the therapeutic morality and the encouragement of indiscipline inherent in contemporary culture undermine the sense of respon-sibility that was grounded in earlier religion-based or secular-rationalist-based cultural paradigms. And that this in turn has contributed to a crisis in the work ethic. This absence of sufficient production is the other side of demand overloads, resulting in Bell's famous 'cultural contradictions of capitalism'. This problem area has partly receded from popular controversy, given the apparent low inflation post-Fordist recovery of ad-vanced capitalist nations, accompanied by the displacement of the stereotyped narcissist by the equally typed workaholic Yuppie, and the narcissist's polymorphous sexuality by the iconographic abstinence and familism of the late 1980s post-AIDS imagery. Yet the problem of the connections between culture and the work ethic remain unsolved. And the clichéd figure of the Yuppie brings us no further. Does not his/her workaholism, in the stereotype, structure itself around consumer-ism and brutal careerism rather than moral responsibility and any possible vision of work as redemption? The Anglo-American literature on the culture of work has fundamental issues. Such issues have, on the other hand, become topics of heated debate in Germany – for example the delinkage of work ethic from labour markets and community versus individualist regulation of work.[62]

(b) *The decline of meaning* Postmodern culture has often been understood as having its effectivity not via meaning but via *impact* on its audience. This can be understood via an economic model. Meaning is only achieved by the connection of signifieds to signifiers. If there is an oversupply of such signifiers – as there appears to be in today's constant bombardment of images and sounds – and only a finite number of signifieds to go round, then large numbers of signifiers will persist with no meanings attached, and be literally experienced as such. In this, one does not purchase on any sort of market the signifiers – from billboards, ghetto blasters, TV sets, etc. – that bring on this oversupply. They are perhaps mediated by commodities one purchases on markets, but the signifiers themselves are in fact more part of the 'built environment' than of markets. On the contrary when one purchases, unmediatedly, a cultural experience – or a set of signifiers – for example, cinema tickets, or the entry price to an art gallery, or buys a novel or book of poetry, or tickets to a classical or pop concert, then one enters, so to speak, an artificially isolated environment in which one precisely will not be subject to such sensory overloads from external sources. This latter type of cultural consumption is the consumption of cultural services. But increasingly, we purchase or rent material commodities such as TVs, video recorders, compact disc players, video and audio tapes which themselves produce these cultural services. We are, in the realm of culture too, becoming what Jonathan Gershuny has called a 'self-service' economy. With this transition from services to self-service the contemporary overload of signifiers results.[63]

(c) *Culture as an economic sector*   To what extent can culture be considered as an economic sector? How significant is this sector in contemporary political economies? To what extent and in what proportion are the signifiers produced in this sector 'postmodern'? I think we can speak of a cultural sector in today's political economies. In this sector, entities (goods or services) which are primarily cultural, as distinct from primarily material, are produced. The difference between cultural and material goods (I want to use the word 'cultural goods' here as Bourdieu uses it, to include both goods and services) is simple to explain. Both cultural and material goods possess both use-values and sign-values. In material goods, the use-value lies in the material properties of the good, and the sign-value in its signifying properties. In cultural goods both use-value and sign-value are

43

inherent in the object's signifying properties. The signifiers in cultural goods, we shall see, can be either (1) representations or (2) symbols or (3) information.

The main branches in the cultural sector are: (1) education, (2) audio-visual, (3) publishing, (4) tourism, and (5) advertising. All of these branches have a turnover which matches those of significant industrial branches. The 'sales figure' of education would be the annual expenditure of institutions of higher, secondary, and primary education. The education sector produces signifiers which primarily are those, not of *representation* or symbolism, but *information*. Audio-visual would include (a) the annual income and expenditure of TV stations, (b) total annual revenue of film production and distribution, including revenue from videos, (c) music – revenue from sales of records, compact discs, audio and video tapes, and concerts. The signifiers in this sector are primarily representations, except in TV, which carries a high proportion of information.

Publishing would include books, newspapers, and magazines, and all revenue from these sources. In this sector signifiers would function primarily as information, though in fiction and poetry they would be representation. Pleasure in tourism is obtained progressively more and more through culture. Fun parks and pleasure beaches are becoming displaced by or converted into 'theme parks'.[64] Increasingly, better-educated tourists gain pleasure from the flavours of local culture rather than merely from sun and sand. The whole of the booming museum trade would come under the branch of tourism. Culture consumption in tourism would be primarily of symbols, not of representations or information.

Culture as a sector has an enormous multiplier effect in especially the electronics industry and the building trades. Whether the manufacture of TV sets, video recorders, stereo equipment, etc., should come under the culture sector is a matter of debate.

Cultural goods and commodification

Finally, regarding cultural goods themselves, any political economy of culture, and in particular postmodern culture, must be able to account for the following.

(a) *The different types of cultural good; representation/ symbol/information*   As mentioned above, the main distinction between representation and symbol is that the former points somehow more or less to a referent, while symbols can never refer to reality but only to a meaning or a signified. Hence clothing styles and architecture are symbolic but are not representations; i.e. they cannot refer to reality. Information, it might be argued, is carried by representations. But information is for immediate use in the sense that representations are not. Telephones, computers, fax machines, telex, teaching, TV news and newspapers, and most nonfiction books consist of signifiers whose primary function is to carry information. Pop songs, soap operas, films, paintings, plays, novels, and theories in the sciences and social sciences consist on the other hand of representations. The differences are: (1) information is much more directly for use than representations – people will act immediately on information, which they won't typically do on the basis of 'representations'; (2) representations have a relationship to reality which is in principle understood as a better or worse fit and can be contested. They are self-consciously, as it were, mimetic in a sense that information is not self-consciously mimetic. When representations are false they somehow are deficient in mimesis. When information is false, it consists of lies. Representations are, in brief, aesthetic 'utterances', while information consists of descriptive utterances. Though neither representations nor information, significantly, is grounded in Habermas's sense in the argumentation mode of discourse.

(b) *Cultural objects as commodities*   First in this context 'commodification' must be addressed. It would be wrong to think of the history of the past few centuries just in terms of commodification. A countervailing process of decommodification has also been going on – perhaps most importantly with the rise of the welfare state, but also in culture in, for example, romanticism. Romanticism and trends within modernism come closest of all to Benjamin's notion of 'aura'. Postmodernism, or at least one side of it, e.g. Pop Art, the architecture of the new financial districts, seems to represent a recommodification of the aesthetic sphere, in that there is an at best ambiguous and ironic stance taken towards the commodity. The left critique of the bureaucratic welfare state still would endorse decommodification, while the right critique would advocate the commodification of welfare services. But the left, decentralized critique might be comprehensible as I indicated above, in terms of 'decommodified markets'. The real question here is: Is the concept of decommodified markets a contradiction in terms? Claus Offe would imply so. In his analysis of work he speaks of two 'allocation problems': the allocation of labour power to tasks and that of resources to individuals possessing labour power. His view is not only that neither of these should be commodified, but that both should take place as much as possible outside of the market.[65] Should this be the same for the allocation of social services? Are there non-market mechanisms that will produce need-responsive and decentralized allocation? In principle there can be: for example, the mediaeval guilds[66] and their corporate bound mutual funds. Can these sorts of bodies constitute 'mini-public spheres' in contemporary civil society? But in contemporary societies there are a host of problems with the distribution of welfare services via a guild model: for example, the centralized training of social workers. In the mediaeval model, supply and demand were geographically side by side, so there was no need for a mechanism of allocation. In advanced capitalism a mechanism of allocation is necessary. If not a centralized bureaucracy and if not the market, what then?

Cultural markets, however, would work a lot differently than the markets which distribute social services. They are partly a means of getting what was previously auratic, and only available to elites, out to the broader sections of the population. In important ways cultural markets resemble – more closely than the market for welfare services – the markets for consumer commodities such as cars, TV sets, and clothing: i.e. in which needs, unlike in social services, are *not* in the same way collectively defined.

At stake here is commodification and cultural objects. And it must be realized that commodities and markets are not necessarily the same thing. For Marx a commodity possesses a number of characteristics. Perhaps key is that commodities are entities that possess exchange-value. This means that they are sold on the market. Labour power, means of production, and objects produced are not commodities in pre-capitalist societies. Before capitalism these entities possess only use-value. Later in capitalism, means and objects of production come also to possess value and exchange value; further, labour power comes to possess exchange-value. For Marx, exchange-value is quantitative unlike use-value which is only qualitative. *Value* is also quantitative and is the amount of 'congealed homogeneous labour-time' in a commodity. For Marx, value as 'abstract labour-time' is the 'social substance' of the commodity.[67] In places in which there is no such social construct as abstract labour-time, goods or the products of labour do not have value (but only use-value) and are hence not commodities. Marx says that 'value' (i.e. abstract homogeneous labour) is the 'common factor in the exchange relation'. 'Exchange-value', on the other hand, is 'the necessary mode of expression, or form of appearance, of value'. The value in a product of labour stands in relation to its exchange-value much as the use-value of the labour incorporated into the product stands to the use-value of the product to its user. All products of labour have thus a complex nature – the use-value of the labour they contain plus the use-value they are to its consumer, and the value of the labour they contain plus the exchange-value they have from the point of view of the consumer.

Hence the commodity for Marx has not a 'two-fold nature', but a four-fold nature. They have two 'supply side' characteristics – (1) value and (2) the use-value of the labour power they contain – and two 'demand side' characteristics – (1) exchange-value and (2) the use-value to the consumer. Marx begins the first chapter of *Capital*, entitled 'The Commodity', with discussion of the 'supply-side' characteristics in particular in the section on 'The Dual Character of the Labour Embodied in Commodities'. Then he shifts to an extended discussion of the 'demand-side' of exchange value. And he concludes the chapter by attempting more or less successfully to bring it all together in the well-known section on commodity fetishism. In this, one of the commodity's four characteristics, exchange-value, is somehow reified and takes on powers which suppress its three other characteristics. At the same time the exchange-value of the commodity suppresses much that is human in work and in social interaction more generally.

47

Thus, to speak of commodification, is to speak of the sphere of consumption rather than the sphere of production. But, for Marx and in the present context, the sphere of production is also important. The 'auratic' work of art is somehow primarily a use-value from the point of view of labour, in that the labour gone into it is concrete, particular, and distantiated from markets, while the non-auratic work of art from the point of view of production is primarily an embodiment of value, of abstract, homogeneous labour-time. It *does* then make sense to speak of commodification from the production as well as from the consumption side. Benjamin of course speaks in effect of commodification from the supply-side in his discussion of mechanical reproduction.[68] For him, one and the same work of art can entail auratic production and mechanical (or electronic) *re*production.

From the consumption-side, commodification comes from a concern of the consumer not with the concrete and specific use-value of a product, but with the price that a product will fetch on the market, i.e. with its exchange-value, an abstract and general quality. Commodification also entails that the consumer is qualified to consume a given product because of his/her ability to pay. The 'sign-value' of a product is yet again something else and not necessarily related to commodification. Products have sign-value also in precapitalist societies as well as in contemporary consumer capitalism.

Commodification also means, as Marx underlined in the section on commodity fetishism, the power of things over people and the importance attributed to commodities in capitalism as opposed to human beings. This power is mostly due to the qualities that products possess as exchange value. Exchange-value, unlike Marxian use-value, is also a social construction.

The commodity is thus an *ideal-type*. In its pure form it has a set of production- and a set of consumption-side characteristics. It is difficult, empirically, to find products of labour which are purely commodities. For example if a product is acquired less for its exchange-value than for its use-value or 'sign-value' then it is not in any sense fully a commodity. Think for example of a painting which may be purchased for a combination of these three factors. Or even privately purchased welfare services like health care or education. Though commodities in the sense of the consumer's ability to pay, they are not commodities in the sense that they are above all consumed even by the rich primarily as use-values. To the extent, for example, that houses are purchased with an eye to re-sale, they are purchased as exchange-values; otherwise they serve both as use-values and sign-values. All these are, of course, matters empirically to be determined. Thus it makes sense to speak of goods and services as being more or less commodified, rather than as commodities or non-commodities full stop.

It is still useful to speak of commodification and de-commodification as goods take on more or relatively fewer characteristics of the commodity ideal-type. Commodification, given this, is a process which begins in the sphere of exchange, with the exchange first of consumption goods and then means of production, of first luxury goods and then necessities on the market. Finally, labour power itself takes on an exchange value and becomes what Marx called 'variable capital'. The trend is for commodification to pervade the sphere of exchange before it enters that of production, as mechanical and then electronic production techniques increasingly render abstract, first through deskilling and then through reskilling, the 'supply side' of the commodity.

The process of commodification is probably more complex in the sphere of *reproduction* than it is either in that of production or exchange. Labour-power is reproduced through the consumption of material and cultural products. In terms of reproduction through consumption of material products, a general process of commodification takes place, affecting the working class only on a large scale with the advent of mass production. Of material, as distinct from cultural, products only welfare payments and services are more complex to analyse. It has been argued that the development of the welfare state is a process of decommodification. But this is not the case. The four main welfare payment and service categories – unemployment insurance, pensions, public provision for health care, and supplementary benefit (to 'dependent children' and the long-term unemployed) – had never, prior to the welfare state, been on any important scale commodified. They were regulated by guilds, parishes, families, and charitable organizations. There has more recently been a process of welfare commodification going on. And surely decommodification is now an important objective for the Left. But there was never any original 'commodified' state of affairs before the development of the welfare state.

Let us then consider the reproduction of labour power through the consumption of cultural goods. The two key categories in this are education (including training) and leisure. The development of public education was also not a process of decommodification. Education and training had never been commodified, but had come under the *gemeinschaftlich* and traditional auspices of guilds and craft organizations, the family, the parish church, etc. In the past decade or so there has of course been a movement towards commodification. How about leisure? First, a lot of so-called leisure time is devoted to non-market forms of production. Most important here is housework and childrearing. But also the skilled work involved in repairing automobiles, pointing the outside of one's house, etc. Or putting together a local pop band, or an amateur theatre production, or a local football or basketball team. Some of these activities can be 'hired out' via the market. That we include them somehow in the sphere of 'leisure' rather than the sphere of production is an indicator of how commodified our very notion of leisure is. And our notion of work.

Where has commodification, in any event, been making advances in the sphere of 'leisure'? Not so terribly importantly in, for instance, childrearing, except perhaps in-so-far as we begin to follow the abstract norms of the manuals of the Spocks and others in our childrearing practices. The best clue here might be to return to our discussion above of culture as an economic sector, and in particular the audio-visual, publishing, and tourism industries. In these there has surely been a commodification of consumption. The narratives and information we consume, the melodies and songs we hear, and the images we see come in increasingly commodified form, we buy package tours from companies that specialize in these, and book our flights with specialized agencies, and so on.

Commodification, by some accounts, penetrated high and popular culture at about the same time, towards the end of the nineteenth century. At this point took place the end of the patron system in painting. But much of the shift here, in painting and music, was towards, not a market, but a *state* mode of governance. The 'abstract rationality' of market and state in this context 'colonized' *high* culture (even the old patronage system in painting had substantial market elements) well before it colonized the culture of the masses. When commodification penetrated mass culture towards the end of the nineteenth century – in music halls, popular spectator sports, the fish and chip shop in England, vaudeville, etc. – this was the birth of popular culture itself. Commodification of mass culture is in effect three simultaneously occurring processes:

(1) the creation of a specifically working-class (as distinct from artisan or peasant) culture,
(2) the shift from 'folk culture' to popular culture,
(3) the commodification of the culture of non-elite groups.

Thus commodification is importantly present in both the origins of (1) modernism and (2) popular culture, both beginning in the last half of the nineteenth century. In the origins of high modernism, the bohemian painter or poet was in part reacting to the decline of the patron system and its displacement by the market, and in doing so producing consciously an 'auratic' work of art whose method was directed against the commodity form. Among the masses commodity and culture were much more closely integrated.

Does, however, the culture that the masses consume become progressively more commodified? The place of television is central here. To buy a TV set is to enter into commodity exchange, but the impact of TV is rather another matter. That is, there are few commodities which cost so little and which users get so much (at least quantitative) use from. If our leisure is spent more than anywhere else in front of the 'telly' then is this commodified consumption? Not necessarily; TV is only a medium. What we watch through it can be more or less commodified. All TV shows are commodified, in the sense that they are mass distributed. But their production can be more or less craftsmanlike, or, as it were, 'auratic'. So can their content. Surely to watch Bergman's *Seventh Seal* on TV, or a nature show, or a documentary on women in Algeria is not the commodified consumption that is the viewing of *Miami Vice* or *Dallas*, or a succession of MTV pop videos. It can however be argued that what we are exposed to on TV is *increasingly* commodified. But even in this context the most fascinating development is, with the spread of higher education, the use of privatized TV – the paradigm example is Britain's Channel 4 – for the *market* distribution of *non*-commodified images.

But is the consumption of images on *Miami Vice* and on MTV reducible to the consumption of commodities? This question is much the same as asking if postmodernist de-differentiation is the same as the process of intensive commodification of culture in contemporary societies. The immediate answer that can be given is no. After all, commodified cultural objects can foreground differentiated signification just as well as they can foreground the 'spectacle' of de-differentiated signification. Then let us ask a more nuanced question. Is there something implicit in the logic of commodification of culture which at a certain point produces a mass culture of the image, of spectacle, that can be called postmodern? This is a serious question indeed. This is presumably the sort of mass culture, with its commercialization, its advertising, etc., which is evoked by Adorno's postwar critique and became central to 'mass culture' theory in general.[69] Baudrillard operates from a not dissimilar model, in which commodity and image are both 'simulacra', but in which the image is a 'higher order' simulacrum than the commodity. The Adornian critique also implicates high culture. Similarly postmodernization in large measure represents the triumph of commodification not just in mass culture but in the previously auratic, and potentially critical, culture of elites.

This position, which identifies postmodernization with commodification, must be taken very seriously indeed. But with the provisos that: (1) the postmodern culture of the image and spectacle must be seen not so much as a *continuation* of commodification, but as a different 'order' of commodification; (2) commodification is one among several processes of de-differentiation in postmodern culture; (3) there are progressive and reactionary versions of postmodernism.

Part One

POSTMODERNISM
AND SOCIAL THEORY

Chapter Two

GENEALOGY AND THE BODY: FOUCAULT/DELEUZE/ NIETZSCHE[1]

INTRODUCTION

Anglo-American commentators in the human sciences have for some time now taken Michel Foucault at his word, that he has been, as archaeologist and as genealogist, most fundamentally a Nietzschean. It is as a genealogist, In *Madness and Civilization, Discipline and Punish,* and *The History of Sexuality,* that Foucault has had the greatest impact. But what *is* genealogy? The problem is of the utmost import. Genealogy cannot only potentially serve for sociology, taken in its very broadest sense, as a method. It has not only, as Habermas (1981) has noted with some vexation, provided a theoretical counterpart to 'postmodernist' developments in the arts. It has, moreover and most of all, been understood by its main proponents to be a possible successor to Marxism as a doctrinal basis for the multiplicity of 'micro-struggles' in today's fragmented capitalism.

Genealogy patently, all are agreed, concerns knowledge; it concerns power; it concerns probably above all the body. But there are two central shortcomings in the otherwise very useful work of the growing legions of Foucault commentators and exegetes (e.g. Sheridan 1980; Dreyfus and Rabinow 1982; Racevskis 1983). We are given first and foremost to understand that only Foucault among contemporary French analysts in the human sciences is a genealogist. Gilles Deleuze, we shall see below, can justifiably claim equal status as a genealogist with Foucault; the works of the one are inextricable from, indeed inconceivable without, the works of the other. Yet the now standard and highest-quality commentary on Foucault (Dreyfus and Rabinow 1982) mentions the name of

Deleuze only once, and at that only *en passant*. Moreover, the oeuvre of Nietzsche is, in most of the secondary literature, given insufficient consideration for questions of genealogical method.

The task of this essay is to develop a notion of the body in broadly (not just Foucaultian) genealogical framework. The means towards this end, and subsidiary aims of the essay, are several. They are: to provide a more critical understanding of Foucault through a consideration of Deleuze's influence; to begin to flesh out a broader concept of 'agency' in genealogy, through the systematic scrutiny of the notions of 'desire' and the body in Deleuze and Guattari's *Anti-Oedipus*; to present a consistent and in-depth account of Nietzsche's consideration of the body, which I shall argue below are at the same time functionalist and heavily privilege action over structure.

FOUCAULT: THE BODY AS PASSIVE

(i) *Pessimism, Classical and Modern*

Foucault's chronology of history, which puts at centre stage the transition from the 'Classical' to the Modern, revolves mainly around two different modes through which discourse acts upon the body. In the Classical period, heralded by Descartes and absolutism, when souls and discourse are separate from bodies, knowledge relates to bodies from the outside, through represen-tation and direct repression. The point of entry to the Modern was provided by the French Revolution, the usher was Sade. We Moderns have witnessed the cementing of souls back onto bodies; the breaking of discourse with representation to enter bodies themselves; the constitution, individuation, and normalization of bodies; the recruiting and drilling of bodies, acting through incarnate souls, in the interests of the reproduction of society.

In *Madness and Civilisation*, whose orginal Plon edition was entitled *Folie et déraison* (1961), reason and unreason were separated during absolutism; that is, at a point in time when words were disengaging from the sensuous, the bodies of madmen were enclosed and separated from the light of reason. Modernity, in contrast, saw the dawn of the psychiatric hospital, whereby discourse, operating via families and 'bad conscience', began to normalize and mobilize the bodies of the mad. In *Birth of the Clinic* (1963), *Classical* medical texts were entrenched in the philosophy of representation, and inferences about organisms were deductive; the study of anatomy was king, as words referred to parts of the body; the light of the medical gaze itself ended at the surface of bodies, whose shadowy interior remained unknown and unknowable. *Modernity* witnessed the advent of the clinic, the disappearance of the signifier, as doctors came to know the body and its organs as 'in-themselves'. Corporeal penetration through physiology meant that experimentation replaced deduction and that bodies were to be regulated, their interior movements made calculable.

In *The Order of Things* (1966), whose French title literally translates as *Words and Things*, bodies disappeared altogether, but Foucault's Classical episteme circumscribed a two-world conception of words, ideas, and the subject, on the one hand, and things, which were understood as real and material, on the other. In the 'sciences of man' in the Modern episteme, there is no longer a clear hegemony of words over things. Now what is broadly conceived along the lines of the body (or the material) is at the centre of discourse, quintessentially in Marx and in Freud, while the cogito has retreated towards the periphery. *Discipline and Punish* (1975), Foucault's first full-length text in a genealogical framework, has a quite pronounced focus on the body. While Foucault was writing the book, his series of lectures given at the Collège de France was entitled *La volonté de savoir*, the will to knowledge, which was also to be the title of the French edition of *The History of Sexuality*. Nietzsche often spoke of a will to knowledge, but, as we shall see below, one which is functional for the prosperity of individual bodies. Foucault, in his genealogical text on punishment and sex, speaks almost only of a will to knowledge which disintegrates bodies while reproducing the social. In *Discipline and Punish*, which drew most directly on *The Genealogy of Morals*, Foucault used to great advantage Nietzsche's concept of 'memory'. Here punishment and discipline, through a sort of socialization process, create a 'memory' for offenders and for society in general. This memory, which exists at the level of the unconscious, is at the same time an agent of social control, and functions in the interests of social reproduction. In Foucault's narrative, memories were engraved directly on bodies in the seventeenth and eighteenth centuries through the ghastliest and cruellest rituals; through a 'mnemo-nics of pain', which functioned as spectacle for the audience and towards the reproduction of absolutist rule. From the nineteenth century as the Word loses its dominance over things, power is no longer separated from the social field. Previously, penal practices affected the body directly and negatively in the reproduction of a power which was transcendent in relation to the social. Now penal discourse reproduces a power which is immanent in society; for this purpose it individuates, normalizes, and mobilizes human bodies; it operates on bodies not through direct physical cruelty, but via a gaze that has its effects on the soul, via the 'bad conscience' which is attached to bodies.

If Classical punishment consisted of the physical engraving of a memory directly on bodies, in Modern punishment it is discourse which creates such a memory. Thus the applied sciences of Man (penology, psychiatry) and the 'pure' sciences of Man (psychoanalysis, economics), which characterize Modernity, function as structures in the engraving of memory. In opposition to 'memory' and to 'discourse' Foucault has proposed the con-struction of a 'counter-memory', of a 'non-discursive language'. Most of Foucault's discussion in this context concerns how literature can serve as a non-discursive critique of the often oppressive rationalities of discourse in the human sciences. But there is evidence that Foucault has intended such non-discursive language (he seems to view his own work under this heading) to be part and parcel of everyday life. If the discourse of the social sciences has made possible the subjection of the body in a number of institutional settings, then non-discursive language can help create a counter-memory as a resource for resistance to such subjugation (cf. Bouchard 1977, pp. 8-9; Foucault 1964).

Nonetheless in the corpus of Foucault's work, in each case and in each period, bodies are acted *upon* in discursively-constituted institutional settings. Resistances are rarely constructed, strug-gles are not engaged. This bodily passivity, this pessimistic vision of agency, is perhaps even more pervasive than elsewhere in *The History of Sexuality*. In his demolition of the 'repressive hypothesis', Foucault shows that sexuality has never been more the object of discourse than in Modernity, and that the function of discourse on sexuality from the early nineteenth century through Freud and Lacan, has been to normalize and recruit bodies and thus to facilitate social reproduction. Previously, we shall see below, Foucault worked closely with Deleuze; now he attacks even him and views 'desire' as part and parcel of Modern discourse (Foucault 1980a, pp. 81–90). Barthes in *The Pleasure of the Text* (1975) celebrated '*jouissance*' which he defined in terms of the *absence* of 'desire'. Foucault likewise argues against *scientia sexualis*, and for an *ars erotica* based on an amorphous, unstructured body, from which desire is excluded. Deleuze's 'desire' is conceived along the lines of Nietzsche's 'will to power'. To argue as Foucault does that 'desire' is a servant of power, is effectively to break with Nietzsche. More important it is to endorse a cipher-like delibidinized vision of agency that would be incapable of constructing resistances, incapable of mobilizing resources.

(ii) *A Genealogy of Bodies*

'Nietzsche, Genealogy, History', observe Bouchard (1977, p. 22) and Dreyfus and Rabinow (1982, pp. 106–14), is perhaps Foucault's key methodological essay after his break with archaeology. In it he underlines Nietzsche's opposition to any idea of 'origins', and instead emphasizes that genealogy is a question of two processes – of 'descent' (*Herkunft*) and 'emergence' (*Entstehung*). It is under the category of descent that Foucault begins to introduce systematically a notion of the body. *Herkunft* is here the equivalent of 'stock'; 'it is the ancient affiliation to a group sustained by the bonds of blood, tradition, or social class' (Foucault 1977c, p. 145). Equally, 'descent attaches itself to the body' (Foucault 1977c, p. 147). When Foucault thus mentions 'stock' and 'blood' he should be taken *à la lettre*. He writes, 'the analysis of *Herkunft* often involves a consideration of race or social type'; in developing the idea of a 'double soul', nineteenth-century 'Germans . . . were simply trying to master the racial disorder from which they had formed themselves' (Foucault 1977c, p. 145).

Violence is not done to our common-sense notion of genealogy, whether we conceive of 'descent' in terms of a genealogy of morals, of things, or of attributes. Descombes's (1980, p. 157) definition, as a search for antecedents, 'with an eye to establishing the baseness or nobility of lineage', could refer to any of these entities. Nietzsche (1956b, p. 210; 1966, p. 818) seems to lend credence to such an unfocused conceptualization when he, for example, writes, 'Thus the whole history of a thing, an organ, a custom becomes a continuous chain of reinterpretations and rearrangements, which need not be causally connected among themselves, which may simply follow one another'. But Foucault's idea of 'descent' suggests not a genealogy of morals but a genealogy of *bodies*. This itself is a perfectly justifiable, indeed very insightful, conception. The problem is that it draws on only a selection of Nietzsche's writings which offer a very partial treatment of the body. Foucault is in particular overly dependent on *The Genealogy of Morals*. Here, for example, in speaking of the value distortion and resentment which the ascetic priest arouses in his suffering followers, Nietzsche explains, 'the wish to alleviate pain through strong emotional excitement is, to my mind, the true physiological motive behind all manifestations of resentment'. And further, 'sinfulness is not a basic human condition but merely the ethico-religious interpretation of physiological distemper'. For Nietzsche (1956b, pp. 263–5; 1966, pp. 867–70) such a physiological 'cause may lie in an affection of the sympathetic nerve, or an excessive secretion of bile, or a deficiency of alkaline sulphates and phosphates in the blood'. Morals and psychology may be explained then by an understanding of the body or physiology.

This is not the fully-formed, both functional and activist Nietzschean theory of the body which we will explicate below. But the body here, if not a conscious actor, is at least a *causal* agent. Curiously enough, however, Foucault reads even this partial theory (which is the only theory of the body enunciated in *The Genealogy of Morals*, and the theory which is associated with 'descent') in a rather backwards manner, whereby cause largely becomes effect and the body becomes passive. For Foucault thus (1977c, p. 148), 'the body is . . . a volume in perpetual disintegration. Genealogy, as an analysis of descent, is thus situated within the articulation of body and history. Its task is to expose a body totally imprinted by history and the process of history's destruction of the body.' And, 'The body is moulded by a great many distinct regimes; it is broken down by the rhythms of work, rest and holidays; it is poisoned by food or values, through eating habits or moral laws; it constructs resistances'

(Foucault 1977c, p. 153). We are then provided by Foucault with a body largely deprived of causal powers.

(iii) *Foucault and Deleuze*

It is well known that May–June 1968 fuelled Foucault's adoption of genealogy in the place of archaeology. Three central 'methodological' essays prepared the way for the new approach which was first put into practice in *Discipline and Punish*. Two were written in 1970. One of these was *L'ordre du discours*, his inaugural lecture at the Collège de France. In this, after outlining a relatively archaeological definition of discourse, Foucault adumbrates the 'rules of exclusion' from discourse in a Nietzschean context (cf. e.g. Major-Poetzl 1983). He then continues almost literally to equate discourse and slave moralities, observing that the birth of discourse took place as Socratic philosophers replaced Pre-Socrates poets (Foucault 1971, pp. 16–17). The other benchmark article of 1970 is 'Theatrum Philosophicum' and is a review of two of Deleuze's books, *Logique du sens* (1969) and *Différence et répétition* (1968). It is here that Foucault (1977d, p. 165) famously commented, 'perhaps one day this century will be known as Deleuzian' and spoke of Deleuze as proceeding 'with the patience of a Nietzschean genealogist' (Foucault 1977d, p. 181). The third essay was 'Nietzsche, Genealogy, History' published in 1971, and was, we shall see below, as much influenced by Deleuze's writings as through Nietzsche's concept of 'descent'. During the period between the publication of *The Archaeology of Knowledge* (1969) and *Surveillir et punir* (1975), Foucault's only other publications of any scale, that looked forward to his genealogical writings, were the 'Presentation' and 'Les meurtres qu'on raconte' in *Moi, Pierre Rivière*, which were not methodological essays. The remainder of his output of this period – on Cuvier, Bachelard, a response to Derrida, the essay 'What is an Author?' – treated topics central to his books of the 1960s.

There is a good bit of further evidence of the centrality of Deleuze's influence. In *The Order of Things* (1966), Nietzsche and Mallarmé are treated as a sort of epiphany of postmodernity and counter-memory; this echoed resemblance noted by Deleuze in 1962 (cf. Deleuze 1983, pp. 32–4). Foucault and Deleuze collaboratively wrote the introduction to Pierre Klossowski's 1967 translation of Nietzsche's *Fröhliche Wissenschaft*; they were interviewed together in 1972 on the relationship of intellectuals to power; Foucault wrote the preface to the 1977 English translation of *L'Anti-Oedipe*. More generally, it was Deleuze who was by most accounts the prime mover in the French Nietzschean renaissance of the past two decades (cf. Leigh 1978); a recent book on Foucault rather matter-of-factly states that in France, Deleuze has stood to Nietzsche as Althusser has to Marx and Lacan to Freud (Major-Poetzl 1983). Probably most important is that *The Anti-Oedipus* was, as Turkle (1979, pp. 148–53) has argued, the intellectual culmination of 1968 in France. This is true in terms of its widespread popularity; its thoroughly Nietzschean, playfully eclectic, and extremely influential reconciliation of Freud and Marx; and most of all in its spirit of irreverence that stood in counterposition to the sober back-to-Marx-and-Freud of Althusser and Lacan, and that captured the '*sous les pavés la plage*' ambience of the May–June events. It is likely then that Foucault's conversion to genealogy was catalysed by – indeed was effectuated through the prism of – Deleuze's infectious interpretations of the May–June days. Foucault's subsequent practical involvement with the prison information movement even seems to emulate Deleuze's involvement with anti-psychiatry militants. The 1970s, Descombes (1980, pp. 136–90) has suggested, were largely Deleuzian years in intellectual France. Late 1970s intellectual celebrities like Jean-François Lyotard have taken a number of cues from Deleuze. The parameters of Barthes's late period of *The Pleasure of the Text* and *A Lover's Discourse* were largely set, for better or for worse, by Deleuze, and *nouveaux philosophes* such as Bernard Henri Lévy continue to write extended anti-Deleuzian tracts.

Foucault in his commentary on *Différence et répétition* praises Deleuze – and the unnamed opponent seems to be Derrida – for breaking with a tradition which has understood 'difference' as a difference within something; it sought, instead, he concurs, to be treated in terms of an irregularity of '*intensities*' (Foucault 1977a, p. 182). This quantitative difference of intensities is a figural distribution of points on bodies. It is, for Deleuze, given rise to by another quantitative difference; a difference between 'active' and 'reactive forces' which yield values, 'events', and bodies and their properties. The active and reactive forces are themselves constituted through the 'affirmative' and 'negative' qualities of the will to power (Deleuze 1983, p. 50). The unity of a body is then, Deleuze (1983, pp. 40–41) states, 'a plurality of irreducible forces' and 'what defines a body is this relation between dominating and dominated forces'. We should note here that for Deleuze the will to power is prior to the 'forces', which themselves are prior to the body. Nietzsche on the other hand, we shall see below, defined the will to power in terms of a drive of the organic to increase the 'quanta of power' under its disposition. He could not, as Deleuze does, conceive of the will-to-power as logically prior to, and distinct from, the body. Deleuze's systematic valuation of 'forces' at the expense of the body is also pervasive in the *Anti-Oedipus*, where it is 'desire', a 'flux', which will assume centre stage and not the body. The important point for us here is that Foucault rather uncritically accepts Deleuze's very undynamic view of the body.

In 'Nietzsche, Genealogy, History' (Foucault 1977c, pp. 148, 154–5) and 'Theatrum Philosophicum' the concept of 'event' plays a central role. In the latter, Foucault endorses a concept of the body that Deleuze developed in terms of 'phantasms' and 'events'. Phantasms are 'figures' on the surface of human bodies. They arise between the surfaces of bodies and constitute a sort of 'incorporeal materiality'; they can only be characterized 'quantitatively', by a multiplicity of points of given intensities (Foucault 1977d, pp. 169–72). The term 'phantasm' comes from Freud's analyses of phantasy in, for example, his discussions of 'phantasmic castration' (Foucault 1977d, pp. 179–87). Yet phantasms are neither Freudian images nor Lacanian signifiers; they are on the contrary *real* and material (Foucault 1977d, p. 177).

'Events are produced by bodies colliding, mingling, separating' and also are created on the surface of bodies. They as well are non-corporeal; events are not causes, not states of things and cannot verify or falsify. They do not take the adjectival form of qualities, but verb forms such as 'he is dying'. Events and meanings coincide; events take place simultaneously on the surface of bodies and the surface of words (Foucault 1977d, pp. 173–5). We can speak of the 'series' of phantasms and the series of events. The phantasm however is 'excessive' in regard to the singularity of the event. 'Thought' produces phantasms, which have 'primal appendages', in a theatrical vein. Phantasms are intoned by the body through the mouth, as the objects of thought; the corresponding event is 'I am thinking' (Foucault 1977d, pp. 176–9). Phantasms, unlike signifiers which are constituted through the identity of a language, are pure difference in the sense that 'intensities are pure difference'. Thought therefore is 'intensive irregularity'. The production of 'meaning-events' takes place through the repetition of a phantasm. The event then is 'displaced and repeated difference' (Foucault 1977d, pp. 182–3).

Deleuze and Foucault have rescued the notion of phantasm from its psychoanalytic usage in the understanding of illusion. Bodies (and not subjects) 'think' not through concepts, nor categories, nor even language, but through phantasms. Philosophy becomes schizophrenia, it becomes theatre. Deleuzian phantasms, we shall see below, are constituted at the interface where society meets human bodies. Inscribed on the human body by means of the social they govern not only our thought events, but our political practices, our sexuality. Under capitalism, for example, the marking of phantasms through oedipalization organizes our sexuality and use of language in forms conducive to the reproduction of capitalist social relations. In competition, for Deleuze, with the capitalist social formation for the creation of phantasms on the human body, is, of course, 'desire'. Deleuze's body is then an object of competition, for whose control the active forces of desire and reactive forces, mobilized by capital, engage in struggle. The problem is that Foucault, unlike Deleuze, operates without a developed notion of desire or its equivalent; thus Foucault's body is only the prey of *reactive* forces – normalizing and individuating forces – and Foucault's geneaology remains incomplete.

Foucault approvingly mentions that the concept of the body advanced in Deleuze's *Logique du sens* is a near-polar opposite to that of Merleau-Ponty's theory. For Merleau-Ponty, wrote Foucault, 'the body-organism is linked to the world through a network of primal significations, which arise from the perception of things, while according to Deleuze, phantasms form the impenetrable and incorporeal surface of bodies', and give rise to 'something that falsely presents itself as a centred organism'

(Foucault 1977d, p. 170). Foucault writes similarly in 'Nietzsche, Genealogy, History', 'the body is the inscribed surface of events (traced by language and dissolved by ideas). The locus of a dissociated Self (adopting the illusion of a substantive unity)' (Foucault 1977c, p. 148). There is here an extraordinary convergence between this definition of the body and the 'body without organs' in Deleuze and Guattari's *Anti-Oedipus* (see discussion below). The 'body without organs' as well is a surface on which figures of varying intensities are inscribed. It is the locus of a dissociated self, insofar as it is separated from desire. It gives rise to the illusion of a unified subject. It is moreover operated on by discourse. Deleuze and Foucault seem here to have less in common with Nietzsche than with Merleau-Ponty, whose 'lived body' was also a body without organs (Dreyfus and Rabinow 1982, pp. 111–12).

DELEUZE: BETWEEN DESIRE AND SOCIETY

There is rather broad agreement that Deleuze and Guattari's *Anti-Oedipus* dissimulates, under a reconciliation of Freud and Marx, a Nietzschean critique of both Freud and Marx (cf. Seem 1977; Turkle 1979, pp. 148–53; Descombes 1980, pp. 173–80).[2] The book is divided into two parts: the first develops the notion of 'desire', the main locus of agency, in a psychodynamics – but, we shall see, a very sociological psychodynamics – whose main components are desire, the body and the subject; the second part is an account of how desire is 'coded' in different historical periods. It is only the first part which we will deal with here. Perhaps I may be forgiven for the following rather detailed treatment, which can, hopefully, serve as an aid to the reader in coping with what is a very difficult text. My central goal in this discussion, however, is to show how Deleuze and Guattari's 'schizodynamics' are part of the project to provide us with a 'counter-memory', how their de-oedipalized notion of agency constructs resistances to institutional psychiatric practices; how their de-familized unconscious is at the same time an attack on phallocentricism. In short to underscore how the *Anti-Oedipus* is integral to the whole genealogical enterprise.

(i) *Schizodynamics contra Lacan and Freud*

Deleuze and Guattari have two central objections to Lacan. The first concerns the notion of 'desire'; the second is the question of the mode of investment of desire. The *Shorter Oxford English Dictionary* defines 'desire' as 'the fact or condition of desiring; that emotion which is directed to the attainment of possession of some object from which pleasure or satisfaction is expected; longing, craving; a wish.' Lacan's notion of desire is rather close to this every-day usage of the term in so far as it entails the absence or lack of the object of desire. Lacan's concept diverges from our ordinary usage in so far as he specifies that desire must be unconscious. Here the category dovetails with Freud's concept of 'wish', which in *The Interpretation of Dreams* is *inter alia* seen as developing from a need that was satisfied in the past but not in the present; hence from a lack. Lacan distinguishes desire from 'need' and 'demand'. The infant at first cannot distinguish need from demand. With separation from the mother and identification with the father, demand and need become distinct and desire is born. Demand is conscious, desire is unconscious. Desire is, then, from the outset a question of lack; it is desire to have the mother and desire to be the phallus (Wilden 1968, pp. 185, 189). 'Desire' for Deleuze and Guattari (1977, p. 26), in contrast to this, corresponds to Freudian 'libido'. It does not entail the absence (or presence) of objects. It consists of flows of energy created by the id.

Lacan, it can be argued, also works with some sort of notion of psychic or sexual energy. The point is that – in contrast to Freud, on the one hand, and Deleuze and Guattari on the other, whose understandings of libido are more-or-less physical – Lacanian psychic energy is structured by language. And the manner in which the latter is structured by language is based on absence or lack. Lacan's tripartite overarching schema consists of the Real, the Imaginary, and the Symbolic orders. The Imaginary comes into existence at the same time as desire (Wilden 1968, pp. 295–6). Desire, though born in the unconscious with the advent of the Imaginary, is, in connection with the castration complex, reconstituted in the Symbolic. Classical psychoanalysis distinguishes between imagination on the one hand, which conceives representation of objects and events not actually present, and symbolism on the other, in which the unconscious substitutes one image for another, the latter being a representation of a repressed object (Rycroft 1972). In poetics, 'metonymy' is a figure in which an attribute of an entity is substituted for the entity. In this context Lacan speaks of the Symbolic as operating on the model of metonym. The entity which operates in such a fashion for Lacan is the 'signifier of signifiers', the phallus. The phallus 'represents . . . vital thrusting or growth . . . which cannot enter the domain of the signifier' (Lacan 1958a, p. 252, cited in Wilden 1968, p. 187). This 'transcendental' phallus none the less appears as metonym in each of the signifiers which structure the unconscious and constitute desire.

If libido has its basis for Lacan in the Symbolic, for Deleuze and Guattari (and for Freud) its grounding is in the Real; its foundations are material, even biological. Freud's libido has its basis in the id and exists in various forms corresponding to biological – oral, anal, and genital – 'part objects'. What Deleuze and Guattari call 'desiring-machines' closely resemble Freud's id. Desiring-machines produce desire. The 'parts' of desiring-machines are the 'part objects' of psychoanalysis (Deleuze and Guattari 1977, pp. 6–7). Deleuzian desire is also conceived as the equivalent of Nietzsche's will to power (Descombes 1980, p. 173), and it is significant as we shall see below that the will-to-power doctrine is pre-eminently biological.

The first point, then, on which Deleuze and Guattari are in disagreement with Lacan, concerns the constitution of desire. The second point concerns the way in which desire is invested. Here too the main bone of contention is a matter of Deleuze and Guattari's attribution of primacy to the Real in contrast to Lacan's focus on the Symbolic. On this matter Lacan is found in Freud's corner, inasmuch as classical psychoanalysis has stressed the investment of psychic energy in imaginary and symbolic objects. For example, in a feminist commune, classical psychoanalysis might view the cathexis of an older woman by a young woman at least partly in terms of symbolic cathexis of the mother. Deleuze and Guattari (1977, pp.84ff) would prefer to understand this simply as a real and material investment of libido in the older woman. They would thus reject the 'oedipalization' of desire. Oedipalization, the authors claim, is a product of capitalism. With the breakdown of tradition-bound relations of precapitalist societies – what the authors refer to as 'decodification' – a problem of social control arises. The only way in which capitalism can ensure its reproduction is for the family through oedipalization to take on functions of social control (Deleuze and Guattari 1977, pp. 284-6). They maintain, as Foucault did in *Madness and Civilization* and *The History of Sexuality*, that psychoanalysis only continues and strengthens a process – social control through the familial codification of desire – which preceded it by a century.

(ii) *The body without organs*

The first elements of schizodynamics is, as we noted, desiring-machines. The second element is the body. Deleuze has gone farther in thinking out a notion of the body than the other French poststructuralist theorists. Let me briefly outline this concept of the body, drawing not just on *Anti-Oedipus*, but on Deleuze's work more generally. Although Deleuze's desiring-machines are modelled on biological lines, his view of the body, unlike Nietzsche's, is not at all biological. Deleuze, following Artaud, speaks of a 'body without organs'. Here he and Guattari are also influenced by Freud's (1958) most considered account of schizophrenia in which the schizophrenic's body was experienced as ungendered. By 'body without organs' Deleuze means that we do not experience our bodies in terms of their biological organization, or, more precisely, that we *should* not so perceive our bodies. Deleuze recognizes the convergence between this non-organic view of the body and Merleau-Ponty's 'lived body', only he does not want to attribute the unity, coherence, and intentionality to the body that Merleau-Ponty does (Deleuze and Guattari 1980, pp. 185-204; Deleuze 1981).

Deleuze's body is conceived as a sort of hollow sphere, whose surface is structured in four ways, through each of which it is marked by a pattern of intensities. First, 'figures' are recorded on the surface of bodies which correspond to the part objects (the anus, the breast, the penis) of desiring-machines themselves (Deleuze and Guattari 1977, pp. 60-1). Here Deleuze and Guattari agree with Melanie Klein (1932) about the importance of libidinal investment in such entities; they, however, reject Klein's understanding of such cathexis as symbolic and in terms of the Oedipus complex. They advocate instead a real investment in such objects, which would then promote a sexuality free of the phallocentricism and normalization entailed by oedipalization (Deleuze and Guattari 1977, pp. 70-5). Second, figures are recorded from the outside world on the body; an example of this would be the illustration in regard to the feminist commune which I gave above. This is the point at which the third element of schizodynamics, 'the subject', is introduced. Deleuze and Guattari (1977, p. 100) propose, in opposition to the unified subject constituted through the oedipus triangle, a 'decentred ego' which serially identifies with a number of real and historic subjects in whom psychic energy is invested. The third type of zone of intensity which circumscribes bodies is the 'phantasm', which was discussed above. The fourth is the sense organs themselves. Deleuze suggests in this context that we should confront art in a manner similar to that in which the hysteric perceives his or her body. This means that for example when we listen to music, the ear should be distorted to take the shape of a 'polyvalent organ' which not only hears, but sees and feels (Deleuze 1981, pp. 36-7, 79-80).

There are innumerable problems in the work of Deleuze and Guattari. They present insufficient argument for their thesis concerning capitalism and oedipalization. They seriously under-estimate the extent to which the family has already declined as an agent of libidinal coding and investment. At points they push their theory of desire and the body just a bit too far for belief. Finally, I would reject their (and Foucault's) anti-Marxism, both for its conservative political resonances and because their theor-etical arguments against Marxism are at best sloppy. We should not, however, let these shortcomings lead us to underestimate Deleuze's contributions, which are not inconsistent with a neo-Marxist perspective. He has contributed importantly to the development of a non-organic concept of the body. He and Guattari have given us a set of prescriptions for the investment of libido which is condemnatory of hierarchy and sexism and enabling of healthy diversity. Most of all, their genealogy puts in the place of Foucault's passive body, the active forces of desire.

NIETZSCHE: BODIES AND THEIR RESOURCES

For Nietzsche the 'body' is not hypostatized as a concept, as it is in Foucault and Deleuze. It is spoken of in a rather more mundane manner as one of a set of biological terms, such as 'physiology', 'the organism', 'the sense', 'the sensuous'. The key point here is that – unlike Foucault, whose bodies are riddled and cross-cut by the power of knowledge, and by the use of knowledge by power – for Nietzsche knowledge is functional for the body; indeed the capacity to acquire knowledge is the most important 'organ' of the human body.[3]

(i) *Organic processes*

Nietzsche saw his 'post-Darwinian epoch' as one in which philosophers have begun to speak of bodies rather than souls. He did not consider his focus on the body, then, to be particularly original. Where he differed from his contemporaries was in his rejection (1) of their Whiggish understanding of the body's ever-increasing perfection in favour of his theory of eternal recurrence and (2) of the primacy they placed on feelings of pleasure and pain as fundamental causes; for Nietzsche (*Will to Power* (*WP*), pp. 347, 353, 357–8) these were instead *effects* of the will to power.

Nietzsche understood the human body or 'organism' in the context of the bodies of all organic beings. The body in any species is 'a multiplicity of forces, connected by a common mode of nutrition'. These forces include 'resistance to other forces'. To a mode of nutrition belongs 'feelings' and 'thoughts'. An organic species is 'an enduring form of processes of the establishment of force' and relations of force. 'Life' refers only to what is organic, and is the organic process through which the will to power of the dominant forces extend their boundaries (*WP*, pp. 341–3). To all organic beings, to all organisms or bodies – from amoebae to humans – the will to power is basic. This is more than a 'will to preservation', but a drive to absorb and dominate other organisms, other bodies, and thus add to the body's 'quanta of power' (p. 345). In other words the will to power is a drive towards 'expanded reproduction', with which bodies are possessed. In this supremely functional model the body is both agency and structure; agency in so far as it initiates reproduction, structure in so far as it is reproduced.

What are the functional elements, then, of organisms, of bodies? They are the organs themselves. The body, writes Nietzsche, is a 'political structure', in which 'cells and tissues' 'struggle'; in which lower organs are subdued by higher ones, and the former serve as 'functions' for the latter. A body's organs, as well as the whole multiplicity of events within an organism, are an effect of its will to power (*WP*, pp. 348, 355). Sense organs in animals and humans serve as means of 'interpretation' (p. 360). These organs can never reproduce 'truth' itself, but can only, in interpreting the environment, yield 'errors' which are more or less functional for bodies. Thus in general 'truth' is that species of error which is most functional (i.e. contributes most to its expanded reproduction) for a given body. And human sense organs are more highly developed than those of animals in so far as they can provide interpretations, whose errors are particularly functional.

The same theme informs his differentiation of the Overman, as 'a higher body' from Man:

> perhaps the entire evolution of spirit is a question of the body; it is the history of development of a higher body . . . The organic is rising to yet higher levels. Our lust for knowledge of nature is a means through which the body desires to perfect itself. (*WP*, p. 358)

Organs, and especially sense organs, are then absolutely fundamental to Nietzsche's notion of the body; this stands in sharp relief to the body 'without organs' of both Deleuze and Foucault.

(ii) *Bodies and knowledge*

Nietzsche's central theme here is that human bodies develop 'beliefs' as adjuncts of their sense organs. One subset of such beliefs concern knowledge, in which 'truth', the 'subject', and the logical categories are far from *a priori* or unconditioned. They are instead inscribed on a body's organs only in so far as they serve as resources which contribute to its expanded reproduction. Nietzsche attempts to demolish the whole conceptual apparatus of epistemology through his critique of the subject. His case against the 'I' (treated as the equivalent of 'ego', 'subject', and 'will') is better and more clearly put than it is by contemporary poststructuralists (cf. e.g. Deridda 1978a, pp. 45–51). Descartes, he notes, begins from the assumption that 'thinking' exists. This itself, Nietzsche remarks, is a 'strong belief', at best 'question-able', hardly 'indubitable'. This shaky assumption is followed by the *non sequitur* that the 'I' exists. Even if thinking was indubitable, the argument for the 'I' would depend on another assumption – that there must be a 'substance' which thinks, which itself, observes Nietzsche, is dependent on a belief in 'substance' (*WP*, p. 268). Nietzsche may have, with justification, added that there is no necessity that such a substance be the 'I'.

The subject, for Nietzsche, must be understood in terms of perspectivism and interpretations; it is an apparent unity on the 'surface' of a body characterized by multiplicity. The later Nietzsche is an anti-positivist; he will allow no facts, only interpretations. There is no subject, no interpreter behind the interpretations; it is instead our 'drives and needs' that interpret the world, 'each one (with) its perspective' (*WP*, p. 267). It is the same with 'events'; we should be able to understand events as activities without subjects; we should be able to think of 'flashing lightning' without thinking 'lightning flashes' (WP, p. 288).[4] The 'ego' then is a 'perspective illusion', an 'apparent unity that encloses everything like a horizon'. The 'evidence of the body (however) reveals a tremendous multiplicity; (we are to study these) richer phenomena as evidence for the understanding of the poorer' (*WP*, p. 281). The reason that we believe in the subject stems from our perspective; that is, such belief is functional for the expanded reproduction of human bodies. The ego's stability lends to our interpretation of the world an unchanging, ordered nature, which (though it has no necessary relation to reality) 'has helped us control and dominate over our environment'. If the ego is not in a state of being, but in a 'state of becoming', then all logic falls apart (*WP*, pp. 280–1).

(iii) *Negative doctrine*

In the *Nachlass* that became *The Will to Power*, the body is discussed least of all in its negative doctrine, the critique of our highest values. These latter 'slave' values are promulgated by weak bodies, or by 'classes', 'races', 'ages', 'peoples' (pp. 226–8) of weak bodies. At the same time these belief-systems assign a low value to bodies in comparison with 'spiritual' entities; that is, their ethos is spiritual rather than bodily. In spite of their overall life-destroying character such values serve as resources for the expanded reproduction of weak bodies.[5] If weak bodies can convince strong ones to accept such valuations, then their life-destroying power will enable the weak to dominate the strong. Nietzsche and Nietzsche-commentators sometimes rather misleadingly speak of such slave values as forms of the will to power, and thus maintain that the will to power can be a drive which fosters a 'diminished reproduction', so to speak, of bodies. There is a confusion in such formulations of the drive (the will to power) with the *resources* over which it disposes. The drive is always towards the expanded reproduction of bodies to further the latter; the strong and the weak will make use of antithetical sets of resources.

Life-destroying value-systems can be moral, cognitive, or aesthetic. In terms of morality, for example, in the Christian 'type the excitability of a degenerate body predominates'. The Christian in turn disregards the 'demands of the body', 'reduces bodily functions to moral values', 'mistreats the body (a necessity for the Christian) and prepares the ground for the sequence of "feelings of guilt"'. For this 'one has to reduce the body to a morbid and nervous condition' (*WP*, pp. 131-3). As with morality, cognitive and aesthetic realms consist of valuations. We speak, for example, of judgments or propositions, in terms of their 'truth-value'; we evaluate research programmes as more or less progressive, more or less degenerating. In art, Nietzsche contrasts bodily and non-bodily values. He criticizes his early work (in *The Birth of Tragedy*), as inscribed in a 'two-world' conception, as an 'aesthetic justification' – or 'aesthetodicy' – in which a 'will to beauty' is counterposed to the ugliness of this world. Against such Romantic, or even Modernist notions, for the later Nietzsche 'the eternally-creative' appears as the 'compulsion to destroy . . . associated with pain, (where) things assume the form of the ugly' (*WP*, p. 224). Artistic creation should, for Nietzsche, enhance the quanta of power at the disposition of the artist's body. It must function towards the expanded reproduction of bodies of consumers of art (cf. Nietzsche 1982, p. 28). Its form and content should be consistent with the bodily ethos of the Dionysian.

(iv) *Summary*

We have isolated, in the previous discussion, the following characteristics of Nietzsche's conception of the body.

(1) All organisms or bodies are driven by a basic instinct for their own expanded reproduction, a drive towards the increase of quanta of forces under their disposition. This drive is the will to power.

(2) Whether such expanded reproduction ('life-enhancement') will take place depends on a body's struggles with other external bodies, and on relations of force between struggling entities (organs, structures, values) within the body.

(3) Our beliefs in 'the subject', 'truth', and the categories of logic have no objective validity. We hold these beliefs in so far as they function towards the expanded reproduction of bodies.

(4) Such beliefs lend a certain (false) stability to the external world. This yields interpretations of the world that are functional for the prospering of human bodies. The beliefs attach themselves so to speak to our sense organs, to the 'surfaces of bodies'. Thus the 'I' doesn't think, but bodies think through the 'I'.

(5) The spiritual (in knowledge, art, and morality) is born out of the bodily. These two principles, in the spiritual and the bodily, then co-exist in a state of irreconcilable tension within the body.

(6) The balance of forces between these principles underpins cognitive, aesthetic, and moral discourse. For example, a Nietzschean aesthetic would value artistic creation wherein the production of art will lead to the expanded reproduction of bodies of both producer and consumer. Such art would break with the predominance of the (Apollonian) signifier to carry a bodily message through bodily forms.

(7) Slave moralities which are non-bodily in content, attach themselves to weak bodies or groupings of weak bodies, because they function in *their* expanded reproduction. The weak are able to impose such value-systems on stronger bodies who are enfeebled and thus come under the domination of the former. Such moralities are life-destroying, however, for the species. Given values can be life-destroy-

ing (for the species) at one point in time and life-enhancing at another.

CONCLUDING REMARKS

A theory of the body is important for social theory, and in particular for action, as distinct from structural, approaches to sociology (Lash and Urry 1984). In (at least) Continental philosophy, there has been a shift in the locus of agency from the mind to the body. Thus we can understand Merleau-Ponty's theory in which the body is an intentional agent. Sartre, as well, criticized his own earlier position as being overly Cartesian in nature, and in *The Critique of Dialectical Reason* and subsequent work on Flaubert adopted a number of Freudian precepts which in effect relocated the bases of action towards the body. Even theology was not untouched by this shift as Karl Rahner re-read Aquinas partly through Heideggerian spectacles, entailing an anti-dualism which involved a fundamental revaluation of the body. To stress the centrality of the body or the unconscious for *sociological* action theory is hardly novel. Parsons, crucially influenced by Freud, came to understand the unconscious as the interface of structure and agency. Goffman consistently maintained that the 'presentation of self' took place largely apart from, and even in spite of, our conscious strategies. The influential action theory of Pierre Bourdieu features the notion of the 'habitus' which is conceived along lines of the body.

I think that the importance of 'genealogy' – of the work of Foucault, Deleuze, and Nietzsche – is partly by way of its potential contribution to the development of such a sociology of action. To work out such a theory is beyond the scope of this paper. But let me briefly draw on the three writers discussed in the essay to delineate a few guidelines. Such a theory should first of all enable us to account for the effects of social structures on agency, and at the same time provide a critique of extant social structures. It is here that Foucault's special genius lies. On a number of counts Nietzsche and Foucault are engaged in the same enterprise. For both, one important effect of such powers of discourse is to individuate, to 'invent subjects', which are attached, so to speak, to bodies. Nietzsche's indications of how power acts on bodies are, however, even on a generous reading, incomplete. He, first, mainly discusses the body *not* in the context of how discourse acts on it, but in terms of how it can use discourse. Moreover, even when values are dysfunctional for bodies, Nietzsche does not relate them to forms of society, but sees them restrictively as values of slave classes. Foucault provides remedies for both of these insufficiencies. It is by substituting power (power not in Weber's sense of the Same being an extension of the Other's will; but power as the Other itself, be it as absolutist monarch or 'the people') for the slave classes that Foucault can avoid the aristocratic ethos of Nietzsche's genealogy, as well as Nietzsche's brand of 'methodological individualism'. It has been necessary, thus, for Foucault to 'twist Nietzsche out of shape' in order to provide bodies with practical and critical weapons – resources which he has most visibly supplied to those in penal institutions and their advocates, but also for bodies in psychiatric institutions, and those subject to medical discourse in general. It may be that Foucault's genealogy in the end will be of greatest use to feminists, especially in struggles around sexuality. Taken together, *Madness and Civilization* and *The History of Sexuality* can yield a portrait of the female body which has, since the onset of Modernity, been structured – by discourse on mental health and sexuality – along familial lines. The effects of such structuration have been, arguably, to invent a female sexuality and subjectivity (and the inventors surely have been men) which in turn acts as a bad conscience or 'soul', as a 'prison-house' on the bodies of women. Such a framework can be extended to account for the effects of rather more recent discourse of 'sexual liberation'.

Second, in such a theory the body should possess some positive, libidinal driving force. That such a force is largely absent, as I argued above, in the work of Foucault, is confirmed by the latter in a late interview (Foucault 1983). Here he described his oeuvre in terms of recounting the price man has had to pay for his pursuit of self-knowledge. Foucault put this characterization in context by contrasting it with the life's work of Deleuze, which he saw as working out a notion of more positive force in the concept of 'desire'. For Deleuze, the body is the surface of intersection between libidinal forces, on the one hand, and 'external', social forces on the other. It is the interplay of these forces which gives the body its shape and its specific qualities.

For Deleuze and Guattari libido itself is socially structured by the global characteristics of the social, acting through the mediation of significant groups, like the family. The authors of *Anti-Oedipus* have added to genealogy's critical power by their alternative prescriptions for the investment of psychic energy. The central proposal here is that we should *not* understand libidinal investment in non-familial persons and objects as symbolic investment in the family. The uses of these notions are not confined to the criticism of orthodox psychoanalysis and psychiatry. The gay movement can find a resource in such a non-normalized understanding of identification and cathexes, feminists in the alternative provided to Lacanian phallocentrism, and anti-racists in its censure of the segregative subject and its alternative serial identification.

I think that Nietzsche's biological view of the body should be rejected, partly because we do not experience our bodies in such terms. A theory of the body should include, however, some set of mechanisms with which the body reproduces itself. This is the value of Nietzsche's contribution, which is at the same time a criticism of Merleau-Ponty's understanding of the body. Here we can conceive of the body's unity and intentionality as resources created by the body in the interest of its own reproduction. Moreover, Nietzsche's Dionysian aesthetics of the body look forward to postmodernism in the arts, in which – from Dali and Bunuel to Sylvia Plath and Peter Brook – the unconscious has come to be the dominant organizing principle.

Acknowledgement

This chapter was first published as an article in *Theory, Culture and Society*, Volume 2, Number 2, pages 1–18, September 1984, and is reproduced by permission of Sage Publications, London.

Chapter Three

POSTMODERNITY AND DESIRE

Western social theory over the past fifteen to twenty years has been marked by a paucity of communication between Germanic-critical and Gallic-structural inputs; moreover, relations between those Anglo-Americans who drew inspiration from the former and those influenced by the latter have been characterized frostily by silence. It is to the credit of Jürgen Habermas to have recently broken seals on hermetic casks and opened debate. In this context, Habermas's intervention brings into sharp relief the problematic nature and political implications of modernist and postmodernist culture.[1]

Habermas initially aims his critical arrows at cultural neo-conservatism in the USA and West Germany against the claims of writers such as Daniel Bell that cultural modernity has come into contradiction with social modernization. But the main focus of his attack is, as Habermas's critics have noted, postmodernist culture itself, and especially the 'postmodernist theory' of Nietzsche-influenced contemporary French writers. For Habermas, cultural modernity comprises theoretical, practical, and aesthetic spheres, which attain autonomy from one another from the end of the eighteenth century. The assumption here is that social modernization is accompanied by such a tripartite differentiation in the cultural sphere. The negative consequences of this for Habermas lie in the autonomization of the aesthetic realm. In this context, the aesthetic realm is wholly separated from everyday life. Worse, there is a drainage of theoretical and especially of moral-practical content from 'aesthetic reason'. Aesthetic modernity in effect *undermines* theoretical and practical reason.[2]

Habermas's attacks on French postmodernist theory follow from those on aesthetic modernity. He claims that the privilege attributed to the aesthetic sphere by the neo-Nietzscheans tends to undermine theoretical and practical rationality. He contends that such a primacy of the aesthetic entails an absence of social mediation and especially a lack of articulation between cultural modernity/postmodernity and every-day social practices. He notes a certain convergence between the French postmodern theorists and neo-conservatives, implying that the renunciation of any notion of substantive rationality by the former paves the way for the 'decisionism' advocated by some of the latter.[3]

This chapter has two basic aims. The first is – partly by way of response to Habermas's explicit criticisms – to elucidate the concept of cultural postmodernity that can be found in French theory. Here we shall see, in a treatment of Michel Foucault, Jean-François Lyotard, and Gilles Deleuze – probably the three most prominent French writers in this context – that the postmodern is inextricably bound up with a theory of desire; a theory whose broad outlines I also attempt to paint.

In this discussion we shall see that the neo-Nietzscheans indeed have conceived of their work in terms of social mediations, in terms of the shift towards a 'post-industrial capitalism', and in close conjunction with the micro-politics of the new social movements. Equally, we shall find that their view of the aesthetic realm is in no way a transcendental aesthetics. For the French theorists the aesthetic is paramountly a matter of political practice. Theory is not here devalued; indeed theory operates itself as an important critical weapon in the indictment of both contemporary political subjugation and the discourses that surround and justify it.

My second objective is a critical assessment of the principles at issue in the controversy between Habermas and the 'poststructuralists'. Both the former and the latter view social theory as very centrally involved in a combat against forms of domination and subjugation. Here I look at the spirit of Habermas's work – rather than the letter of his reproaches at the postmodernists – and attempt to show that he operates with a core notion of moral or natural rights that is systematically excluded by the theoretical framework of the French theorists. Such a systematic absence, we shall see, opens the door to the possibility of domination. Then I turn to a thorough consideration of the incisive criticism to which Lyotard has subjected Habermas, and argue that the strong notion of consensus – and the relegation of the aesthetic – in communicative action theory is similarly problematic in regard to the issue of power and subjugation.

Although Habermas sometimes glosses the distinction between aesthetic modernity and postmodernity, I think it is a crucial one. Aesthetic modernity is, by the conventions of most art historians and literary critics, dated from the last decades of the nineteenth century. It constitutes a break with representation, hence a certain self-referentiality and above all a set of *formalisms*. Commentators such as Foucault and Richard Rorty have noted similar phenomena taking place approximately concurrently in epistemology, moral philosophy, and the social sciences. The *post*modernity of the 1960s on the other hand, consider for example Peter Brook in theatre and Plath's poetry, means a break with formalisms, a break with the signifier; it means a new primacy of the unconscious, of the bodily and material, of desire, of libidinal impulses.[4] The work of Foucault, Lyotard, and Deleuze not only clarifies this new aesthetic substrate and indicates its ethical and political implications; the work of these writers is part and parcel of theoretical postmodernism itself.

Although the material covered below might appear to be wide-ranging, my claims are not over-ambitious. This chapter does not contain systematic argument for a periodization of the arts and literature, nor a thorough discussion of the possibility that the theory of desire, or indeed of communicative rationality, can provide thematic underpinnings for 'postindustrial' political culture of the social movements. The apparent breadth of scope of this article, then, is a matter of drawing on a number of sources as resources for the two above-delimited aims.

SOCIAL THEORY AS DESIRE

We turn, then, to considerations of how the neo-Nietzscheans have provided us not only with an aesthetics but an ethics of postmodernity, which has counterposed 'dissensus' and 'invention' to hierarchies and subjugation. Perhaps most important is that they have begun to outline a postmodern social theory. Theoretical, like aesthetic, postmodernity has meant a break with formalisms. If aesthetic postmodernity has entailed the supersession by the unconscious and the bodily of the hegemony of the symbolic in literature, in the fine arts, in music, then postmodern theory has meant, for Foucault, Lyotard, and Deleuze, to turn narrative or 'the story' against discourse. Theoretical postmodernity has been above all a matter, for the French theorists, of a divorce with *structuralisms*. It has proposed, in strong contradistinction to the many incarnations of the latter, an end to the primacy of discourse, the text, the word, the signifier; the demise of the hegemony of 'writing'. At the risk of being overly schematic it could be said that recent French social theory is divided into two camps: the moderns and structuralists such as Barthes, Lacan, and Derrida, whose inspiration is Saussurean; and postmoderns, Foucault, Deleuze, and Lyotard whose inspiration is Nietzschean. For numbers of French student activists the clash with authority of 1968 was at the same time a clash with the structuralisms purveyed by their teachers. It was a bursting out of the 'prison-house of language'; for feminists and others, the 'end of the sovereignty of the phallic signifier'. If under the paving-stones was the beach (*'sous les pavés la plage'*), then surely under the signifier, under language, was desire.[5]

An aesthetics of transgression

Michel Foucault has described the corpus of his work as recounting man's quest for self-knowledge and the price that has had to be paid as a consequence of the successes of this quest.[6] Man's quest for self-knowledge has resulted in a number of 'discourses'. Foucault in the 1960s developed a notion of 'non-discursive language', which could be used to counteract and construct resistances against discourse. It is in 'non-discursive language' or 'counter-memory', with which Foucault identifies his own work, that we can find a concept of the postmodern. 'Discourse' and 'non-discursive language' are elements of a sort of 'spatial model' with which Foucault seems to have worked in the 1960s.

This model can perhaps be most helpfully conceived in terms of the Same and the Other. The space of the Same is characterized by light; it is the space of discourse. The elements that characterize the space of the Other – the realm of darkness for Foucault – are those that have been excluded by discourse (and the Same);

these are the figures of madness, sexuality, desire and death. In what Foucault calls the Classical period (c. 1650–1800), signs were constituted and referents identified in the world of the Same. At this point there was a persistence of quite literally Manichean arrangements, with the discursive practices of ever-garrulous princes of light set against the silence of knaves of darkness. But in the Modern period, with Kant's aesthetic establishing the possibility and Sade the realization, a new and third world invented itself; or more appropriately, we should say a new space or a new 'fold'. That is, with what Foucault called the 'birth of literature' a 'vertical' space was established at the limit of where light met darkness; a space that opened up that limit. This is the space of non-discursive 'literature', where language takes on an opacity, and 'ontological weight'. It is in this *pli*, this fold, that the postmodern is constituted. It is here where Mallarmé, Nietzsche, Bataille, and Blanchot wrote and where Klossowski and Foucault write. It hardly attests to Foucault's modesty when he qualifies – referring of course to his privileged position within this literary space – his entire opus as 'fiction'. The new language of this vertical space is able to offer a wholly new description of discourse and the Same. It can also speak about the Other (madness, sexuality, death) in a qualitatively different way than that of which discourse is capable. From time to time figures from the Other are able to cross over into this fold of non-discursive language and speak – sexuality and death in Sade, madness in Artaud, woman, arguably, in Molly's soliloquy and recent feminist history.

In *Madness and Civilization*, the mid-seventeenth century heralded a new relationship between words and things, which was the condition of existence for a different discourse on madness; one that systematically excluded the mad into the realm of the Other, into a space previously occupied by death. In the sixteenth century, words and their referents, both of whose consistency was of a certain substantiality or materiality, were connected through similitude. Serious speech acts functioned to preserve life by keeping death, and not the mad – who were not in any case wholly excluded from discourse – at bay. This sixteenth-century episteme that Foucault characterized in terms of 'hermeneutics' – in contradistinction to 'semiology' – did not advocate the realist notions of truth that could separate the world into

82

realms of light and knowledge, on the one hand, and darkness and madness on the other. The Cartesian synthesis of the seventeenth century, surely, as Adorno and Horkheimer emphasized, promoted man's ability to control his environment. But at what price? The new discursive space, in which words were cipher-like signs bearing lamps connected to things that had lost their depth, was made possible through the transsubstantiation of madness from opacity into darkness and its exclusion into the realm of the Other. More recently in the vertical non-discursive language that has opened up space for itself between the Same and the Other, into this fold that is also a space of 'physical suffering' and 'terror', the postmodern in the form of Artaud has stood up and 'hurled words at the fundamental absence of language'.

The Other on this spatial model is inhabited by figures of madness, sexuality, and death and bears strong resemblances to Freud's unconscious. The non-discursive language in the space between the Same and Other persists in a struggle against death. Postmodern cultural practices draw on madness and on sexuality for their sustenance, and level a critique at the realm of discourse and the types of subjectivity that are constituted by discourse. Elements of this model, as we just saw, are visible in *Madness and Civilisation* and *The Order of Things*. The model is, however, most fully developed in Foucault's writings on literature in the early and middle sixties.

In 'Language to Infinity' Foucault develops some of Maurice Blanchot's themes on the connection between death and writing. For Ulysses, Blanchot noted, language was a resource 'poised against' death. He is able to escape the fate that is presented to him by 'pursuing [his] fictive speech . . . into this space which borders death, but is also poised against it, [the space in which] the story locates its natural domain'.[8] Language escapes death through becoming self-reflexive; through opening up a space on the limit of death and pursuing itself to infinity. Time, Heidegger saw, was socially constituted and a function of language. Language itself, in its reflection on death, and against death, constitutes for us, operating exclusively in dimensions of space, an infinite past and an infinite future. Language does so 'through a murmur which redoubles itself, through setting up an endless "play of mirrors" '.[9]

One of the most influential themes of *The Order of Things* is that of the 'birth of literature'. In 'Language to Infinity', prior to the birth of literature, at the beginning of the nineteenth century, religion occupied the space that was poised against death. For literature to be born, it is not enough that men become atheists; language must through the ultimate transgression – paralleling the regicide of *Discipline and Punish* and parricide and matricide in *I, Pierre Rivière*,[10] – murder God and thus take the place of the Word.[11] But the birth of literature means more than the death of God. It means that language, through the agency of its midwives such as Sade and Hölderin, must set fire to discourse and 'persist in transgressing' the limit of discourse into the realm of the Other (death, madness, sexuality).[12] It must do so through its 'excess', which is the 'act of naming through transgression'. In the Classical period, Rhetoric, which is part and parcel of the philosophy of representation, is king. Literature begins where rhetoric ends, at a 'moment . . . when a language appeared that appropriates and consumes all other languages (i.e. religion and Classical discourses) in its lightning flash, giving birth to an obscure but dominant figure where death, the mirror and the wavelike succession of words to infinity enact their roles'.[13]

If Foucault sees Blanchot in terms of the postmodern poised against death, he understands Georges Bataille in terms of such non-discursive language's drawing on sexuality. Here the key concept is 'transgression'. In Christian mysticism, Bataille observed, sexuality, rapture, and ecstasy were not divided from spirit but existed 'at the heart of the divine'.[14] In the nineteenth century, as the concept of sexuality became an object of discourse, sexuality itself was excluded into the space of the Other, or relegated into the unconscious. In transgression, the sensual makes its reappearance and speaks through non-discursive language. Transgression means not only to communicate through sexuality,[15] it is at the root of the latter. Through transgression sexuality opens the 'excessive distance [which is] at the heart of the limit'. Transgression, whose precursor is Christian mysticism, and whose epiphany is found in the words of Georges Bataille, is both a profanation of the sacred and the marking of a new sacred. Its language of eroticism, which for Foucault is a language of the future, [16] is to 'overcome the limits to the death of God'; 'in a world which no longer recognizes any positive meaning in the sacred . . ., transgression supplies the sole manner of discovering the sacred in its unmediated substance'.[17] In the 'excessive' act of killing God, it is not God nor religion that is transgressed but the 'limited and positivistic world', the world inscribed by discourse.

Crucial to transgression in Bataille's novels and for Foucault is 'the eye'. The eye, which inhabits the opened limit of non-discursive language, is the space from which Bataille speaks. The eye is 'a figure of being in the act of transgressing its own limit'.[18] Through transgression the eye looks inward and outward. As it looks inward it illuminates the night of the Other, 'yet it owes to the dark the stark clarity of its manifestation'.[19] The upturned eye links language with death. As it looks outward it functions as lamp and mirror. A lamp, the darkness of its core 'pours out into the world' and lights it up. A mirror, it 'gathers up the light of the world into its black spot'.[20]

Blanchot and Bataille were Nietzscheans. So, above all, is Pierre Klossowski. In the foregoing paragraphs we have seen the space of the Other to be inhabited by madness, death, and sexuality. In Foucault's essay on Klossowski it is inhabited by the diabolical.[21] The essay is called 'La prose d'Acteon'. Acteon, trained as a hunter by the immortal centaur Cheiron, spied on Artemis (Diana) in her bath and was promptly turned into a stag to be devoured by his own hunting dogs. Klossowski's prose in so far as it transgresses – in so far as its eye transgresses the goddess Diana, in so far as his words transgress the limits of discourse – is la prose d'Acteon.

Non-discursive language, and its counterpart in social action in postmodernity can be characterized in terms of 'simulacra', in so far as essence and appearance, signifier and signified are no longer of relevance. Klossowski's prose and Acteon's action comprise simulacra; and what is addressed in Diana's bath is not Diana but a simulacrum of Diana.[22] The simulacra of Acteon's words and of Diana are both mediated through 'the demon'. The simulacrum that appears through Diana's 'theophany' is at the same time the demon, who thus 'mediates between the gods and men'. And Acteon's (Klossowski's) non-discursive prose re-enacts gnosticism and dualist versions of Christianity in so far as the diabolical leaves the space of the Other.[23] The spectre of the simulacrum – the imitation of an essence that is itself an interpretation – inhabits thus for Foucault (as he says it does for Gide, Klossowski, and Borges) not only the realm of words and things, but also that of human beings and of social action.[24]

Foucault has, at least in the 1960s and 1970s, to my knowledge never used the term 'postmodern'. The closest he approaches to using this term is in *The Order of Things*, in which he hints that the non-discursive language of Nietzsche and Mallarmé constitutes a critique of the Modern and points to an epoch that is somehow beyond the Modern.[25] Foucault's aesthetic, as outlined above, is, however, distinctly recognizable as a *post*modern aesthetic, in so far as it breaks with formalism and has its basis in the unconscious. This is confirmed in so far as the writers whom Foucault draws on to formulate his notion of non-discursive language – Nietzsche, Artaud, Blanchot, Bataille, Klossowski – have been among the foremost purveyors of the postmodern aesthetic. Cultural postmodernity is portrayed in Foucault, as discussed above, in a model of 'exclusion and transgression'. Here, figures such as madness, death, sexuality, and the diabolical are excluded by discourse into the space of the Other or the unconscious. Cultural postmodernity, or non-discursive language, arises in the space between discourse and the unconscious. The figures of the unconscious through such non-discursive language then transgress the limit into the space of discourse. It should be clear then that, *pace* Habermas, what is at stake here is more than an aesthetic. Foucault has, first, drawn on aesthetic postmodernity as a basis of what is for him a *theoretical* intervention. When theory acts through transgression on the realm of discourse it mobilizes a critique – of discourse, of forms of subjectivity – that is pre-eminently practical and political. The practical and political nature of such a critique is clear in Foucault's conscious relation to the social movements and micropolitics of the 1970s. If anything, Foucault's cultural politics of transgression are a sort of non-rational simulacra of Habermas's communicative rationality or practical reason. Foucault's aesthetics are, in brief, as Said has noted, an 'ethics of languages'.[26]

A few important qualifications in regard to the work of the late Michel Foucault must be entered at this point. In many important ways Foucault's oeuvre departs significantly from a problematics of desire. First, it should be noted that the French tradition of Georges Canguilhem in the history and philosophy of science has an influence on Foucault that arguably came close to matching the Nietzschean input into his thought.[27] Second, the work of Foucault's 'middle period' had important structuralist resonances. In *The Order of Things* and especially *The Archaeology of Knowledge*, the power relations and libidinal (madness, the body) vision of agency of the early and later work were mostly absent, to be replaced by a search for the structural preconditions and structural characteristics of discourses. Structuralism and aesthetic modernism – in the strict sense that I have used the latter term here – are both formalisms in the sense of sundering the transparent connection between signifier and content or signified. Foucault's ambiguity towards structuralism is echoed in his oscillations between the valuation of the postmodern and the modern. The above-mentioned reading of Klossowski had elements of the modern and of the postmodern. The much criticized essay on Magritte, *This Is Not a Pipe*, centres on the latter's juxtaposition of the discursive and the figural and his break with the resemblances of an aesthetics of representation for an aesthetics of 'similitude';[28] this is clearly a 'modernist' reading of Magritte. Indeed the ideal types of the Apollonian modern and the Dionysian postmodern are never found in reality; consider, for example, Joyce's *Ulysses* where a lyrical hypostatization of the formal is interspersed with the tones of Bloom's murmuring id. In fact, both Lyotard and Deleuze mix in elements of the modern with their largely postmodernist aesthetic. Having said this, we should note that Magritte is conventionally taken to be a postmodern in the sense that the term is being used here.[29] Indeed surrealism as a genre is, in the common wisdom, understood as a rejection of formalisms and the Apollonian for a focus on the dream, id impulses, and the unconscious. And Foucault has chosen an inordinate number of surrealists, or those who have shared the concerns or surrealism, as subjects of his aesthetics essays – not just Magritte, but Bataille, Roussel, and Artaud.

Third, in an interview published in *Telos* in 1983, Foucault seemed to separate himself from the 'Deleuzian notion of desire', noting that if Deleuze were a Nietzschean in the sense of the will to power, then he, himself, was a Nietzschean in the sense of the 'will to knowledge'.[30] I take Foucault here, as is conventional in France,[31] to have equated desire with the will to power. The 'will

POSTMODERNISM AND SOCIAL THEORY

to knowledge' on the other hand is mentioned in Nietzsche's fragments and notebooks that were posthumously published as *The Will to Power*. The concept is however consistent with that of 'slave moralities' in *The Genealogy of Morals*. Though departing, of course, from the elitism of Nietzsche's concept, Foucault is here understanding the will to knowledge as discourse, as that inimical to the will to power, or to desire and the body. In this sense, Foucault's statement that he and Deleuze have been involved in different projects does not entail that they are not indeed complementary projects. Yet even, in the half-decade or so subsequent to 1968, when Foucault was closest to Deleuze, he never articulated a positive theory of desire and the body, the latter constituting a sort of passive vector on which discourses operated. And in the first volume of *The History of Sexuality* Foucault seemed to regard 'desire' itself as part of discourse,[32] agency now being located in a body whose resistances might only be based on the pleasures of an *ars erotica*. In the late 1970s and in the 1980s Foucault moved even further away from the theory of desire; this was due partly perhaps to a change in his politics from a *gauchiste* to a rather liberal/centrist position; partly perhaps to contacts in the USA with scholars sympathetic to analytic philosophy, on the one hand, and to Weber and the Frankfurt School, on the other.[33] Granted, then, a pronounced and lasting ambiguity of Foucault towards the problem of desire. Let me stress, though, that I have not argued above that Foucault was a theorist of desire. I have only claimed that in Foucault's work can be found the elements of a theory of desire, and it is the latter that I have attempted to explicate.

In addition to the ambivalence towards desire, Foucault has maintained a rather idiosyncratic view of what constitutes the modern. Through the major part of his output Foucault distinguishes a modern period, dating from approximately 1800, from a Classical period, whose duration is from 1650 to 1800. What I take to be the four basic characteristics of the modern here are: (1) the break with epistemological dualisms towards an immanent relationship of concepts and their referents, (2) power begins to operate immanently and positively rather than 'transcendentally' and repressively, (3) the birth of the human sciences, (4) the elevation to a position of priority of the social. In the very suggestive *Telos* interview Foucault seemed to prefer to speak not so much of the modern as of a series of 'formalisms' that were characteristic of the twentieth century. Herein he moved much closer to the common wisdom among art and literary critics,[34] albeit extending the formalistic framework to the theoretical realm. The claims I have made above in regard to a postmodern ethos in some of Foucault's work would be applicable to either his earlier idiosyncratic but immensely insightful view of the modern, or a more conventional view that sees modernism in terms of formalisms. In either case the non-discursive language of desire, madness, and dream would transgress and disrupt discourse. Interestingly, Foucault, towards the end of *The Order of Things*, situates formalistic structuralism as merely an apparently metamorphosed continuation of the central themes of the modern in the human sciences;[35] the suggestion here is that Foucault himself might begin to help provide a theoretical counterpart to the non-discursive language of Mallarmé and Artaud, and thus help point the way to what might come after the modern.

Finally, it might be asked why Foucault did not respond, as did Lyotard, to Habermas's criticisms, either by way of a (self-) defence or a criticism of Habermas's project. Here one can only speculate. It is probable that Foucault did not have sufficient familiarity with Habermas's work to be fully confident of making a reply; it is known that in the late 1970s and early 1980s he was particularly cautious in this type of intervention.[36] Second, Foucault made a practice of not commenting, or at least not directly commenting, on the work of his contemporaries. Third, as I suggested above, Foucault was moving closer towards a positive assessment of Weber and the Frankfurt School. Moreover, often the criticisms from theorists of Foucault's and Habermas's status of one another is not of the greatest fruitfulness, each being too fully engaged in his or her own pursuits to take another fully seriously. The above-discussed ethics of transgression, which forms part of the ethos of Foucault's work, is, I think, as applicable a critique of Habermas's work as it is of other discourses situated in the modern. It is, apparently, up to us practitioners of 'normal' human science, in whose ears the gods do not whisper, to work out implication, critique, and counter-critique in this *Auseinandersetzung* of 'transgressive' and communicative social theory.

Libido and language games

Many of the contributors, including Habermas, to the postmodernist controversy, cite Jean-François Lyotard's *La condition postmoderne* as the foundational work for the debate; yet none of the contributors give any idea of what Lyotard's book is about, or directly address the issues raised in it. If this volume of Lyotard's is the benchmark text for Habermas and Critical Theory, his earlier work[37] was the crucial catalyst for what was possibly the most influential book of postmodernist theory in France – Deleuze and Guattari's *Anti-Oedipus*. Below we turn to *La condition postmoderne*, and in particular its treatment of the relationship between post-industrialism and postmodernist forms of knowledge. First, however, let us turn to Lyotard's earlier work in so far as it bears on art and criticism in postmodernity.

If Foucault's critique of discourse is made via playful and non-discursive theoretical language that draws its impetus from desire, the object of his studies is, however, not desire but the discourse of the human sciences. Lyotard is, in contradistinction, unchallenged as 'the metaphysician of desire'. Lyotard's desire is Freud's libido. Freudian libido 'solidifies' to make up a psychic apparatus: Lyotard's flows of desire are similarly embodied in libidinal (or 'pulsional') 'dispositives'. For Freud and for Lyotard, human behaviour is a matter of such embodied psychic energy working on and transforming flows of psychic energy. Freud mainly considers variation in the qualities of the psychic apparatus in terms of individual patients in the here and now. Lyotard, on the other hand, is concerned with types of cultural practices, hence his libidinal dispositives vary mainly between spheres of culture and over history.[38]

A work of art – and its corresponding dispositive – has value for Lyotard in proportion to the intensity of energy it transmutes to the consumer of art. The less representational a work of art is the more it transmutes libidinal impulses to the consumer. This is because (for example in painting) a representational libidinal dispositive would invest energy in the object that was being painted, whereas a modern dispositive would invest energy in the 'support', the painting itself. Inasmuch as it is the latter that transmutes energy towards the consumer of art, it is the modern painting that would maximize such flow and intensity. Pure representation corresponds for Lyotard roughly to Foucault's classical, partial representation and partial energetic 'positivity' with the modern, while aesthetic postmodernity approaches the type of fully free-flowing and continually metamorphosing energy.[39] Lyotard's systematic anti-semiotics refuses to speak of signs, symbols, or even images, but only of the 'real' and 'material' transformation of psychic energy. His theoretical dispositive would thus have little use for the modernist formalisms of the signifier, whether in the poetry of Eliot or in the literary criticism of Saussureans such as Barthes and Derrida.

Lyotard, as Foucault, presents us with any number of mutually contradictory periodizations in this context. Let us, however, retain the conventional modern/postmodern distinction adumbrated above. In music, Lyotard views Schoenberg, as composer, and Adorno, as critic, as moderns – with one foot in an aesthetics of representation and the other in a libidinal economy. Schoenberg's compositions are surely modern in their 'audible abstraction, the indifference to putatively natural frequency differences, . . . the universalization of the principle of the series to all dimensions of sound'.[40] But this 'new radical dispositive', which emerges through a 'critique from the heart of the old, the classic', itself remains 'liturgical'. It is Schoenberg's formalism that is typically modern in comparison with Classical representation and postmodern 'energetics'. The scepticism of Schoenberg's music-as-critique must be formalist in so far as, in it, all is relation. Schoenberg's chord structures are no longer related to our senses but are only 'monads held together by the domination of a plan'. He carries to the extreme Romanticism's movement away from 'the theme'. Lyotard in this context makes use of Benveniste's distinction between 'discourse' and 'narrative' (*récit*). Schoenberg's music is in this sense discourse in comparison to the narratives of classical music. Yet it is a 'discourse of faith' in that it 'desensitizes the material', and 'leads to the effacement of the libidinal body'.[41] In Schoenberg's 'magic square is . . . the emergence of structure, the neutralisation of differences in intensity'. Lyotard's postmodern alternative is the aleatory music, the prepared instruments of John Cage. He wants a 'music of intensity, a sonorous machine without finality . . . a music of the surface, without depth, precluding representation'. Such a music would be 'a politics of intensity, rather than one of tragedy'.[42]

Cage's postmodern double in the realm of theory is clearly Lyotard himself; Schoenberg's modern compeer is Adorno. Adorno had a great deal in common, maintains Lyotard, with the pessimism and nihilism of Freud's and Schoenberg's *début-du-siècle* Vienna. Adorno understood that human subjectivity was being destroyed by capitalism and took this process as a defeat. He also understood the lack of content in modern art as a result of the alienated subjectivity of the artist. Lyotard wants to affirm both this destruction of subjectivity and disintegration of aesthetic content. Adorno (correctly argues Lyotard) underlined the similarity between Schoenberg's music-as-critique and his own theoretical critique. Thus as modernist he applauds the departure of Schoenberg's compositions from the sensible in that it approaches knowledge in its abstract qualities. Adorno's *Philosophy of the New Music* appeared within months of Mann's *Doktor Faustus* whose protagonist, Leverkuhn, was partly based on Schoenberg. Mann, one of the trinity of great Moderns of the novel, portrayed in narrative what Adorno described in discourse. Leverkuhn can only bring about his qualitative musical critique through the disease he contracted in his visit to the brothel. Aesthetic modernity can only then appear as illness.[43]

Painting and writing for Lyotard are forms of 'inscription', in which energy, through the hand (mediated by a dispositive), marks a 'support'. In both the energy emitted from the medium – which is inscribed on the support – is transmuted through the eye of the individual in the public. Such transmutation will then, it is hoped, positively affect the libidinal dispositive of this individual. Writing is for Lyotard non-chromatic inscription, painting chromatic inscription.[44] Lyotard points to the 'over-codification' of energy in Renaissance painting, in which colour, instead of constituting the region of libidinal investment, only 'marks the invested region'.[45] For Premoderns thus the canvas (as support) was a 'transparent window, . . . giving a view on a spectacle'. With modern painters, however, there is positive transformation of energy from the hand of the painter through the medium. In Cézanne, for example, not only does the medium inscribe the support, but there is even inscription of the medium as medium.[46]

Cézanne, however, attributed to the subject a status that showed he was still to a certain extent a purveyor of an aesthetics of representation. Warhol, on the other hand, is properly a Postmodern. To present objects such as soup cans that 'are exchangeable, obsolescent, that will disappear, be consumed, that have no importance' is at the same time to 'indicate what is important. [And this is] the energetic, fluidity, desire in its deplacability; . . . it is the metamorphoses which count, not the object itself; . . . there are thus elements of liquification in Pop Art'.[47] Postmodern Art is in this sense flux; it is the multiple and 'polymorphously perverse' cathexes of partial objects of infantile sexuality. But even the Postmoderns have not – inasmuch as their exhibition in museums bespeaks the residues of codification – gone far enough. The only solution to the limits of today's painting, Lyotard argues, is to 'explode this limit and take art out of the museums, even out of inhabited places; to paint walls, mountains, bodies, the sand'.[48] For its part, the role of postmodern art criticism should be 'to transform the energetics which the "painting" puts into play', not into a theoretical dispositive, 'but into a sort of liquification, a sort of aleatory production'.[49] Lyotard wants criticism, then, neither to pose nor to solve, but to 'dissolve' the theoretical question of painting.

In *La condition postmoderne*, Lyotard most directly addresses the question of postmodernity, in the context now, not of aesthetics, but of the problem of knowledge. The shift to postmodernism in the sciences and social sciences is for Lyotard crucially connected with the development of post-industrial 'information societies'. Such a shift is most of all marked by a change in the way that knowledge here is legitimated. In Modernity, the natural and human sciences are legitimated through what Lyotard calls 'the great metanarratives'. The crisis of the sciences of the early twentieth century was circumscribed by an incredulity before such universalist legitimations. Postmodern science finds itself face to face with new sets of legitimations; with a system-induced 'performativity', on the one hand, and with legitimation through 'invention', on the other.[50]

All knowledge, for Lyotard (and for that matter all social relations), is a question of language games; games in which the

most important properties of statements are their uses. Statements are thus 'moves' in the game, in an agonistic of language,
in which 'to speak is to do battle'.[51] The Nietzsche in Lyotard's
Wittgenstein is, however, a gentle Nietzsche, for there is one
move Lyotard will not allow in such contests, and that is what he
calls 'la terreur', the elimination of one or more of the
participants from the game.

Lyotard's own pragmatics hinge on the qualitative distinction
he makes between scientific or discursive knowledge (con-
naissance), and knowledge in general (savoir). Scientific
knowledge is composed of denotative statements and the 'metaprescriptive' statements of the scientific community. Knowledge
in everyday life in addition to these comprises ethical, aesthetic,
technical, and other types of statements. The legitimations of
such statements – in other words the criteria for competence of
given statements of performances – are constituted by the
participating interlocutors. The pragmatics of scientific
knowledge vary vastly from the pragmatics of every-day or
'narrative' knowledge. In scientific pragmatics statements are
mainly denotative. Here the speaker A must convince his
interlocutor B that statement C is true by means of proofs. The
interlocutor B is in fact the scientific community of equals, who
are 'partners in a general agonistics'. The partners operate
through metaprescriptive rules into whose framework – through
the university – new participants are from time to time
introduced.[52]

Scientific knowledge up until quite recently has, however,
depended on narrative knowledge for its legitimations. It has
been, not given denotative statements, but the game itself that has
needed legitimation through narrative.[53] The differentia
specifica of the science of modernity was its legitimation by the
great metanarratives of the nineteenth century. Lyotard speaks of
two such metanarratives, the first of which is the Enlightenment's popular 'right to science'. Here everyone has a right,
through education, to be a scientist, and knowledge must be
functional for the social. This is legitimation through
knowledge's popular function, through narrative of liberty. The
second legitimating metanarrative is, for Lyotard, 'speculative
spirit' or idealism. In Schleiermacher, for example, the subject is
not the people, but a notion of autonomous rationality. We can

94

view Hegel's dialectical development of spirit similarly as a legitimation of scientific discourse. This took – in *The Phenomenology* and elsewhere – not the form of propositions for which argument was advanced, but that of a narrative itself, a *metarécit*. The speculative autonomy of the German university, notes Lyotard, on which the American university beginning after the Civil War was modelled, was based on such a metanarrative.[54]

The ethos of modernity's legitimation through the metanarrative, in this case the 'popular' metanarrative, continues, Lyotard maintains, right through to 'the crisis of sociology' of the 1960s, in both functionalism and Marxism. Here Parsons and his colleagues wanted knowledge to function towards the expanded reproduction of society as it was; the Marxists of the Frankfurt School want knowledge to serve as critique of society as it is, and as a basis for society as it should be.[55] There is a crucial difference, notes Lyotard, between Parsons and the German neo-functionalists of the late 1970s and early 1980s, and this is that the latter's view of system is not, as in Parsons, coextensive with the social or the people. Parsons believed in legitimation forms consistent with popular sovereignty, which he hoped would coincide with system needs. Luhmann believes in legitimation through 'performativity' which he hopes will coincide with what the people choose.[56]

The legitimation crisis of the modern sciences came, via Nietzsche and Wittgenstein, through the self-reflexivity of the sciences themselves. Why should we, asked Nietzsche, believe in the great metanarratives? Wittgenstein – not to mention Moore several decades earlier – bore witness to the autonomy of prescriptive from denotative statements, thus questioning the legitimation of knowledge through the prescriptive statement of the language of emancipation.[57] With the end of the *metarécits*, postmodern knowledge is faced with two competing principles of legitimation. The first is performativity; that is of science adapting itself to system needs. This is, argues Lyotard, fostered by the growth of 'information society'. The development of computers, data banks, circuits of sounds and images have led to a quantification,[58] in which knowledge becomes an exchange-value as the use-values of *Bildung* disappear. 'Informationalisation' facilitates power using knowledge for its own purposes. This phenomenon is registered in the work of Luhmann, whose

Hobbesian ethos, transmitted through the influence of Carl Schmitt, has underlain his interest in the reproduction of the state rather than of society. For Luhmann, who devaluates prescriptive utterances, there is 'a replacement of the normativity of laws by the performativity of procedures'.[59]

Lyotard rejects Luhmann's solution as terroristic in that it eliminates players from the largely denotative game of science; indeed it would seem to eliminate the game itself. He applauds Habermas's valiant attempts to take Luhmann to task, but concludes that he ultimately fails. This is, first, because Habermas's advocacy of legitimation through the dialogue of intelligent and free wills is dependent on the validity of the great metanarratives (of human emancipation).[60] Second, Habermas's search for legitimacy through a universal consensus – his notion of justice whereby the 'emancipation of humanity will come about through the regularisation of permitted moves in all language games' – is potentially a threat to the autonomy and inventiveness of the sciences.[61] Lyotard would then perceive his own views of postmodern legitimation to be in competition with Habermas's as an alternative to the systemic neo-conservatism of Luhmann or the cultural conservatism of Bell. Indeed this is what the postmodernity controversy is all about: a competition between the principles of substantive rationality à la Habermas and neo-Nietzschean 'desire' to serve as legitimations of resistance to power in contemporary capitalism. Lyotard does not mince words in his attack on Habermas's attempt at legitimation through 'consensus obtained by discussion'. Habermas 'ravages the heterogeneity of the play of language', Lyotard writes, 'and would do away with the dissent which is at the root of inventions'.[62]

Lyotard's answer to Luhmann is that the pragmatics of scientific knowledge are such that they cannot be subordinated to the demands of performativity; that they are indeed 'the countermodel of a stable system'. It is that science does not play the same language game as society, the latter whose heteromorphic variety of utterances contrasts with science's simpler model of denotative and metaprescriptive statements. The pragmatics of science in which new ideas are encouraged by the interest of players of the game is on the model of the 'open system'.[63] Postmodern science, having broken with the metanarratives, justifies itself in a number of *local* settings, through the second postmodern principle of legitimation, 'paralogy'. This means imagination, inventiveness, dissensus, the search for paradoxes. The only way in which society can impose legitimations of performativity on science is to destroy the scientific enterprise itself. Lyotard extends this notion of postmodern legitimation through paralogy from science to society itself. He wants a system of justice that is based not on consensus, but on dissensus; one that resists the necessity of even the milder 'terror' that he sees entailed in the Procrustean bed of communicative rationality.

There is prima facie disparity between Lyotard's analysis of knowledge through language games and legitimations and his above-discussed libidinal aesthetics. Some connections between the former and the latter are clarified in a book of interviews, given contemporaneously with the writing of *La condition postmoderne*, on the problem of justice. Here Lyotard's summary prescription, pointing at the same time to 'invention' in language games and to desire, is 'let us be pagans'.[64] But other parallels should be clear. Legitimation through paralogy is at the same time advocacy of the decoding of libido in the sciences and elsewhere. Language games are themselves agons whose moves are governed by the libidinal economy, which they in turn help structure. We should then – in art, in science, in every-day life – be pagans, but, Lyotard enjoins, let us be gentle pagans.

From signification to sensation

After a political thematization of the postmodern in *Anti-Oedipus*[65] Gilles Deleuze addressed its aesthetics in *Francis Bacon, Logique de la sensation*.[66] Here he delineates for us the elements of a fully developed postmodernist aesthetic, one based on notions of the 'body' and 'forces'. Francis Bacon as a painter is known for his creations of distorted human figures. His style closely resembles that of renascent (in the 1980s) figurative expressionism. Deleuze understands Bacon's paintings and his own theory of desire as inscribed in a 'logic of sensation'. 'Sensation', Deleuze proposes, occurs when 'forces' act on the body. The body, which differs from the organism, is 'traversed by a wave which traces levels and thresholds according to variations in their amplitude'.[67] 'Sensation' is the meeting of forces with these 'waves'. Sensation takes place when, for example, a force, such as light, meets with the body's waves by means of an organ such as the eye.[68]

To paint, as Klee noted, is not to render the visible but to render visible; or as Lyotard repeated, painting should be, not 'figurative', but 'figural'.[69] What this means for Deleuze is that time, inertia, sound, thermal qualities – in short, forces not accessible to the eye – should be made visible in painting. If classical painting reproduces forms, and modern painting invents them, postmodern painting should do neither; it should instead render forces as forms.[70] Thus the agitation in Bacon's heads comes not from movement but from the pressure of forces. In each successive face of, for example, the triptych, *Three Studies for a Self-portrait*, the zone where forces happen to strike is marked by deformation. When Bacon paints bodies he paints forces. Whence the extraordinary bodily passivity in Bacon. Bacon does not reproduce the spectacle of a body undergoing torture, but the isolated body – wanting to vomit, wanting to sleep – on which forces act. For Bacon – as he does in his re-interpretation of Velazquez's *Innocent X* – to paint a pope's cry is again not to paint the spectacle that gives rise to it, but to paint the invisible forces which are its condition. But this assumption of passivity, this pessimism, is only one side of sensation. The other side is the optimism of a cry that is itself the struggle of the visible body against the invisible, decomposing force. It is the body whose figure *renders* the force visible. The cry is thus 'life', 'desire', in struggle against the forces.[71]

The postmodern, for Deleuze, means a culture of sensation, not only for the painter and the painting, but for the consumer of art and the science of criticism. 'Presence', Deleuze writes, 'is the word which first comes in front of a Bacon painting.'[72] What Deleuze calls a 'clinical aesthetics' is thus extended to the consumer of art, who is also conceived on the model of hysteria. Forces – the lines and colours of the painting – invest the eye, or, more accurately, *create* the eye as polyvalent organ on the surface of the body. The eye is in the stomach, it is aural, it is tactile, as it is invested with a range of non-visible forces that have been rendered visible in the form.[73] It is the congealed intensity of the figural in postmodern painting that releases forces that convert 'normal' organismic bodies of consumers of art into bodies without organs. It is these forces that create hysterics out of the psychodynamically conventional through the release and establishment of excesses of presence. Bacon's object is thus to deregulate the senses in order to attain an intensity of sensation. Deleuze's *clinique esthétique* compares music with painting. In music, in which the ear becomes the polyvalent organ, inertia is taken away from the body; music 'disincarnates the body', makes it immaterial; music 'inserts itself on lines of flight which traverse the body, but which find their consistency elsewhere'. What music is to raging schizophrenia, Deleuze argues, painting is to hysteria. Painting meets the body at angles 'where the body escapes itself, but in escaping itself, discovers the materiality of which it is composed, the pure presence of which it is made'.[74]

Cultural postmodernity: towards an ideal type

Let us rehearse the main lines of the framework of postmodernity, the elements of which I have traced above through treatment of Foucault, Lyotard, and Deleuze. Such a framework gives us an account of the production, the content and mode of consumption of postmodernist art forms, as well as a delineation of how the latter may be appropriated by the human sciences. It presents us with guidelines for the understanding of the postmodern forms of knowledge and of micropolitical struggles of the every-day world. (1) Postmodern art draws on uncoded and semi-coded libido in the unconscious to produce a literature and fine arts that break with the classical aesthetics of representation and with the formalism of modernity. It penetrates to underneath the signifier, to the real, the material, to sensation, to what Barthes many years ago described as the 'degree-zero of writing'. Postmodern art not only draws on desire, and operates from a position of sensation; it also embodies desire. The intensity of libido embodies in a work of art – hence transmitted to the consumer – increases proportionally with the extent to which it departs from the representational.[75] Moreover, the form and content of postmodern art, for instance in the theatre of Peter Brook, is bodily and, in some sense, of the unconscious. (2) The effect on the consumer, the spectator, the 'public', is equally by means of the unconscious. The flows of libido embodied in the book, painting, or piece of music produce forces that give rise to 'sensation' when they strike the bodies of consumers, through the now polyvalent eye or ear. Via such mediating organs, these forces foster the decoding, and thus maximize the flux, of libido in the consumer. Such effects on the unconscious are maximized – and hierarchy is diminished – to the extent that not just the separation of stage and audience is cancelled, but the walls of the theatre destroyed to erase the distinction between inside and outside. (3) Aesthetic postmodernity is also critique: critique of social scientific discourse as well as representational and formalist trends in art. Culture criticism, and more generally the human sciences in postmodernity, are to supplement such critique. The natural sciences in postmodernity are to oppose the criteria of 'performativity' imposed by political decision-makers in 'information society', an opposition that follows directly from the agonistic of language games interior to the sciences themselves, the latter produce the valorization instead of 'invention', of 'dissensus'. (4) For all of our authors this critical weaponry that is created by postmodern culture is directly political; it is often understood in quite concrete connection with the 'micro-politics' of the various social movements; it is sometimes understood in the context of post-industrial society. The political here, we should note, means more than opposing one type of high culture to another. For example, Foucault's notion of transgression also circumscribes the practices of 'deviants' and others subjugated by the effects of discourse in every-day life. Deleuze and Guattari's work describes the highly political battles over the structuration of the unconscious in the every-day world.

HABERMAS VERSUS THE NEO-NIETZSCHEANS

The problem of rights

The above discussion was partly framed as a reply to Habermas's explicit attacks on postmodernist theory and aesthetics, attacks that even a number of those working sympathetically to critical theory have found to be somewhat exaggerated.[76] There is, however, in Habermas's oeuvre material for a much more fundamental critique of the theorists of desire, a critique that would by implication extend to French structuralists such as

Barthes, Derrida, and Lacan as well. This critique can, I believe, be very usefully launched around a notion of 'rights' that is at points explicit, at points implicit in the theory of communicative rationality. Let me first then attempt to explicate this doctrine of rights, and then use it as a *point d'appui* for criticism of the neo-Nietzscheans.

Although Albrecht Wellmer, among others, has taken Habermas to task for the procedural nature of his theory of practical discourse, I believe that the latter can be understood effectively as a theory of natural rights. Habermas's project can be seen as one of the development of a plausible theory of substantive rationality. He sees this as the ultimate goal of modernity, which for him – in contrast to the above-discussed writers – is the project of the Enlightenment. Modernity is thus for him an *'unvollendetes Projekt'*, whose telos passes through formal rationality – of which the Habermas of *Theorie des kommunikativen Handels* sees Max Weber as a key proponent – to the possibility of a substantive rationality.[77] The search for such a substantive rationality was the guiding framework, Habermas notes, of the work of the 'Classical' Critical Theorists, at least until 1941, and it is this goal to which Habermas's oeuvre has been devoted.[78] The theory of substantive rationality of the early Frankfurt School has, however, been noticeably lacking in plausibility. First, because of a notable absence of systematic argument on its behalf. And second because it is grounded in a nineteenth-century philosophy of consciousness, a 'meta-narrative' few find credible today. Habermas, recognizing this, wants to present us with a convincing theory of substantive rationality. His method of doing this – and surely this is Habermas's most profound insight, one that shines in even greater brilliance to those of us who have come to Habermas after a more Gallic-oriented theoretical education – is through a twentieth-century philosophy of language. That language, not consciousness, is the human *differentia specifica* is at the basis of his theory of universal pragmatics.

Habermas's view of language here is one with which Saussureans such as Derrida, and semioticians such as Eco (who has adapted Saussure in the construction of a Peircian pragmatics) would have little to quibble.[79] Unlike the empirical realism of the early Wittgenstein, for whom language replaces consciousness as a 'mirror of nature', Habermas's signifiers do not directly latch on to referents in the external world. Unlike some of the more naive statements that can be found in the text of Saussure and Barthes, Habermas eschews any notion of 'sign', in which signifier stands in some natural connection with signified or concept. Understanding in communication between inter-locutors is brought about instead through an attachment of signifier to signified that is conventional and rule-bound. The only disparity with Saussure – and there is arguably no disparity at all with Eco – is that rules replace the play of differences of elements, and focus is on *parole* instead of *langue*.[80] To students of French theory, it is as if Habermas had, not only stolen the bats and balls of the structuralists/poststructuralists, but used them to blow the whistle on their whole anti-Enlightenment ballgame.

Habermas's universal pragmatics did not, of course, draw on the French theorists but instead on the writings of Austin and Searle. For Habermas the substantively rational goal of Critical Theory – a life-world free from forms of subjugation – is inherent in the 'truth', or intersubjective validity with regard to which all speech acts are situated. Speech acts, taken generically, are intended to bring about a specific set of interpersonal relations. Speech acts, for Habermas, are like offers; that is they can be accepted or rejected by the hearer. Speech acts are accepted by hearers if they are recognized as valid. In this sense speech acts as offers are accompanied by validity claims. Besides the point that speech acts must be comprehensible to the hearer to be recognized as valid, validity claims include assertions about the truth of expressions in regard to the extralinguistic world. They involve thus claims to the truth of expressions in connection with the external world; claims to the rightness or appropriateness of locutions in connection with the social world; and claims to the sincerity of locutions in regard to the subjective world. More specifically, Habermas speaks of 'constative' speech acts in relation to the external world, of 'regulative' speech acts in relation to the world of social norms, and of 'expressive' speech acts in regard to the subjective world.[81]

Constative and regulative speech acts stand in a special prox-imity to a world that is located apart from and adjacent to Habermas's world of action. This is the world of 'discourse' or of 'argumentation'. If a constative act is rejected, and attempts at its empirical grounding are also rejected, then we are likely to move into the world of 'theoretical discourse'. If a regulative act is rejected, and the extant social norm in which the speaker attempts to ground it is also rejected, speaker and hearer may move into the world of 'practical discourse', in which arguments are put for the validity of the norms themselves.[82] Since my claims are about the convergence between Habermas's communicative action and natural rights doctrine – and about the validity of such as a Habermasian critique of structuralism/poststructuralism, my interest is, of course, in practical discourse.

Let me, then, list several reasons that lead me to believe that Habermas's practical discourse is for all intents and purposes equivalent to a doctrine of natural rights.

(1) The substantive rationality that serves as objective for early Critical Theory and Habermas should be understood as entailing substantive natural rights. This is because both incarnations of Critical Theory want to apply reason first and foremost to the normative sphere or the social world. Rights and obligations are inherent qualities of all norms. This is true in the sense that all norms contain an imperative, whose binding nature stems from a source that is external to the norm itself; and all obligations entail the existence of rights. And the rational justification, as distinct from the institutional justification, of rights and obligations is the *differentia specifica*, in contradistinction from legal positivism, of natural rights theory.[83]

(2) Correlatively, early Critical Theory and Habermas want the Enlightenment-type formal rationality of social norms to be extended and developed into substantive rationality. Weber spoke not only of formal and substantive rationality, but in *Wirtschaft und Gesellschaft's Rechtssoziologie* of 'formal' and 'substantive natural law', associating the former with the bourgeoisie and the latter with the working class.[84] Formal natural rights here would be discursively redeemable but still leave intact a number of unnecessary forms of domination and neglect the realization of important sets of human needs. Substantive natural rights are addressed as a remedy for this and a fulfilment of these two normative goals of Critical Theory.

(3) The young Marx's critique included, as a negative doctrine, a set of objections to bourgeois 'formal' natural rights in *The Critique of Hegel's Philosophy of Right*, and – as positive

doctrine – a theory of human needs, whose fulfilment was promised by the norms of a future communist society. Inasmuch as there is present in Marx's work a number of arguments for the validity of such norms, it is plausible to speak of a doctrine of substantive natural justice to be implicit in Marxism. The importance of human needs, often in conjunction with notions of a universalist or substantive justice, assume a position of centrality also in the work of Lukács and the early Frankfurt School. They are central to Habermas as well, inasmuch as the justification of norms in practical discourse that he advocated consists of a set of arguments addressed to generalizable human needs.[85] In this sense what I am arguing is that Habermas's theory of natural justice is a signal contribution to the development of a Marxian ethics, a project that writers well apart from the tradition of Critical Theory, such as G. A. Cohen, have also addressed in reference to doctrines of natural justice.[86]

(4) Enlightenment natural rights doctrines, however, are, with the end of the great metanarratives, rather implausible today. Either they make inferences from descriptive to prescriptive statements and are based on initial assumptions about people in a state of nature that most of us will not accept; or, as in Kant's *Metaphysical Elements of Justice*,[87] such theories of natural law are based on a strong foundationalism and a strong version of transcendental argument that are acceptable to few today. The elements of a philosophy of consciousness are of course present in Kant, just as they are in Hegel's practical discourse as well as the natural-rights thematics of the young Marx, Lukács, and the earlier work of Horkheimer, Adorno, and Marcuse. Consequently, such theories also are lacking in credibility. It is Habermas's capital contribution to offer us a doctrine of natural justice (practical discourse) that breaks with both Kant's strong foundationalism and with the philosophy of consciousness. Habermas's theory is, as is now well known, procedural. But in an age in which we would reject the substantive assumptions of any of the just-mentioned doctrines, it seems to me that any plausible natural rights theory must be procedural. The renaissance of natural law doctrine for the English-reading public has been most importantly catalysed by the work of Rawls. His doctrine is highly procedural in content, and has been compared in a rather detailed manner with Habermas's by

more than one Anglo-American philosopher.[88] The juris-prudential application of Rawls's political philosophy has taken place above all through the writings of Ronald Dworkin, who in debates with legal positivists, has defined natural or moral rights quite literally in terms of the discursive redemption of rights inherent in legal norms. Dworkin's natural rights are defined in contradistinction to both the legal rights that characterize the laws of the state, and rights inscribed in institutional norms; they are instead rights that are supported by reasoned discourse.[89] It is a similar type of thinking on Habermas's part, that, I suspect, leads him to draw rather on Searle's theory of speech acts rather than on Austin's because of the latter's assumptions that speech acts are institutionally situated.[90]

(5) Habermas, Rawls, and Dworkin proffer a procedural theory to the extent that norms are accorded validity to the extent that they are chosen by rational autonomous individuals. In their defence, it might be recalled that a number of Enlightenment-type natural rights are also procedural rights: for example, due process in the courts, guarantees of the generality of the law, and the right to choose political representatives.

(6) Finally, in the context of sociology of knowledge, it is hard to believe that Habermas was not affected in his youth by the large number of (secular and Christian) natural rights doctrines that were in circulation in postwar Germany in reaction to the experience of the Third Reich.[91]

I have, I hope, reasonably established that Habermas's 'practical discourse' can be understood as a theory of natural rights. Such a theory is, I think, a necessary element of any conceptual framework whose objective is to counteract subjugation and domination. I should now like to turn to the French theorists, and argue that structuralism/poststructuralism systematically excludes any such conception of rights. Habermas obliquely comments on this when he defends the constitutional rights stemming from the Enlightenment against what he sees as the anti-rationalist ethos of aesthetic modernity. Richard Rorty, himself far from an unconditional friend of the Enlightenment, has levelled a similar reproach at Foucault, who in an interview with French Maoists on popular justice, objected to even the slim residues of legality that remained in the people's courts of Mao's China. 'What need for any kind of courts?' Foucault seemed to be saying.[92] To the extent that Foucault was, like Lyotard and Deleuze, an *anarchisant* advocate of the revolution of desire against any kind of structure, legality – whether bourgeois or proletarian, formal or substantive – ought to be dispensed with.

But there is a more systematic exclusion of any notion of rights by the several varieties of poststructuralism/structuralism. In Foucault's genealogical version of a philosophy of history, the Classical period (1650–1800) is associated with dualist (whether rationalist or empiricist) epistemologies and a dualist paradigm of power that Foucault has labelled 'juridico-discursive'. In the Modern period, dualisms disappear; discourses are immanentist and power operates immanently, no longer operating repressively and negatively from above, but positively and, as he puts it, in 'the capillaries of society', as a normalizing and individuating force.[93] If we understand rights in terms of the justified powers that are ascribed to individuals,[94] then there must be a second and separate instance, typically the state or political doctrines themselves – as in natural rights theory – that does the justifying. But for Foucault any such notions are associated with the Classical period and badly outmoded. Foucault has also referred to a juridico-discursive model, though this time rather elliptically, in his criticisms of the Soviet state.[95] In his eager and thoroughgoing anti-Platonist hostility to any two-world conceptualizations, Foucault has thrown out the liberating (moral rights) baby with the statist bathwater.

A similar rejection of rights is integral to the historical periodizations of Deleuze and Lyotard. For the *désirants*, capitalism and modernity result from a process of the decodification of desire; in premodern societies desire is heavily symbol-laden; in capitalism symbol becomes sign and desire is only codified by the commodity-form. Bourgeois natural rights in this context would arise through the coding of desire by the commodity-form. Deleuze and Lyotard have not advocated, as Habermas has, the reinforcement of formal natural rights and their extension to include substantive rights in a possible post-capitalist society. Instead for the *désirants*, the end of capitalism would be associated with the complete decodification of desire and the absence, hence, of both formal and substantive rights.

Consider then French theorists such as Barthes and Derrida who write in semiotic, and arguably structuralist, vein. The great advance of the theory of desire over the semioticians lay in the former's – catalysed by the 1968 events – supplying a theory of power that was notably absent in the latter.[96] In the absence of a conception of power – power over persons or powers over things – and since rights by definition assume such powers, no notion of rights is possible.[97] As well, the anti-dualism inherent in Derrida's attacks on a 'metaphysics of presence', on the identity of signifier and signified, of speech and concept, preclude, as I've argued above, the possibility of rights. Hazily-formed notions of justice, based on calls for the free play of the signifier, of desire or of language-games issued by the French theorists are no substitute for the thoroughgoing theory of substantive rights that pervades Habermas's notion of practical discourse. Calls by writers such as Lyotard for the freedom of invention of artists and scientists from state power are not at all the same thing as guarantees for ordinary individuals against public violation of their autonomy, or guarantees to a certain level of fulfilment of human needs. The neo-Nietzscheans, in their implacable hostility to state power, have broken with any concept of the discursive justification of norms, which then leaves the individual without protection from the difficult-to-wish-away state.

A problematic consensus: Lyotard versus Habermas

In a more recent article Lyotard, responding rather more directly to Habermas's attacks on the theoretical and aesthetic postmodernity, upped the ante in the postmodernity controversy. Shifting registers from his work of the early and mid-1970s and consciously following Walter Benjamin, he argued that aesthetic modernity/postmodernity lay in the unstable and contradictory nature of forms of art that corresponded to the disharmonic and paradox-ridden condition of late nineteenth- and twentieth-century society. Rather at odds with his previous attacks on the signifier, but only *en passant*, Lyotard distinguished an aesthetic modernity whose content registers the breakdown of identity and totality (his examples are German Expressionism and Proust), from a postmodernity, in which instability and experimentation are registered also in form (his examples are Picasso and Joyce). More to the point here, he uses Benjamin as it were against

Habermas. He understands trends of the early 1980s both towards a new representationalism and towards an eclectic kitsch, as an onslaught against the experimentation of aesthetic modernity/ postmodernity, an offensive that attempts to restore belief in the unity, consensus, and harmony of in fact paradox-riven capitalist and socialist societies. Habermas's work, and especially what Lyotard sees as Habermas's attacks on innovation in arts and the literature, are then understood as part of this consensual effort.[98]

In *La condition postmoderne* and 'Qu'est-ce que le postmoderne?' we can distinguish five interrelated lines of criticism that Lyotard makes against Habermas, all centred on Habermas's problematic notion of consensus.

(1) Habermas's theory is based on the great metanarratives. This point is not wholly valid. As we saw above, Habermas's practical discourse has gained such wide credibility precisely because it breaks with the strong foundationalism of the meta-narratives. However, because Habermas refuses to separate his descriptive theory of society from his ethical doctrine, he must bring in another *metarécit* in the form of his theory of social evolution. And so far the evidence that he has presented for his identification of moral development with the evolution of societies is very thin.[99]

(2) Habermas seeks the regularization of language games. Lyotard originally brings this up in his discussion of science; a discussion that suggests a different twist to the argument for value-freedom and against Critical Theory's refusal to separate the normative from the theoretical. It is an argument for *Wertfreiheit* that is not based on any hoped for objectivity in the natural or human sciences, but that calls, in the very name of an ethics (of freedom and inventivity), for freedom from political interference (be it consensually constituted or not) in the various language games of science.[100] Habermas has partly responded to this type of criticism, at points suggesting that communicative rationality is situated in a number of autonomous spheres of social life, and more consistently insisting on a Kantian separation of the aesthetic, the practical, and the theoretical as a defining characteristic of modernity's project. Lyotard is willing to give Habermas the benefit of the doubt here, but then asks, in reference to the strong notion of universality in Habermas's oeuvre as well as his insistence on the pervasive interarticulation

of the aesthetic, the normative, and the theoretical, 'how, then, is Habermas able to realise their effective synthesis'.[101] This leads one to pose the related but central question not of how the conditions of achieving communicative rationality are problematic for Habermas, but the normative question of why should we consider an ethics of communicative rationality to be desirable in the first place? Habermas's ethics heavily draws on Kohlberg's developmental psychology. Communicative action is so conceived to be a higher stage than stage 6, the highest stage in Kohlberg's schema. Stages 4 and 5 here correspond, as Steven Lukes has pointed out, to ethical doctrines, to which large numbers of contemporary political philosophers with very good arguments subscribe. How can Kohlberg and Habermas then, often unproblematically, assume the superiority of stage 6 and communicative ethics?[102]

(3) Lyotard points out that Habermas's call for the artist to relate much more closely to the experiences and practices of every-day life can have negative effects on the creativity of the avant-garde,[103] and in this respect does not differ significantly from the cultural conservatism in the West or in the East.

(4) Habermas ravages the heterogeneity of language. This is a stronger version of the weaker claim that Lyotard and others have made that Habermas wants to bring about a fully transparent society.[104] Habermas has rejected this reproach, but his arguments supporting this rejection are tangential, allusive, and hardly convincing.[105] Lyotard's stronger claim here is that Habermas's advocacy of transparency, which supports the identity of signifier and signified, is supportive of the realist and totalizing cultural strategies of contemporary political power.

(5) Lyotard states that it is possible that Habermas 'confuses Kant's notion of the "sublime" with Freudian sublimation and that the aesthetic for Habermas is still a question of beauty'.[106] What Lyotard seems to mean here is that in effect Habermas would reject Kant's notion of the sublime as the basis of a modernist aesthetic and instead adopt (also) Kant's notion of beauty. Lyotard notices that modernist criticism no longer equates aesthetic value with beauty. He recommends a modern/ postmodern aesthetics of the sublime, the elements of which can be found in Kant's *Critique of Judgement*. This Lyotard understands in terms of the mixed feelings of pleasure and pain that

arise from the contemplation of art that 'presents the unpresentable', or presents what Kant understood as entities that lack form.[107] The Freudian analogy here stems, it seems to me, from Lyotard's understanding of the 'unpresentable' in terms of the play of libidinal forces. This specific criticism of Habermas badly misses the mark. Habermas does not subscribe to an aesthetics of beauty. Yet Habermas's theory of self-reflection, which suggests the cognitive control of the 'constraints' and 'illusions' of the unconscious, and the rendering transparent of the latter in order to help 'subjectivity' emancipate itself from these constraints, would surely be anathematic to Lyotard's Kantian aesthetic.[108] Indeed is not the richness, creative unpredictability, and community-centred communicative-exchange of the life-world anchored in such 'constraints' and 'illusions'?

SOME CONCLUDING COMMENTS

Lyotard's criticisms are important, or at least should be important, to Habermas. They amount to the charge that Habermas, in trying to implement Critical Theory's objective of emancipation from unnecessary forms of power, in fact ends up reinforcing, through his ethos of universality and consensus, that very power and thus undermining the aims of Critical Theory. The reproaches, on the other hand, that can be levelled from a Habermasian perspective at the absence of a concept of substantive justice in neo-Nietzschean theory are, as I have tried to argue, also quite valid. This does not preclude, however, the possibility of a theory of social action or agency that is coherent and consistent, embraces the positive contributions of both theoretical trends, and avoids the pitfalls that I have underlined. The presentation of such a theory is well beyond the scope of this chapter. But it should be noted that a theory that embraces and assigns centrality to notions of natural justice, as does Habermas's, *can* dispense with a theory of evolution, and strong notions of consensus and universality. If Habermas is convincing in regard to the question of rights and moral reason, it is not because but rather in spite of these latter qualities of his problematic.[109] While I would disagree with the subordinate (indeed subjugated) role Habermas assigns to the aesthetic and the sensual, surely Lyotard and the other neo-Nietzscheans do not have to break so radically with

substantive justice and rationality in order to stress the importance of desire and aesthetic creativity. Habermas's work is
suggestive of a tripartite quasi-Kantian notion of agency, in
which a cognitive 'faculty' stands in a position of dominance *vis-
à-vis* moral and especially aesthetic-sensual faculties. Habermas
would here, not unlike Kant, understand the relation of these
components of agency along lines of a 'heteronomous' and
autonomous legislation, in which 'self-reflection' describes the
cognitive component's relation to moral and aesthetic-sensual
components. But in a strange sense, Lyotard and many French
theorists present mirror images of this schema, and would
understand autonomous agency in terms of the aesthetic-sensual
component's legislation to the cognitive and the moral elements.
I think that it is preferable to break with both of these Kantian
legislative models, and view agency more 'dialogically', in which
the cognitive (and the moral) are enriched and underpinned by
the aesthetic-sensual, and in which the latter is continually
restructured by theoretical and practical reason.[110] Perhaps, in
this vein, William Morris had the right idea in his conception of
domination of capitalist over worker in the labour process in
terms of the obstruction of aesthetic creativity; a conception that
evokes an aesthetic understanding of the moral advocacy of
substantive rights in the conditions of production.

This said, we should also note a number of points of convergence between Habermas and the French theorists. Perhaps
foremost, both break with the relativisms that have been so
preponderant in social theory of recent decades. Against
relativisms, both theoretical trends subscribe to a (more or less
weak) form of foundationalism. This is rather apparent as we
described above in especially Habermas's theory of normative
foundations. But what Habermas has said of Marcuse – namely
that he came to reject a practical discourse founded on reason for
one founded on the instincts[111] – could be equally applied to the
French writers. Also against the relativistic implications of
cyclical or contingent notions of history, both communicative
rationality and the problematics of desire are inscribed in a linear
notion of historical time; Habermas here is the Whig, Foucault
the mirror-image of the Whig, and the *désirants* optimistic
readers of history as an evolutionary process of decodification.

Further, both stand in a similar position in respect of

Marxism. Both Habermas and the neo-Nietzscheans have come to occupy, indeed to dominate, centre-stage in social theory in concurrence with the very rapid decline of Western Marxism in the 1980s. Neither assigns a very conspicuous role to the working class, and both are quite attractive as doctrinal sources for the social movements. Yet neither will spell out the possible role of such forces for social change, an absence that, it seems, it associated with a sort of elitism that pervades both bodies of thought. Habermas has rightly accused the French theorists of such an elitism, in which a 'transcendental' aesthetic realm is not at all sufficiently interwoven with the social. Though I have defended the neo-Nietzscheans against Habermas's charge that they lack an ethics or a politics, such elitism is pervasive and especially patent in Lyotard's dismissal of popular culture in Adorno-like resonances.[112] On the other hand Habermas's 'seminar' model of social change hardly lends itself without qualification to the social struggles of the every-day.

A final point of comparison concerns the neglect of Habermas and the French writers to attach sufficient importance to the uses of symbol. Both Critical Theory and the neo-Nietzscheans take as point of departure, and normative underpinning, the importance of resistance to forms of domination. Notions of substantive rationality and the associated idea of substantive rights, developed largely through critical reflection, have been important resources for resistance to domination by, for example, labour movements, anti-racism, and feminism. The labour history literature contains numerous examples of bodies of workers who have understood Enlightenment notions of formal natural justice in terms of more substantive notions of justice, which then served as ideological resources in industrial and political struggles.[113] The problematic centring on desire and the body, on the one hand, and codification or repression through structure on the other has also had explanatory potential (and meaning) for resistance to domination in the late 1960s and again in the rebourgeoning social movements of the 1980s.[114] Neither of these interpretations of power and resistance, however, seems to understand the importance of the resistance of subordinated groups through ritual or the construction of collective identity through symbol. This sort of analysis, with the renascent influence of anthropology and the new central role of cultural

112

studies,[115] is coming to assume a position of central importance in the human sciences of the late twentieth century.

Theory and Society (1985)

Acknowledgement

This chapter first appeared as an article in *Theory and Society*, Volume 14, Number 1, pages 1–33, 1985, and is reproduced by permission of Kluwer Academic Publishers, The Netherlands.

Chapter Four

COMMUNICATIVE RATIONALITY AND DESIRE

ROY BOYNE AND SCOTT LASH

Over the past decade a debate has been opened in which Habermas's theory of communicative rationality has been counterposed to the 'aesthetic-sensual forms of subjectivity' advocated by certain French theorists, who have come to be known as the 'poststructuralists'. Among the latter, the most significant figures are Michel Foucault, Jean-François Lyotard, Gilles Deleuze, and Felix Guattari. This confrontation between theories of desire and theories of communicative rationality is perhaps only just beginning, but already it has made a creative contribution to the development of social theory, and more importantly, it has helped – in conjunction with the new social movements (feminism, the peace movement, the ecology movement) – to clarify some *practical* issues involved in the task of building a new political culture. It is in this general context that we should like to intervene in the 'postmodernity controversy' in order to show that the positions of Habermas and the poststructuralists are not as antithetical as is commonly conceived. At the same time we feel that it is necessary to make some critical points with respect to the account of the work of Deleuze and Guattari, provided by Manfred Frank.[1] It is not our intention to provide a full-scale exegesis of Deleuze and Guattari's work, but given the quite critical status of their *Anti-Oedipus*, its significance, in other words, for understanding the poststructuralist theories of desire and the body, the more important of Frank's misconceptions will be corrected as we proceed to examine the compatibility or otherwise of the standpoints of desire and communicative rationality.

When comparing Habermas and the poststructuralist, three

kinds of affinity can be discerned. In the first place, there are shared characteristics, both positive and negative; next there are compatibilities such that although the theoretical constructs may differ they are far from mutually antagonistic; lastly, their politically significant audience is identical, and so we may speak of them as sharing certain principles, and as being able to operate within the same delimited cultural field. Let us expand on these three levels.

Habermas and the French theorists owe a common debt to Hegel's formulation of the master-slave dialectic. Habermas, of course, has conceived master and slave to be connected through *both* labour and language. The poststructuralists, however, reject the Marxist connection through work, to focus only on the Nietzschean one through language. The radical heritage of the master-slave conception is taken up on both sides: emancipation from the tyranny of work is paralleled with emancipation from the tyranny of language. Furthermore, the master-slave dialectic figures as a point of theoretical departure for both camps; this hardly needs demonstrating in the case of Habermas, but it may be less obvious for the French theorists, in which respect, as Wilden has pointed out, the ubiquitous opposition of the Same and the Other is based on Hegel's master and slave.[2] Two examples of this theoretical lineage come to mind straight away: Lacan's presentation of the relation between the conscious and unconscious mind, and Foucault's account of that between words and things. A word of warning is, however, in order here: an awareness of the poststructuralist debt to Hegel may be thought to warrant the inclusion of Derrida and the deconstructionists within the poststructuralist category, a move which Frank makes in referring to Deleuze as a practitioner of deconstruction. But such an assimilation would be misleading, because the deconstructionists locate themselves within the domain of the text, while the poststructuralist enterprise is defined in opposition to such textual incorporation of the body and desire. The point to be made, then, is that while Habermas and the poststructuralists share a link to Hegel, this is only theoretically significant as part of the whole ensemble of relations between them. One further comment should be made, before we leave the topic of Hegel, and this relates to the question of subjectivity. If the influence of Hegel is important, then we would expect both

Habermas and the poststructurlists to be elaborating a theory of the subject. Clearly, in Habermas's case, such a theory is being developed through the interanimation of the ideas of communicative rationality and those of moral identity. But Frank has suggested that two central figures in the poststructuralist camp, namely Deleuze and Guattari, do not contribute anything to a theory of subjectivity. Now, if this is right, any assertion of a significant connection between Hegel and the poststructuralists is thrown into considerable doubt. But it is not right; whether or not it is felt that they succeeded to any extent, there can be little doubt that Deleuze and Guattari, in *Anti-Oedipus*, were seeking to theorize a different, 'nomadic' notion of subjectivity in contradistinction to the normalized and hierarchic forms of subjectivity which have been constituted through territorialization and the commodity form.[3]

A second feature, shared by Habermas and the poststructuralists, concerns their dismissal of the working class as the main agent of emancipatory social change. The visibility within the field of theory over the last few years, on both sides of the Atlantic, of Habermas and the French neo-Nietzscheans, is partly a result of the quiet removal from centre-stage of Marxism and theories of class struggle. For all the faults of Marxist fundamentalism, this reaction may well have been excessive. A neglect of class stratification is politically reprehensible in times of increased unemployment and social inequality, and it is intellectually unjustifiable in the absence of an empirically informed theoretical demonstration that the working classes do not still remain a highly important force for social change. This bears tangentially on Frank's elision of Deleuze and the neofascist right; Deleuze's libertarian and anti-hierarchical appeal to the activists of the new social movements, his arguments against racist interpretations of Nietzsche, and his role in the public debate on the question of the silence of the left-intellectuals,[4] all show Frank's suggestion to be irresponsible.

The third shared characteristic is the featuring of agency over structure. Rationality is a concept primarily applicable to agents, whether individual or collective; it is the pivotal notion for Habermas's project, and defines it as action-theoretic. This is, of course, the conventional understanding of the matter. The point here is that the world of Deleuze, Lyotard, and the later Foucault is also action-theoretic; that is to say, the theory of desire and the body stands in basic contradiction to the derivative nature of the social actor in *all* structuralisms, whether of mode of production, of *langue*, text, or *écriture*.

A typically action-theoretic reticence with regard to postulating either contractual fictions or transcendental constraints may partly explain why neither Habermasian Critical Theory nor poststructuralism has sought to formulate a theory of rights, especially moral or natural rights. Most guilty on this count are the poststructuralists, and Rorty, among others, has already taken them to task on this. But the same accusation can be made against Habermas, who accepts the irreducible centrality of constitutional guarantees won in the bourgeois revolutions, and who speaks of communicative rationality and of substantive rationality, but who rarely speaks of substantive rights. The action-theoretic form in Habermas leads to the situation where the implicit right for the actor is the right to language, whereas for the poststructuralists, it is the right to desire. In each case, and in opposition to the spirit of both enterprises, an implicit reliance on a formal right is paralleled with a disregard for the question of substantive rights. It cannot be emphasized enough that both projects urgently need to develop a vocabulary for the discussion of such topics as rights to welfare, safe working condition, education, and a thousand other things. Of course, the individual theorists make statements and hold opinions on these sorts of questions; but the important thing is to try and integrate the theme of substantive rights into the respective theoretical machinery. The radical projects of both the poststructuralist theory of desire and Habermas's communicative rationality would be strengthened if the advice of G. A. Cohen were to be followed. He points out that neo-conservatism has made considerable cultural capital out of notions of individual autonomy and individual rights. Two examples of which illustrate this nicely are Margaret Thatcher's use of individual-rights language to legitimate a whole range of economic and social policies, and the use by jurists, at the European Court of Human Rights, of individual-rights arguments in order to diminish effectively the possibility of union protection for workers. Cohen argues that this weapon must be taken from the Right and made to serve other ends, emphasizing that the discourse of rights is invested with considerable meaning for contemporary society.[5]

The lacuna represented in this discussion of rights might seem to support a view of poststructuralism as morally relativistic. Indeed, Manfred Frank makes exactly this claim with respect to the work of Deleuze and Guattari. There may be something in this, but the position is very much more complex than Frank allows, since he considers only one side of the matter. To assess the position more adequately, we need not only to consider the lack of substantive ethical considerations, but also we must take account of the poststructuralist hostility to the formal relativisms of modernism and structuralism. In explaining this a little more fully, we will be able to demonstrate a further shared feature of Habermas and the poststructuralists, for Habermas, too, is hostile to the modish relativisms of the immediate past.

There are many definitions of the modern and of the postmodern, but one quite conventional usage is the one adopted by both Barthes and Foucault, which differs little from the definition of aesthetic modernism found in many standard texts. Here the modern begins towards the end of the nineteenth century and is characterized by a break with the aesthetics of representation. This departure from the mimesis of the 'classical' epoch is coeval with the repudiation of the previously dominant 'mirror-of-nature' theories of knowledge, which now come to be opposed by the sociologistic epistemologies of Durkheim, Weber, and Nietzsche. Post-mimetic aesthetics and epistemology are marked by a certain autonomy *vis-à-vis* the 'real', and this issues in expressions of relativism, subjectivism, self-referentiality, and, in general, a pervasive formalism. Postmodernity begins at the point of emergence out of this immensely self-confident combinatory, whose subversive figures, like Artaud and Dali, had to wait for their time until the 1960s. In the worlds of theory, art, literature, architecture, and music, there is at this time a turn from the formalisms of the modernist period towards new 'essentialisms' from which the old mimesis is not totally absent. Consider, for instance, the avant-garde's emphasis on art with an unconscious or bodily content, whose aim is the decoding of libido in the audience. The affiliation of poststructuralist theories of desire with such postmodern currents is perfectly apparent. In ethics, there is a clear discontinuity between the relativism of analytic philosophy, for example, and the burgeoning of theories of rights, exemplified by the writings of Rawls and Dworkin, and the rediscovery of Leo Strauss in the USA and Germany. Although, as we have indicated, Habermas diverges in certain respects from natural rights theory, the centrality of a rational ethics and substantive rationality in his work makes him, arguably, a part of this anti-relativist grouping which succeeds the relativism of modernist ethics. Do not, for example, his attacks on 'decisionism' stand in much the same political relationship to Carl Schmitt as Leo Strauss's offensive against legal positivism stands to Kelsen's arguments for the existence of legality in the Third Reich? The poststructuralists, like Habermas, oppose a sort of normative foundationalism to such formalist relativisms: this receptivity to the 'ethical' is recognized in Lyotard's notion of 'libidinal metaphysics',[6] a construct which bears comparison with Marcuse's thesis regarding the fundamental status of the instincts for any metaphysic of morals. Although Habermas cannot honestly be presented as Marcuse's unalloyed supporter in regard to the foundational role allotted to the instincts,[7] it is nevertheless instructive to hold in mind the relation between Habermas and Marcuse, when attempting to assess judiciously the debate between Critical Theory II and poststructuralism.

Both Habermas and the poststructuralists, then, are in a position of fundamental mutation in regard to the self-referential relativisms of the modern. Although Manfred Frank seems at points to grasp that it is these new anti-relativisms, essentialisms, and universalisms which separate poststructuralism from the relativist structuralism which accords primacy to writing and the signifier, he is fundamentally wrong to assert that the concept of desire in *Anti-Oedipus* is duplication of Lacan's thematization of lack. The poststructuralist concept of desire is not relativistic. That is the whole point of their work, and in this they are in fundamental harmony with Habermas.

If we now turn to the question of compatibility, the question to be put is this: what is the nature of the inconsistency between the advocacy of communicative rationality and the valuation of the sensual-aesthetic realm? The first thing to note is that the poststructuralist turn to the body, desire, and the aesthetic does not arise from a pessimism that would abandon the world of the social to the power-plays of whatever masters happened to be in control. On the contrary, and against Frank's suggestion that the 'new philosophers' and the poststructuralists share similar orientations (presumably a cosmic pessimism regarding the improvement of the social condition, leading to an inner-directed mysticism – for this is what Lévy, Glucksmann, Clavel, *et al.* purveyed), the reclaiming of the body, desire, the subject, from the Oedipal operations of the social machine is just a first step against the prevailing forms of domination. And further steps are possible, as soon as it is understood that the social order of capitalism is only one of a myriad possibilities, and that its cohesive force is present everywhere as the manifestation of constrained and twisted desiring-machines. Now, it must be admitted that Habermas does not share this vision of a polymorphous future. But the point is that Habermas does have a vision of the future which, as with Deleuze, Guattari, and Lyotard (Foucault has always been extremely circumspect with regard to the future), is understood as a release from the past.

To develop this further, it is worth recalling Habermas's discussion of the ecology movement and other 'defensive groupings', which, he suggested, favoured communicative structures.[8] In this discussion, Habermas endorsed 'the creation of subculturally protected communication groups which further the search for personal and collective identity' and which 'promote the revitalization of buried possibilities for expression and communication'. He suggested that the core of this new 'conflict potential' be understood as 'resistance to tendencies to colonise the life-world', and as resistance to 'developments that visibly attack the organic foundations of the life-world and make one drastically conscious . . . of inflexible limits to the deprivation of sensual-aesthetic background needs'. It is clear, then, that Habermas and the poststructuralists share a concern for the future of the sensual-aesthetic within the life-world. Now, in the case of the poststructuralists, this concern is the one that defines their theoretical task. But, in Habermas's case, the concern has recently manifested itself in disquisitions against postmodernism. This attack on the over-valuation of untrammelled aestheticism in postmodernism has been received as a strong implicit critique of poststructuralist theorizing. But this reception has been, in certain respects, hasty. A concern for some sense of balance between the historic-theoretical and the sensual-aesthetic led Habermas to make rather peremptory remarks about young conservatives, and *this same concern* has led to a somewhat over-respectful treatment of Habermas's case, which although raising an absolutely critical question (what combination of forces – political, theoretical, and aesthetic – should support the move towards establishing autonomous individuals within a sane world?) was not based on an especially rigorous consideration of poststructuralist theory. In short, the critical nature of Habermas's statement that: 'The *Young Conservatives* recapitulate the basic experience of aesthetic modernity. They claim as their own the revelations of a decentered subjectivity, emancipated from the imperatives of work and usefulness, and with this experience they step outside the modern world. On the basis of modernistic attitudes, they justify an irreconcilable anti-modernism. They remove into the sphere of the far away and the archaic the spontaneous powers of imagination, of self-experience, and of emotionality. To instrumental reason, they juxtapose in manichean fashion a principle only accessible through evocation, be it the will to power or sovereignty, Being or the dionysiac force of the poetical. In France this line leads from Bataille via Foucault to Derrida'[9] has served to obscure a potential complementarity, based on shared concerns, between the theory of desire in post-structuralism and the aspiration towards substantive rationality presented in Habermas's work.

If we now turn to the question of the audience for both Habermasian Critical Theory II and the theory of desire, it is significant that the ethic of communicative rationality and that of 'bodily autonomy' correspond to the two main themes characterizing the 'new' opposition since the mid-1960s. The counter-culture of the late 1960s, with its drug-induced normativity and its hazily-formulated philosophy of desire, displays a pronounced affinity with some of the themes of the poststructuralists,[10] while the democratic new left, particularly the SDS of the Port Huron statement, and the mass democratic movement which existed until sectarian schisms closed the decade, would have affinities with the thesis of communicative rationality. Critical Theory II and poststructuralism have a similar relevance to today's peace, ecology, feminist, and homosexual movements and also to the *Bürgerinitiativen* of the 1980s. The writings of Habermas and the poststructuralists are meaningful because comparatively broad sections of the public have *already* highly valued both 'radical-rational democracy' and 'bodily autonomy'; the new social movements comprise very largely those who have been shaped by an expanding and often critical higher education, and these individuals are not infrequently familiar with the latest theoretical formulations, if only through the publications and newsletters of the various movements. The point is this: while Habermas equates poststructuralism with irrationalist reaction, and Lyotard, discussing Habermas in *The Postmodern Condition*, speaks of the conservative implications of a univocally-consensual iron cage of rationality, both theories have the potential to figure as doctrinal bases of a possible political culture for the new social movements. In other words, both theories confront the possibility of practically achieving their own falsely assumed precondition: the fading away of class relations.

We accept that there are basic differences between Habermas and the poststructuralists. We do not call for some theoretical integration. We do maintain, however, that the shared properties which we have identified mean that both are part of a theoretical culture that succeeds the modern. Doubtless there are both left- and right-political expressions within the postmodern domain. But it would seem to be the case that Critical Theory II and the theory of desire occupy different places at the radical end of the postmodern spectrum. The creative tension between them is to be valued.

Acknowledgement

This chapter first appeared as an article in *Telos*, number 62, pages 62–8, Winter 1984–5, and is reproduced by permission of Telos Press Ltd, New York.

Chapter Five

MODERNITY OR MODERNISM? WEBER AND CONTEMPORARY SOCIAL THEORY

Most of those who characterize our times, and Max Weber's times, in terms of the modern are speaking about *modernity*. Conventional usage has habitually spoken of modernity as an era that was ushered in via the Renaissance, rationalist philosophy and the Enlightenment, on the one hand, and the transition from the absolutist state to bourgeois democracies, on the other. What I want to argue in this chapter cuts somewhat strongly against the grain of this position. It is that our times and 'the modern' should be understood, not as modernity, but in terms of *modernism*. Whereas modernity was inaugurated in the sixteenth and seventeenth centuries, modern*ism* is usually taken as a paradigm change in the arts which began at the end of the nineteenth century. I wish to propose, however, that not only contemporary arts but contemporary social practices, taken more generically, can be understood in terms of modernism. Further, my claim here is that modernism registers a fundamental break with the assumptions of modernity.

My arguments to support this claim are drawn from considerations of three of today's leading social thinkers – Daniel Bell, Michel Foucault, and Jürgen Habermas – on the nature of the modern. They are drawn also from consideration of one 'classical' sociological thinker, Max Weber, again on the nature of the modern. In pursuing these arguments I shall at the same time make a subsidiary argument for convergence among these four social analysts. This second claim is that each of these major social thinkers has articulated a position whose logic entails a conception of the modern which is that, not of modernity, but of modernism. Each of these positions thus comprises a view of contemporary sensibility and social practices that foregrounds fundamental *departures* from the Enlightenment and the rationalizing ethos of modernity.

Since the early 1980s the long-standing inquiry into questions of modernity has been joined by widespread debate on the more specific nature and significance of modern*ism* (Giddens 1981; Habermas 1981a). What has remained unresolved in these controversies is whether modernism constitutes a deepening or an undermining of the Enlightenment's project of modernity. I shall argue below that to pose the question of modernism one-sidedly as a deepening of a set of processes set in train by the Enlightenment or equally one-sidedly as an undermining of such a set of processes is falsely to pose the problem. Instead, I shall maintain, aesthetic modernism and its social correlates must be understood as a fundamental *transformation* of this project that includes not only both a deepening *and* an undermining of Enlightenment rationality, but also the transmutation and renewed development of *instrumental* rationality. Modernism is thus a three-dimensional configuration. I shall discuss these three dimensions each by reference to the above-mentioned commentators. I shall look at the modern, first, as a disruption of Enlightenment rationality through consideration of Daniel Bell's concept of modernism; second, as a new departure in instrumental reason – in which former principles of unity and transcendence are replaced; by principles of plurality and immanence – through fairly strict consideration of Michel Foucault's concept of 'the Modern'; third, as a deepening of Enlightenment rationality – or in terms of the development of 'substantive rationality' – through the treatment of Jürgen Habermas's notion of 'modernity'.

Then I shall turn to consideration of Max Weber. Here we shall see that Weber's classical sociology of modernity, like its contemporary sociological counterpart – indeed Bell and especially Habermas have been crucially influenced by Weber – also understands the modern in a sense consistent with modernism. The recent interpretation of Weber by Habermas (1984) and Schluchter (1981) as well as by younger writers – Brubaker (1984) and Turner and Factor (1984) – have understood the conditions and limits of rationality pre-eminently through Weber's essays on the sociology of religion. I shall follow their lead in my treatment below, except that I shall focus instead on Weber's sociology of law. Here it is well known that Weber was a proponent of 'legal positivism'. What is less a matter of common agreement and what I shall argue for below, is the thoroughly modern*ist* nature of Weber's legal positivism and of his sociology of law.

MODERNISM AS ANTI-RATIONALITY

Among sociologists, Daniel Bell's view of modernism in *Cultural Contradictions of Capitalism* (1976) is closest to the standard literary-, music-, and art-critical characterizations of the phenomenon. When Bell speaks of modernism, what he above all addresses is the 'modern sensibility'. The modern sensibility here is an attribute of individual social actors caught between structural changes in society, on the one hand, and culture on the other. All of these changes in the social, in culture and in the individual have been in the direction of an attack on ultimate 'foundations'. Modernist anti-foundationalism challenges and undercuts ultimate (or even enduring) grounds for knowledge, moral action, and aesthetic judgement as well as the stability of every-day life. Modernist culture or aesthetic modernism has for Bell two major dimensions. The first he calls the 'eclipse of distance', the second the 'rage against order'. By 'eclipse of distance' Bell means the dissolution of aesthetic distance between performer and spectator, of psychic distance between author and work of art. This is exemplified in the overwhelming of the spectator through the foreshortening of perspective by expressionists like Munch; or through the new preoccupation with the material in painting, to the point at which brush strokes, the density of paint, and texture are more important than either figure or ground. The eclipse of distance is not only spatial, but temporal, as narrative is disrupted from the succession of beginning, middle, and end, through use of stream of consciousness and general repudiation of continuity (Bell 1976, pp. xxi, 48–9). The 'rage against order' is for Bell even more basic to aesthetic modernism. What is at issue here is not just the often noted modernist war against the sacred, its original difficulty and attempt to disturb the audience, to *épater le bourgeois*; not just modernism's anti-foundationalist revolt and rage against the

125

prevailing style. Key instead is its drive towards self-infinitization; its insistence on the imperiousness of self, on 'man as the self-infinitizing creature' impelled to search for the beyond; its Faustian placement of the self in place of God (Bell 1976, pp. xx, 47, 49–50). The self in modernism's Faustian dimension is for Bell surely not 'abstract man', or a notion of God's replacement by rationalist moralities of humanism. It is instead a Dionysian self rooted in the aesthetic-sensual conceptions of subjectivity. Not only was the formal nature and rational ordering of modernist art in its early decades rooted in a set of valuations that apotheosized the aesthetic realm, but this aestheticism was necessarily linked with an instinct-centred psychology in so far as the aesthetic justification of life meant that the 'quest for the self was to explore its relation to sensibility' (Bell 1976, p. 52).

Bell's account of the modernist sensibility embraces also an implicit aesthetics of reception. Here the receptivity of the audience to the new art forms is conditioned by a set of social structural changes that are equally anti-foundationalist, in which – and the similarities with Marshall Berman (1983) are striking – 'all that is solid melts into air'. What Bell and Berman mean here is that sensibility is not just a question of a relationship to works of high (or even popular) culture, but that it is a relation of our senses to the sounds, images, figures, feelings, even eroticism of every-day life. Perhaps most basic here is a reordering, which is often also a disordering, of the temporal and spatial patterning of our sensations. Temporally, what this means is that with revolutions in transport we are presented not just with a new awareness of motion and speed, but with a jarring increase in the velocity of the succession of images, and succession of much more widely *varied* images. With radio, phonographs, television, video, and now digitalization, it has meant an unusual increase in the frequency of communications (Bell 1976, p. 47), to the extent that meaning is heavily devalued in an 'overload' of communications. The paradigm-shift in our spatial logic of sensations has been even greater, not the least because, as Bell underscores, the old narrative culture has been replaced by modernism's essentially visual sensibility. A temporal organization of sensation reigned at the turn of the nineteenth century in which our cultural equipment was limited to the narrative modes of theology, literature, and oratory. Visual sensation is, of course, temporal and spatial. This is a matter not only of the pervasion of newer visual cultural modes of painting, cinema, architecture, and television, but of the sights of the city itself; of the new spatial juxtaposition of sharply contrasting social classes, ethnicities, modes of appearance and comportment, and sheer numbers of people; of the change from the closed village structure to the impressions of urban architecture – the visual impressions of the 'man-made landscape; cityscape and roads, dams and bridges'. The point here, as Bell notes, is that the 'immediacy of the visual image does not allow for the contemplation of the written word', especially where there is a rapid succession of images (Bell 1976, pp. 106–7).

This reordering/disordering of our spatio-temporal patterning of sounds and images is furthered in the modernist tendency to substitute for a set of ultimate values based on tradition, religion, or reason, a new belief system founded on experience, and sensation. In this sense, as Bell observes, the main source of modernist identity is experience. With the decline of the family and social class, identities are confirmed in the simultaneity of a generation. Our experience and knowledge of increasingly numerous others in increasingly numerous interactions, our multiplied *self*-experience – with the modernist disjunction of person with the number of functional roles he or she fulfils – make our 'sensibility open to immediacy, impact, sensation' (Bell 1976, pp. 88–91).

Bell's cultural-contradictions argument is oriented less to the precariousness of the capitalist economy than to what he sees as the decline of Western civilization, of the civilization of modernity itself. His more embracing claim then is that modernism is undermining modernity. Bell here suggests an account for the rise and decline of Western civilization in the realms of morality and of aesthetics. In the moral sphere, the rise of Western civilization takes place along the dimension of religion-bound asceticism and later a Whig-like secularized sobriety, itself based ultimately on a theological cosmology; the downward slope traces the dimension of modernist hedonism, whose roots were already present towards the beginning of modernity in the Hobbesian psychology of limitless appetites (1976, pp. 80–3). In the aesthetic sphere, the mechanical cosmology of a rational and unified order inaugurated in the

Renaissance is dissolved in the modernist cosmology of disorder, in modernism's conception of a plurality of cultural orders and of a culture-bound subjectivity, which now needed to impose order on an unregulated and chaotic reality (pp. 86, 96). The Renaissance assumption of a well-ordered universe was 'rational' in that formal mathematical principles were applied to painting to impart a geometric lawfulness to artistic space. It was rational also in its rootedness in a scientific cosmology, in which space was understood in terms of depth, time in terms of sequence; in which music was characterized by 'an ordered structure of sound intervals', and narrative by a beginning, middle, and end (pp. 108–9). In literature, for example, the break with such a rationalist cosmology was instanced in the obsession in poetry and prose with the materiality of the word: with attempts to institute a musical principle of simultaneity in, for example, Flaubert, hence disrupting ordered time sequence; with the surrender of narrative control by the rational ego in Proust, in which memories of the past repeatedly incur upon the present (pp. 112–14, 117).

In his depiction of modernist sensibility, Bell has etched a notion of modernism as essentially disruptive of rationality, thus outlining one dimension of modernism as a cultural configuration. The second side of the modernist triangle describes a deepening and becoming immanent of *instrumental rationality*. To elucidate this dimension of modernism we turn to Michel Foucault.

MODERNISM AS INSTRUMENTAL RATIONALITY

Foucault, unlike for example Tönnies or Durkheim, does *not* work in terms of a contrast of tradition with modernity. In most of his writings he speaks instead of two post-traditional epochs: the Classical, which spans the Enlightenment, and the Modern. Foucault's 'Modern', I shall argue, shares many basic characteristics with modernism. His periodization should be placed in the context of French intellectual life already marked by similar models advanced by Sartre and Roland Barthes. The latter two promulgated a chronology of aesthetic forms, in which a Classical period began in the sixteenth century and a Modern in the mid-nineteenth century, the second of these corresponding to the rise of literary modernism (see Lavers 1982, pp. 61–2). Foucault has in effect transmuted this aesthetic periodization into a chronology of theoretical discourses articulated with configuration of power. He has, in other words, changed it into a periodization of *instrumental* rationality. Here Foucault presents an account of instrumental reason in which two basic principles unite what he conceives as the Modern with aesthetic modernism. These are (1) a principle of plurality which contrasts with the Classical principle of unity and (2) immanence as counterposed to the Classical principle of transcendence. Let us address these two principles in terms of knowledge and power.

In the aesthetic realm, as we saw above, modernism departed qualitatively with the ordered unity prescribed by Alberti's Renaissance aesthetic. Foucault's analysis of a similar shift, from the unified operation of power in the Classical to the plural development of 'micro-arenas' of power in the Modern, was addressed above in Chapter Three. A parallel process of change in the realm of knowledge has been less widely discussed. Classical discourse, observes Foucault in *The Order of Things* (1970), was located in a homogeneous field, in which all knowledge 'proceeded to the ordering of its material by the establishment of differences and defined those differences by the establishment of an order': an order that, he goes on to argue, held true not only for the sciences but for mathematics and philosophy as well (1970, p. 346). The unifying framework of this homogeneous and Classical episteme is what Foucault calls 'mathesis universalis' (1970, p. 349). What this presumes for Foucault is a single and universal order of *representation*. That is, the Classical episteme, which established an order of things through classification by smallest differences, is dependent on a relationship between the classifications and the things that is one of representation. The reader of *The Order of Things* is puzzled by the fact that Foucault offers no such single ordering principle to the Modern. The Modern episteme, in contrast, he defines by 'the retreat of mathesis'; the retreat of a view of a homogeneous epistemological space and unified ordering. Foucault's aim is to argue against those who would attribute to Modern knowledge the unifying principle that man has become the object of discourse. Instead he maintains that the epistemological basis on which the human sciences developed was unalterably plural. The appearance of the sciences of man is, for Foucault, conditioned by three new nineteenth-century departures in Modern knowledge: first, a biology whose object becomes the living organism; second, an economics that now gives priority to labour; and third, a linguistics (philology) whose new object is concrete individual languages. The human sciences are for him based on the incorporation into human subjectivity of the objects (life, labour, language) of these new Modern (non-human) sciences. The point is not only that the homogeneous episteme of the Classical is replaced by the plurality of the Modern, but that the heterogeneity of the latter underlies the putatively unified nature of man in the human sciences.

The second transformation in the development of a modernist instrumental rationality is that from the principle of transcendence to the principle of immanence. Modernist art displays immanence rather than transcendence in that it breaks with the dualist model of mimesis and the dualism of figure and ground of pre-modernist art. In addition it is self-referential in its formalistic valuation of the material, of textured layers of paint, of the word. Further, it breaks – in, for example, primitivism – with Western, transcendental, and realist rationalities. Foucault in *The Order of Things* understands changes in the form of knowledge in a parallel vein, in which Classical knowledge (seventeenth and eighteenth centuries) assumes a principle of transcendence, and Modern knowledge (nineteenth and twentieth centuries) a principle of immanence. Perhaps the best way to grasp what Foucault is getting at here is via Hegel. When Hegel criticized Kant for the latter's 'abstract' idea of reason, he was criticizing a transcendental and dualist model of knowledge, in which the knowing subject and reason were radically separate from the object under consideration. The objects of knowledge here, nature and society (in *The Philosophy of Right*), should, Hegel propounded, also be understood as possessing rationality. This conjugation of reason with nature, and *eo ipso* the social, was the very crux of Hegel's dialectic (Taylor 1975). Once nature and the social also were characterized by reason – and Weber's work too would be unthinkable without the previous existence of such a conceptual mode – then reason was no longer transcendent, but now immanent, in the object of knowledge itself.

In Foucault's account of the Modern sciences Hegel's prescriptions seem to have come true. All Classical knowledge here is, as just mentioned, based on principles of representation and classification. This assumes a transcendental model of knowledge based on a dualism of, on the one hand, the knowing subject and, on the other, the object of knowledge. In this, the knowing subject first *represents* the object and its qualities in words (and the original French title of *The Order of Things* was *Les mots et les choses*), and then uses these words to *classify* the objects under consideration. Here, as in Hegel's characterization of abstract reason, both the subject and the words are radically distinct and separate from the object of knowledge. In contrast, Foucauldian Modern knowledge has become based on a principle of immanence, in the Hegelian sense that reason itself has become a quality of the object of knowledge. This has come to pass for Foucault in two senses. (1) Modern science is no longer classificatory, but has engaged with a set of structural interconnections interior to the object of knowledge itself; that is, science has become engaged with a rationality which is proper to its object (Foucault 1970, p. 244). (2) In the history of Modern sciences, first the 'living organism' and then man has taken the place of the object of knowledge. Previously man had been only the subject of knowledge. This Modern immanence, Foucault argues at some length, is characteristic of both natural and social (human) sciences.[1]

This new immanence of Modern knowledge is at the same time a new departure in the operation of instrumental reason. First, it is reason and the development of the human sciences through whose mobilization new forms of power and domination are possible. Second, it is reason and science that provide modes of legitimation for such domination. The point is that immanentist forms of discourse have become at the same time immanentist forms of power. That is, in the Classical, power was lodged in a transcendent juridico-discursive instance, a transcendental state. In the Modern, sovereignty is lodged in the social itself, and power circulates immanently 'in the capillaries of society'; the state is no longer above us but among us. Classical power operates negatively through the exclusion of madmen, criminals, the indigent, and the idle from discourse and from citizenship. Modern power, on the other hand, operates positively; it individualizes, normativizes, and mobilizes (through the *inclusion* into citizenship) bodies in the reproductive interest – both economic and military/demographic – of the social.

Classical power acts on bodies; Modern power, immanently, on souls. What this means is a shift from a coercive to a moral and therapeutic form of power. Classical madness was a matter of 'dungeons, tortures, chains', a 'continuous spectacle' (Foucault 1967, p. 260), a matter of negative and repressive power. In the Modern asylum, however, a therapeutic model has reigned, or more accurately, as Foucault notes, a 'moral' strategy with a therapeutic source of legitimation. The moral strategy has operated through the 'soul' or 'conscience' of the madman; here the doctor 'organized guilt for the madman as consciousness of himself'; the doctor has attempted to build into the madman's consciousness an internalized categorical imperative, and thus mobilized the madman's body through his soul. Through an intricate system of observation, rewards, and punishments, the madman was to come to recognize his 'guilt' and thus 'return to his awareness of himself as a free and responsible subject, and consequently to reason' (1967, p. 247). Thus 'instead of submitting to a simple negative operation that [in the Classical] loosened bonds and delivered reason's deepest nature from madness, one was in the grips of a [Modern and] positive operation that confines madness in a system of rewards and punishments, and included it in the moment of moral consciousness' (1967, p. 250).

For Modern power to act thus on souls, and through moral consciousness, entails a break with Classical juridico-discursive forms of power. This meant most of all the dissolution in the Modern of man as a rights-bearing subject. This disappearance of the transcendental state and the undermining of foundations in the Modern mean *eo ipso* the end of Classical natural-rights doctrine. For Foucault the negative character of power in the Classical left an important sphere of autonomy even to the prisoner and the madman, who in critical respects still functioned as rights-bearing subjects. Thus madness in the Classical comprises a 'symmetrical' and 'reciprocal' relation between the keeper and the madman, in which fear raged on both sides of the gates; in which autonomy was granted to the madman in that 'observation involved only the madman's monstrous surface', in which the sane man 'read in the madman . . . the imminent moment of his downfall' (Foucault 1967, p. 249). The Classical, Foucault observes, involved an 'abusive dialogue between reason and unreason', whose 'spectacle was the very element of the madman's liberty' (1967, p. 261). The Modern, on the other hand, entails an absence of rights, in which the madman loses 'full adult juridical status'. Rights disappear, but legislation remains and deepens, with the asylum and the doctor imparting legislation to the moral consciousness of the insane, which then, itself, becomes the legislator.[2]

One hesitation that there might be in understanding Foucault's Modern in terms of modern*ism* is that he dates the former as beginning at the end of the eighteenth century, while aesthetic modernism is a phenomenon of the last decades of the nineteenth century. But if one is consistently to understand the Modern – as I have argued Foucault does – in terms of a plural, anti-foundationalist, and immanent instrumental rationality, then it would seem to me more appropriate to date it towards the end of the nineteenth century; that is, not at the beginning of capitalism but at the outset of *'organized* capitalism'. The rationalization of management and the shopfloor, the bureaucratization of the capitalist state, the rationalization of extra-institution practices of social workers *vis-à-vis* the mad, criminal, indigent, 'idle', and otherwise deviant were phenomena contemporaneous with the birth of the Welfare State at the end of the nineteenth century. The beginnings of nationalism – hence the priority of the social – as well as the centrality of demographic concerns, and the ethos of social citizenship (cf. e.g. Kocka 1974), as well as the birth of the human sciences themselves, came by most accounts (and even at points by Foucault's) rather at the end than at the outset of the nineteenth century. Foucault is idiosyncratic in his particular chronology because of the earlier rise of nationalism and bureaucracy in France, and because of his focus on the *origins* of Modern discourse (in Kant) instead of on its subsequent *pervasion* in the human sciences and aesthetic modernism, for which the Kantian revolution provided conditions of appearance and existence. In any event, no one has captured with such acuity the specific nature of modernist instrumental rationality, the specifically modernist forms of knowledge/power, as has Foucault. The thematic that runs implicitly throughout his work is one of a great paradox in which the Classical age, the Age of Reason, sets up an epistemology of order against a social reality of chaos, whereas the Modern(ist) age puts forth an epistemology of chaos – while at the same time creating an instrumentally rational and strait-jacketing social reality of organization and order.

MODERNISM AS SUBSTANTIVE RATIONALITY

If Bell has presented us with a portrait of modernism as the crisis of rationality and Foucault as the anit-foundationalist and immanentist deepening of instrumental rationality, then Critical Theory has traced the third segment of the triangle circumscribing the modernist cultural-ideological space and has given us a view of modernism as substantive rationality. By substantive rationality is meant a deepening of the emancipatory side of the Enlightenment's project of reason. Enlightenment reason is – in Hegel's critique – abstract, general, and formal, and deals in 'abstract man' and 'abstract morality'; in modernity reason becomes concrete and substantive. It no longer deals just with man's 'surface' but enters immanently to his external, internal, and social nature.

Adorno, in this context, has provided us with a modernist aesthetics of substantive rationality – that is, an aesthetics of which propounds a deepening of the Enlightenment's project. This rationality is not only embodied in the systematic and formalist working through the aesthetic material in high modernists such as Picasso and Schoenberg, but also in the utopian and critical functions that Adorno assigned to art (see Bürger 1985, p. 122; Jay 1985, pp. 26–7; Wellmer 1984–5, pp. 92–4). Let us, however, turn directly to considerations of the notion of authentic modernity purveyed by Jürgen Habermas.

The first thing that should be noted about Habermas's conception of modernity is that it is a *post*-Enlightenment notion, and is surprisingly close to Bell and Foucault; for all three, cultural modernity is catalysed by Kant and fully crystallizes with the development of aesthetic modernism. Habermas follows Weber and Piaget in dating the onset of the modern as not just post-Christian but post-rationalist and post-foundationalist (Habermas 1981a; 1984, pp. xli, 163; 1985, pp. 195–6). The reality of the modern is in fact that of Weber's 'plurality of gods and demons'. Habermas's aim is, however, to save us from that very foundationless plurality by realizing the project of the Enlightenment and Greek Antiquity (1984, p. 10) on modernism's dubiously friendly terrain. In this quest Habermas goes beyond Adorno's aesthetics into an account of substantive rationality in social sciences and in every-day interaction in the 'life-world'.

In regard to aesthetics, Habermas is in agreement with Adorno's advocacy of the separation of the aesthetic sphere from the life-world (Jay 1985, p. 129). Habermas would also seem to advocate an aesthetics of systematic experimentation. But here he begins to part company with Adorno. First, the importance of works of art for Habermas lies mainly in their influence on the life-world and in their fostering of communicatively rational action. Therefore Adorno's formalism would lead to an over-emphasis on the work of art itself in criteria of aesthetic judgement. Habermas and writers such as Wellmer (1985, p. 109) and Bürger (1985, p. 130) instead have called for a 'semanticization' of art. This is also connected with what they see as a one-sided emphasis on artistic production in Adorno, for which the theory of communicative action (which is at the same time a theory of *inter*action) would complement with a *Rezeptionsaeth-etik*. Primacy here is given to rationalizing effects on the life-world, which would be not just on 'our evaluative language . . . but reach into our cognitive interpretations and normative expectations and transform the totality in which these moments are related to one another' (Habermas 1985, p. 202).

For Habermas, the growth of rationality entails a cumulative learning process and, perhaps first and foremost, the 'discursive redemption' of (descriptive, moral, and evaluative) statements. Because such criteria are not applicable without inconsistency to aesthetic statements, Habermas, unlike Adorno, refuses to speak of 'aesthetic rationalization'. Yet there is an important sense in which the logic of Habermas's theory of communicative action makes it possible to speak of truth and even of rationality of artistic production. Habermas's understanding of modernity hinges crucially on the separation of theoretical, moral-practical, and aesthetic spheres in culture. This separation is mirrored by a decentring of subjectivity in the life-world in which external nature, social nature, and internal nature are respectively differentiated. Here the counterpart of the normative sphere is social nature, and the counterpart of the aesthetic sphere is internal nature. Now internal nature in Habermas's life-world can be more or less rationalized. When it is rationalized it is likely that the 'expressive statements' or the expressive dimension of statements made by social actors will be rational.' Statements are for Habermas rational along the expressive dimension when they are 'candid and self-critical' (1984, p. 43). Cognitive, normative, evaluative, and expressive statements are for Habermas at the same time validity claims. Such claims are plausible and statements are rational when they are 'discursively redeemable'. Behind every type of statement lies, for Habermas, a 'discourse', in which the ground for validity claims come under question. Behind expressive statements then lies 'expressive discourse', in which 'we call someone rational if he makes known a desire, intent, feeling, mood, shares a secret, confesses a deed, etc. and then can reassure critics by drawing practical consequences and behaving consistently thereafter' (1984, p. 15). This is closely related to what Habermas calls 'therapeutic critique', in which 'the argument of a psychotherapist . . . trains the analysand to adopt a reflective attitude toward his own expressive manifestations'. Here sincerity is crucial because 'anyone who systematically deceives himself about himself behaves irrationally' (1984, pp. 20–1). The point in this context is that Habermas speaks in the same tones about the productions of the artist. This is visible in his observations on the rationality of aesthetic discourse; here 'reasons have the peculiar function of bringing us to see a work or performance in such a way that it can be perceived as an authentic expression of an exemplary experience, in general as the embodiment of a claim to authenticity' (p. 20). Thus the rationality of an expressive statement is similar for Habermas to the validity of a work of art, and it is not inconsistent with his overarching framework to speak of aesthetic rationality.

Habermas does state that he wants to oppose the dominance of the 'cognitive-instrumental' dimension of modernity over the moral-practical and aesthetic-expressive dimensions, he indeed seems to depreciate the aesthetic realm. Yet he devalues the expressive-mimetic dimensions of language in favour of its communicative dimension, and is not, as Jay (1985, p. 137) observes, 'cognizant enough of the perhaps more contradictory than complementary nature of cognitive and aesthetic attitudes to nature'. At points Habermas (1981a; 1983) seems almost in agreement with Bell's diagnoses and implies that aesthetic modernity is undermining theoretical and practical rationality, although to be fair Habermas would limit this to specific forms of modernist art. This devaluation of the aesthetic realm is entailed perhaps by the very logic of his break with Adorno's Hegelian framework. The categories of reason, reflection, and consciousness in Adorno have a heavily foundationalist, even metaphysical coloration. Habermas, it is well known, breaks with such a philosophy of consciousness for a philosophy of language. But he needs very much to save a notion of reason. The only way that he can do this in a modernity that has largely broken with realist epistemologies and the metaphysics of natural rights is through understanding reason in terms of discursively redeemable validity claims. This 'seminar' model of rationality poses no problems in dealing with descriptive state-ment of the theoretical realm. But when it is equally brought to bear in the moral-practical and especially the aesthetic realm, as well as the communications of every-day life, it asserts an unavoidable cognitivist bias. Habermas, for example, under-stands what was 'reflection' for the philosophy of consciousness in terms of 'validity testing'. Adorno's Hegelian cosmology allows him to think through the 'unities-in-sublation' of reason and nature, the spiritual and the mimetic, sign and image; syntheses that despite their origin seem to have a considerable empirical fruitfulness, just as does the ultimately Hegelian concept of substantive reason. Habermas, in his very contempor-ary philosophy of language, cannot revert to the old metaphysics, hence he is forced to speak at best rather unconvincingly of a complementary totality of influence of aesthetic, theoretical, and moral-practical cultural spheres in the life-world, and at worst in terms of the devaluation of the aesthetic and the expressive.

Despite his relegation of the aesthetic and focus on discursive redemption, Habermas is indeed a theorist of substantive ratio-nality. In Hegel's sense, Habermas's rationalization of the life-world would be, unlike Kantian abstract morality, the ratio-nalization of ethical substance, of *Sittlichkeit*. Habermas's project is not just for the rationalization of normativity, or of social nature, but his ideas of therapeutic critique mentioned above is a project for the rationalization of inner nature, of our expressive subjectivities. Such rationalization of the life-world is for Habermas the great opportunity that modernity leaves open to us. Let us once again stress here that Habermas's modernity is a post-Enlightenment, post-foundationalist view very like the modern*ism* that we discussed above in Bell and Foucault. Modernization is thus for Habermas a process of 'decomposition and differentiation', which creates a 'decentred' or 'unbound' subjectivity (1984, p. 199). But whereas for Bell this aspect of modernism fosters irrationality and a culture of desire-gratification, for Habermas this very modernist 'plurality of gods and demons' paradoxically opens up the possibility of substantive and communicative rationality (see Alexander 1987, ch. 9).

What Habermas is claiming here is that only in modernity is there sufficient differentiation of subjectivity that communications can take the form of discursively redeemable validity claims. And since Habermas chooses to define rationality largely in terms of such validity claims, it is modernity that promises the brightest hopes for reason. The crux of his argument here is that, prior to modernity, there was too much confusion and conflation of the (cognitive, moral-practical, evaluative, expressive, and hermeneutic) dimensions of communication for the latter to be rational. Habermas cites with approval in this context Piaget's three-stage periodization of mythical-narrative, religious-metaphysical, and modern world-views. In the mythical world-view of primitive society, Habermas notes, there is insufficient distinction between the natural world and the social world, between the inner world and both of the latter, and between language and states of affairs in order for there to be a rationality of communications. This absence of differentiation makes 'internal validity conditions' impossible and leads to contradictions in normative action in tribal societies (Habermas 1984, pp. 46-9, 57-8). Moreover, the assessment of validity claims is contingent on a developed sense of individuality that is impossible in primitive societies because of the absence of a differentiated subjective (or internal) nature; identities are hence not individualized but tied to collective knowledge in myths and rituals (1984, pp. 51-2). But insufficient differentiation for communications of discursively redeemable validity claims persists into the Age of Reason and the Enlightenment itself. Reason, while metaphysics persists, is not yet primarily a matter of rational justification and is not yet differentiated from normative orderings, such as in natural law, or from the ordering of external nature itself. This residual foundationalism makes rational critique impossible. Reason (see e.g. Alberti's aesthetics) is still not sufficiently differentiated as a metaphysical ordering of art for there to be (with several significant exceptions) fully individualized works of art prior to modernism. It is only in the presence of modernist differentiation of spheres, worlds, and dimensions of utterance and discourse that the type of unbound subjectivity is present that for Habermas is the necessary condition of rational critique and of substantive rationality.

I have now at some length, through treatment of three leading contemporary social theorists, put an argument for a sociological periodization. It is one that in particular creates a challenge to the classical sociological periodization of *Gemeinschaft* to *Gesellschaft*, status to contract, mechanical to organic solidarity, or, more generally, tradition to modernity. What I have argued is that after modernity, or perhaps at some point during modernity, something new came into being. This something has often been termed 'postmodernity' (e.g. Lyotard 1979); but because the features of aesthetic modernism also describe its broad parameters, I have called it 'modernism'. I have argued that these three social analysts (through Bell's notion of 'modernism', Foucault's of 'the Modern' and Habermas's of 'modernity') present a view of contemporary Western society which is very much that of modern*ism*.

I have proposed that these analysts have outlined the three main dimensions – anti-rationality, an immanent instrumental rationality, and substantive rationality – of modernist culture. The three dimensions are, I think, intimately interwoven. Discussion of how they are interwoven is beyond the scope of this essay. However, the *plausibility* of such interweaving is suggested by, for example, Freudian theory. This pre-eminently modernist cultural discourse constitutes a break with Enlightenment reason in all three of the above senses. It addresses anti-rationality to the extent that it challenges the assumption that we are rational animals. It involves a deepening instrumental rationality in so far as, for instance, asylums and social work have been influenced by its teachings. It embodies substantive rationality in so far as reason is no longer formal and abstract but penetrates into the human psyche; that is, in so far as it uses reason to understand our very irrationality. Max Weber – and it is probably no accident that classical sociological theory, Freudianism, and aesthetic modernism developed at about the same time – also stands in a crucial relationship to the three dimensions of cultural modernism. It is to him that we now turn.

THE PLACE OF WEBER

Unlike contemporary scholars, Weber could not write with any great self-consciousness of aesthetic modernism. Yet he wrote contemporaneously with the rise of aesthetic modernism, and his writing shared a number of crucial themes with it. Let me touch on a few of these briefly. Modernist art's anti-representational ethos and its concern with the aesthetic material mean that it is essentially self-referential. Similarly, Weber's (and Durkheim's) epistemologies do not assume that knowledge provides a mirror for (social) nature; knowledge instead is self-referential in the sense that its categories and rules take on meaning only within the context of given forms of life.[3] Weber purveys the self-referential thematic not only in his epistemology but also in his ethics. Here, for example, the absolute ethical validity built into Kant's notions of the 'empirical will' and the 'pure practical will' (of the categorical imperative) is sociologized respectively as the instrumentally rational and value-rational social actor. To transform such ethical categories into sociological concepts is to take away their absolute character and make them self-referential categories of particular forms of social life.

The best confirmation of Weber's sociological modernism is to be found in the 'Intermediate Reflections' (Weber 1946, pp. 323–59) of his sociology of religion. In this he discusses the five value-spheres (economic, political, aesthetic, erotic, and intellectual) which have become self-consciously differentiated in the modern. He talks about each sphere in terms of a three-stage periodization, stages that are not dissimilar to Habermas's primitive, religious-metaphysical, and modern. The second of these stages includes the world religions and, by implication, mechanical and rationalist cosmologies. The third stage describes the famous modern 'plurality of gods and demons'. In the case of each value-sphere, Weber stresses the similarities of the modern with the primitive, and the dissimilarities of the modern with the religio-metaphysical stage. What the modern shares with the primitive here are also characteristic of aesthetic modernism; these are a renewed particularism – in comparison with the universalism of the religio-metaphysical – and a break with rational foundations. Thus modernist art departs sharply from the natural-science-based rationalist assumptions of mechanical cosmologies, and each of Weber's spheres becomes once again primitive in its break with the possibility of any ultimate grounding in reason or in rational and universalist religious ethic. The very 'gods and demons' characterization of the modern recapitulates the plural theologies that preceded the world religions and should be understood in three senses: first, that, as in Greek Antiquity, the various value-spheres themselves would be assigned gods; second, that competing gods and demons within a sphere could find no ultimate grounds for legitimation (Brubaker 1984, p. 73); and third – and this is given the most extensive treatment in the *Religionssoziologie* and especially in *Ancient Judaism* – that primitive and modern (but not the Gods of world religions) gods are not universalist in terms of concrete time and space but are gods of particular cities or of particular nations (Habermas 1984, pp. 182 ff.).

In Weber's more general consideration of the value-spheres there is purveyed a notion of modernity which shares at least a dozen characteristics with aesthetic modernism (and the aesthetic modernist sensibility), which was outlined above in the discussion of Daniel Bell. These are: (1) self-referentiality; (2) anti-rationalism; (3) value-pluralism; (4) a new importance of the erotic; (5) a notion of aesthetic aura; (6) the possibility of rationalized modernist aesthetics; (7) a convergence with the primitive; (8) a more radicalized individualism; (9) the disappearance of the sacred; (10) a renewed immanence; (11) anti-foundationalism; (12) a scepticism towards the theoretical in general and grand theory in particular. The germ of such a modernist reading is present in the interpretations of Weber inaugurated especially by Schluchter (1981) and Habermas

(1981b). One area in which such a reading has been notably absent, however, is in Weber's political sociology in general, and his sociology of law in particular. Let me now argue that this pre-eminently non-cultural area can be understood in terms of modernism.

MODERNISM, POLITICS, AND WEBER'S LEGAL POSITIVISM

Weber's sociology of law connects significantly with each of the three dimensions of modernism. As a descriptive sociology it can account for, and opens up possibilities for, each of the three dimensions. As a prescriptive doctrine of jurisprudence it excludes, I shall argue, on the one hand, substantive rationality and, on the other, anti-rationality in the more extreme forms of 'decisionism'. Also as a prescriptive doctrine, Weber's advocacy of 'legal rationality' is tantamount to – as much of the secondary literature has conventionally held – an advocacy of instrumental rationality. It is, however, at the same time a great deal more.

The rationalization of law for Weber was based on two central assumptions, first of the separation of law and ethics and second that law be a deductively rational coherent system. Thus for Weber the historical rationalization of law has consisted of (1) a series of progressive differentiations ending in the differentiation of law from ethics, and (2) a progressive process of formalization. Weber traces this rationalization across what amount to four ideal-typical stages that correspond less to chronological history than to an internal logic of rationalization. The four stages are (1) the primitive, in which the law is formal and irrational; (2) the traditional in which law is substantive and irrational; (3) a 'transitional' stage of natural law, in which law is substantive and rational; and (4) modern law, which is formal and rational (Weber 1978, pp. 809–15, 852–5). For Weber, then, substantive rationality in law is surely a *pre*-modern state of affairs.

Law that is substantive and rational is found, Weber maintains, in theocratic legal systems, in natural law, and in welfare-type social justice jurisprudence. Such law is substantive in that it is based on an ultimate value. It is rational in so far as it is intellectualized and systematized, by university-trained church or legal scholars (Kronman 1983, p. 78). The difference between

142

the univeristy base of rational law and the guild anchoring of irrational English common law was of importance for Weber.[4] Indeed, Weber's whole treatment of rationalization gives inordinate weight to intellectualization, in which the functionaries of the intellectual sphere, be they systematizing theologians or legal scholars (Weber 1978, pp. 883-4), play an 'imperialistic' role in bringing about the rationalization of the other spheres. Natural law jurisprudence – for Weber the 'purest form of value rationality' – effectively bridges the transition from traditional to modern law. Natural law is pre-modern in so far as ethical and legal spheres have not yet been differentiated. It is also premodern in the sense that is assumes a set of fixed legal principles and thus the absence of a process of legal change. This is exemplified in the physiocratic doctrine that politics would be regulated by laws governing the natural order of society, the latter being made known to the monarch by enlightened public opinion (see Turner and Factor 1984, ch. 9). Yet natural law doctrine was intellectually rationalized. Though state law had to correspond to the laws of nature, natural law did promote the principle of enactment, and a sort of procedural legitimation by reasoned argument (Habermas 1984, p. 264). Notwithstanding these rational characteristics, Weber was convinced – and correctly so – that the overall dominance of an ultimate value such as social justice would in the end damage legal predictability and thus legal rationality (Kronman 1983, p. 95).

Natural law theories, and more generally substantively rational legal theories, are hence untenable for Weber in modernity. There have, however, been a number of recent attempts to resuscitate such doctrines which break with the metaphysical assumptions of Enlightenment-based natural law, and instead ground natural rights in reasoned discourse (Rawls 1972; Dworkin 1977). Habermas's theory of communicative action too has been commonly understood as a substantively rational ethics; it can also be seen, I argued in Chapter Three above, as another variant of discursively grounded natural law theory. Anthony Kronman has with special acuity argued that Weber's sociology of law advocates, at least implicitly, a similar position. For Kronman (1983, p. 21) Weber's jurisprudence rests on a guiding assumption that the creation of laws and legal events are 'posits' or acts of choice.[5] Key here (Kronman 1983, pp. 84-5) is that events in regard to law be understood through the logical analysis of legal *meaning*, and that such juristic meaning of the legal event 'expresses or reflects human purposes or intentions'. This differs from pre-modern law, which viewed legal meaning as residing in external sense data. Modern law then for Kronman assumes the possibility for legal actors (whether legislators, judges, legal theorists, or laymen) of 'personality', of Weber's idea of meaningful life conduct. Here legal action is a question of the self-conscious realization of values. And legal actors come under the Weberian principle of *verstehen*, hence meaningfulness, rather than *erklären*, and causality. This view of legal action, as self-reflexive and logical, dovetails significantly with the new discursively grounded theories of substantively rational law. Kronman's use of Weber here opens up fascinating and desirable avenues for jurisprudence. But it is an illegitimate reading of Weber. This is so for two reasons. First, because Weber's notion of legal legitimation excludes self-reflexive behaviour on the part of lay legal actors, whose acceptance of norms is mostly due to 'habit' or 'faith'. Second, because Weber's insistence on the very separation of spheres would allow only legal elements to enter into the self-reflexivity of the legal actor, especially in the sense that Weber assumes that the meta-juristic *grounding* of modern legal *systems* is excluded from rational reflection.

Weber's relationship to the second dimension of modernism, instrumental rationality, is altogether more complex. Analysts such as Mommsen and Habermas (1984) have understood Weberian legal rationality as very much the equivalent of instrumental or purposive rationality. Mommsen's argument here was that Weber explicitly contrasted legal rationality with natural law, and further that the Weberian notion did not even presuppose a parliamentary system (Mommsen 1984, pp. 423-4). One problem with Mommsen's (and Habermas's) interpretation of this is a lack of clarity as to what is meant by 'purposively rational' law. There are several ways in which law can be purposively rational, and these depend on two questions. (1) What entity is serving as an instrument for given interests? (2) For what interests does the instrument serve? The answer to the first question is either a given legal rule or a legal system. The answer to the second is the interests of a nation, a social class, or an individual. Now Weber's sociology of law in *Economy and Society* devotes very little discussion to legal rules or legal systems as an instrument of *any* of these interests. Most of the discussion of law and the economy is devoted not to how law serves as an instrument for economic interests but how certain legal structures function as conditions for capitalist development (see Habermas 1984, p. 256). And even this discussion is secondary to the main theme of the *Rechtssoziologie*, which is the *formal rationalization* of law.[6] In this sense the sociology of law runs parallel to the studies of religion. Though the project of the latter is the discovery of religious pre-conditions of capitalism, most discussion is devoted to the rationalization of the world religions. In the case of law and religion, it is rationalization, and a highly intellectualist process of rationalization, that lays down the 'tracks' on which the battles of interests are fought out.

Yet law is, among other things, for Weber importantly connected to class and national interest. In effect Weber pursues two prima facie mutually contradictory notions of law. The first, as just mentioned, advocates a formally rational legal system. The second is the purposively or instrumentally rational connection of law with interest. Legal thinking that features this latter notion is known as 'sociological jurisprudence' (see Stone 1966, pp. 502–17). This legal doctrine was first importantly developed by Rudolf Ihering (see Turner and Factor 1987), a theorist who exercised a profound influence on Weber. Ihering's idea of law in terms of the objectives of interests was fundamentally hostile to the 'legal-positivist' paradigm in which Weberian formal rationality was grounded (Hunt 1978, p. 104). In Weber, however, there are elements of both doctrines, and I think that these seemingly contradictory conceptions are reconcilable. Although legal positivism insists *contra* natural-law theory that 'the law is the commands of the state', its seamless, rational, clear, and consistent legal *system* must in the end be based on a fundamental norm. This norm cannot, as in natural-law theory, be rationally justified. And this norm – which serves as a guiding principle for the entire system of legal rules – can be such that the system effectively serves class or national interests.[7] Thus Weber's prescriptive legal doctrine, while not in the least reducible to instrumental rationality, is consistent with the latter.

These considerations invite comparison with Foucault. Weberian formal rationality of law would correspond with Foucault's pre-Modern 'juridico-discursive' forms of power. The very generality and impersonality of formally rational law, and the fact that its origins lie in the intellectual abilities of jurists to evolve a progressively more logical and consistent jurisprudence, presuppose a vision of law as transcendent to social interests. Foucault (1975, pp. 52–3) understands (and Weber is in basic agreement) such a general, impersonal, and 'repressive' form of law to give greater dignity to the individual than Modern law, which is largely based on a therapeutic principle. Weberian jurisprudence, in so far as it advocates formal rationality, thus bears in our terms certain pre-modernist traits. In so far as it envisages *instrumental* rationality, Weber's conception would, as judged against Foucault's criteria, be fully modernist. This is because Weberian instrumental rationality entails a connection with social and/or national interest in which law loses its transcendent qualities. Foucault (1975, pp. 210–12) laid particular stress in this context on how Modern legal systems recruit and mobilize individuals in the interest of nations.[8]

To address the third and anti-rationalist dimension of modernism in Weber's sociology of law is necessarily to address the problem of 'decisionism'. Here a system of law would need to rest on ultimate norms whose choice would be a matter of ungrounded 'decision' (Turner and Factor 1984, pp. 43–7). What this means also is that there is no rational basis for choosing one system of law – and discussion here is usually of constitutional law – over another (Turner and Factor 1987). Weber is a decisionist in this sense, and this follows directly from his commitment to value-free social science (Strauss 1953). If, in this context, facts (in social science) must be set free from values, then values too (in ethics and jurisprudence) must indeed be set free from facts. That is, there can be for Weber no ultimate rational grounding of ethical values. The same would then hold true for those ultimate norms in which systems of constitutional law are grounded.

The attacks on Weber as decisionist have surely involved a more serious charge than this. They have involved comparison with Carl Schmitt, Third Reich legal theorist, whose decisionism is based on his reading of Hobbes.[9] What this seems to entail is that a 'decision' has already been made as to a legal system's ultimate norm, and that this norm is *raison d'état* itself. Hence the constitutional form which a nation chooses should be a function of *raison d'état*. The comparison with Schmitt pertains, perhaps more importantly, to a further element of anti-rationality: to Schmitt's counterposition of 'legality', on the one hand, and 'legitimacy', on the other.

Schmitt largely equated legality with parliamentary rule, the representation of pure material interests, the *Rechtsstaat*, purposive rationality, and interest-group pluralism in general. None of this provided a basis, according to Schmitt, for *legitimacy*, by which he meant a more thoroughgoing integration of the masses into a national order. This was to be provided through a presidential 'plebiscitary leadership democracy', which would serve national interests and constitute a 'crystallization point for a new "substantial order" ' (Mommsen 1984, p. 387). As the Weimar Republic shifted away from parliamentary sovereignty in 1930, diverse political forces drew on Schmitt's doctrine promoting a presidential defender of the 'real' German constitution, which was counterposed to the parliamentary constitution of 1919. Schmitt drew here on Weber's advocacy of a strong plebiscitary and presidential principle for the Weimar Republic and from his more general ideal type of charismatic legitimation. Weber himself was, of course, sceptical of the intrinsic value of parliamentary institutions and saw that in Germany they were likely to be little more than a space for the battles of a plurality of pure material interests (ibid., p. 452).

We should, however, not overplay the connection between Weber and Schmitt. First, Weber had more of a commitment to legality and the *Rechtsstaat* than did Schmitt. This was not so much because it would provide a principle of legitimacy to the masses but because it would enhance calculability for economic transactions and provide a certain – though surely circumscribed – space for individual rights in general. Schmitt's subordination of the legal system to a 'substantial order' was such that the violation of Weber's principle of formal rationality was inevitable, as it proved to be in the Third Reich. Moreover, Schmitt's concern for a plebiscitary presidential constitution was far more tied up with the integration and mobilization of the masses than was Weber's. Weber's view of the masses, as we noted above, was of a rather passive force. His élitist ethos did away with the centrality of the *need* for a dominant ideology in organized capitalism (cf. Abercrombie, Hill, and Turner 1980). His advocacy of a strong presidency was mainly rooted in the context of international power politics.

CONCLUDING REMARKS

I have in the above argued that there is a surprising convergence between the notions of the modern advanced in contemporary social thought – in Bell, Foucault, and Habermas – and in Weber's classical sociological formulations. I have maintained further that the conception of the modern in each of these cases has much more in common with the modern*ism* inaugurated in the late nineteenth and early twentieth centuries than with the modern*ity* of the Renaissance and Enlightenment. I have argued that modernism must be understood not only as an undermining of Enlightenment rationality, but also and simultaneously as a process of the deepening of the latter into substantive rationality and as a process of the pervasion of a newly immanent instrumental rationality. I have contended as well, via a discussion of Weber, that modernism is not just a matter of the cultural realm, but that its ethos also extends to twentieth-century law and politics.

These considerations of 'sociological modernism' might, I hope, be cause for reflection, at least for sociologists. What we might begin to ask ourselves is, for example, should we rethink the distinction between the traditional and the modern bequeathed to us by Tönnies, Durkheim, and Simmel? Moreover, should sociology – which has in the past implicitly and now explicitly addressed the issue of modernism – be understood as part and parcel of the phenomenon itself? Classical sociology, as I argued above in the case of Weber, shares a number of essential constitutive characteristics with modernism. Sociology did in fact develop in contemporaneity not with modernity but with (aesthetic) modernism. To pose these questions is to assert scepticism in the face of the still generally accepted Parsonian legacy of a sociology exclusively concerned with modernizing, rationalizing, and civilizing functions. It is to take seriously

Hegel's 'Owl of Minerva' metaphor and to apply it reflexively to sociology itself.

Acknowledgement

This chapter first appeared as an essay in *Max Weber, Rationality and Modernity*, edited by S. Whimster and S. Lash, 1987, Allen and Unwin, and is reproduced by permission of Unwin Hyman, London.

Part Two

POSTMODERNIST CULTURE

Chapter Six

CRITICAL THEORY AND POSTMODERNIST CULTURE: THE ECLIPSE OF AURA

Two ongoing debates have come to assume some prominence in recent years. In 'culture studies', and quickly entering the more proper sociological study of culture, talk has been of modernity versus postmodernity, of modernism versus postmodernism. In social theory and increasingly in sociological theory, a school of writers of German origin, whose leading figures are Habermas, Adorno, and Benjamin, have been pitted against a group of writers of French background, whose leading lights are Foucault, Derrida, and Lyotard, in the controversies between critical theory and poststructuralism. It has been the sometimes unspoken assumption of these two parallel debates – whose spokespersons are often one and the same – that to be on the side of modernity and modernism is to be on the side of critical theory, and that to be a postmodernist is at the same time to be in sympathy with poststructuralism. What I should like to do in this essay is to challenge this assumption.[1]

Of the three just-mentioned most serious and central figures of critical theory, it is Walter Benjamin who comes closest to offering a *sociology* of culture. Jürgen Habermas, by temperament and by his own admission, has devoted relatively little thought to the aesthetic sphere. Theodor Adorno, on the contrary, has produced what are perhaps the most considered, influential, and lengthy analyses of modernist art; yet these analyses tend to be formalist, to ignore the realm of popular culture, and to focus rather singularly on the production of cultural forms rather than on the social bases of their reception. It is only Benjamin, in his writings on the city, his essays on surrealism, and elsewhere in his work, who consistently interconnects the cultural with social phenomena of every-day life. I should like to argue in what follows that Walter Benjamin, probably critical theory's foremost sociologist of culture, is not in any simplistic sense a 'modernist', but that instead his analyses have important connections with the aesthetics, ethics, and politics of *post*modernism. I should like to pursue this argument through the use of Benjamin's conceptual framework in the analysis of postmodernist cultural forms.

Before I attempt to support these claims, however, I should like briefly to sketch some of the broadest parameters of the analysis of art and culture that critical theory of the Frankfurt School proffered. Critical theory differs from more positivist versions of the sociology of culture in a number of respects. First, whereas positivism is concerned with the brute 'facts' of cultural life, critical theory does not want to separate fact from value or theory from practice. That is, cultural forms are also understood in terms of their potential as a critique of existing social conditions. The Frankfurt School analysts disputed what Adorno called the 'identity-thinking' involved in positivism. The latter involved the subsumption by concepts of social reality. Adorno insisted instead that thinking be 'mimetic' and contain a 'utopian moment' from which critique can be launched. The critique of positivist 'identity-thinking' is connected with a second way in which the Frankfurt School diverges from positivism. This is that critical theory offers an aesthetic evaluation of works of art. Here critical theory has also found elements of positivism in the 'social realism' of orthodox Marxist culture analysts such as Lukács. Adorno thus argued that Lukács's aesthetics was an example of identity-thinking, because his realism privileged works of art which correspond with social reality. Adorno maintained that nonrealist art, such as the work of Kafka and Beckett, provided that utopian moment necessary for critique (Slater 1977, pp. 119-46).

Furthermore, critical theory departs form positivism in understanding the facts of culture in terms of a social totality. Culture in this view bears important characteristics of the capitalist social totality, and in the case of mass culture, or the 'culture industry', functions to reproduce labour power and by extension reproduce the capitalist social formation as a totality. This analysis in terms of totalities is rooted in the Hegelian background of the Frankfurt theorists, and is integrally interwoven with the *historical* thinking that is fundamental to Hegel and foreign to positivism. Adorno, Marcuse, and Habermas, like Lukács, work from a similar historical periodization of culture whose fundamental characteristics can be found in Hegel's writings on aesthetics. The chronology involved is one that conceives of culture (and the most often cited example is the Homeric epic) as part of a unified social totality until the rise of capitalist modernity, at which point the cultural sphere gains autonomy and separateness from every-day social life (Kätz 1982, pp. 37-55).

Now I should like briefly to locate Walter Benjamin's cultural criticism in the context of the other Frankfurt analysts. Benjamin was the oldest of the Frankfurt writers and related more directly to the neo-Kantianism of a previous generation of German scholars, which included Simmel and Weber, than did Adorno or Marcuse. Benjamin's pivotal notion of 'allegory' can be understood as similar to the neo-Kantian sociologization of Kant's categories in, for example, Weber's types of social action or Durkheim and Mauss's primitive classifications. In Benjamin's dualistic conception, allegory refers to bits and pieces of every-day life – often discarded objects, sometimes relics – that together constitute 'myths' through which individuals in a given historical period understand the social world. Thus, in his study of seventeenth-century German Baroque tragic drama, ruins, relics, and deathheads were the elements of such allegories. In his writings on Baudelaire's nineteenth-century Paris these elements included the arcades, the faubourgs, detective stories, and prostitutes in the night. The other, more Hegelian, Frankfurt analysts, especially Adorno, were not happy with Benjamin's dualism and extreme subjectivism. Benjamin, Adorno noted, understood 'commodity fetishism' as part and parcel of allegory and both as integral to human consciousness. Adorno preferred instead to see fetishism as part of an objective social totality and not as a characteristic of human subjectivity (Frisby 1985, pp. 233-72).

The second main point on which Benjamin differed from the other Frankfurt theorists, including Habermas, was in his estimation of the role of popular culture. Adorno and Marcuse both argued that popular culture did not have critical potential in that it was not part of an autonomous cultural sphere as were certain high cultural works of art. Popular culture was seen in terms of a 'culture industry' that was not separate from what was becoming a 'one-dimensional' society. Popular culture instead reproduced essentially passive individuals as labour power for monopoly capitalism. Benjamin also understood popular culture as inseparable from the social, but such popular culture forms for Benjamin (who was influenced, on the one hand, by Brecht and, on the other, by surrealism) could have radical political potential for the masses (Rose 1978, pp. 109-35). To Benjamin, the modernization of Paris and the construction of the grand boulevards destroyed the radical and allegorical potential of the older arcades and faubourgs. At the same time, however, modernization created new cultural forms, such as cinema and radio, which could constitute new allegories that themselves had radical possibilities for the populace.

The second difference underscores a radical divergence in the criteria of aesthetic judgement of Benjamin, on the one hand, and the other Frankfurt analysts, Marcuse, Adorno, Horkheimer, and Habermas, on the other. The valuation of high cultural works of art, which sees possibilities of critique only in an aesthetic realm that is separate from the social, is constitutive of the *modernist* aesthetic of critical theory's 'mainstream'. Benjamin's valuation of popular cultural products, which can envisage critique from an aesthetic dimension that is integral to the social, is consistent with a *post*modernist aesthetic. The body of this paper will produce detailed arguments in support of this proposition.

Central to this analysis is Benjamin's (1975b, pp. 219-54) notion of 'aura', which he understood largely in terms of the singularity, the uniqueness of a work of art. This, he observed, came under increasing challenge by new means of mechanical reproduction of art and by the historical avant-garde of the 1920s. What this singularity and uniqueness of the auratic work of art imply is also its *isolation* from the social, both in its inaccessibility and in the absence of political effectiveness (Benjamin 1975b, p. 225). The modernist work of art, to take Adorno's ideal-typical figures of Picasso and Schoenberg, is auratic in each of these respects. The postmodernist cultural form is not (Bürger 1984, p. 122). This departure from high modernism can best be understood through examination of the historical avant-garde of the 1920s, which I think (and shall argue) was the first flourishing of postmodernist culture. In this paper I shall thus look systematically at this break with the aura of high modernist art in the 1920s' avant-garde and in more recent decades.

THE DEMISE OF AURA

Max Weber, in the famous *Zwischenbetrachtungen*, presented his most systematic conceptualization of modernity, which he understood in terms of the *separation* of value spheres and life orders (*Lebensordungen*). He argued that the economic, political, ethical, legal, aesthetic, and erotic value spheres, which previously had been structured according to a unifying principle of the world religions and later of Enlightenment rationalism, now began to march to the beat of different drums (Whimster and Lash 1987). Most basic to Weber's modern and foundationless 'plurality of gods and demons' was this autonomization of the diverse value spheres and particularly the autonomization of the aesthetic value sphere. Many of Weber's contemporaries supposed that with the decline of religion the aesthetic realm might be the only place of retreat for any type of meaningful life-conduct in the face of encroaching purposive rationality (Whimster 1987). The point here is that if cultural modernity is to be understood in terms of the separation and even the transcendence or 'aura' of aesthetic realism, then *post-modernity* would be a matter of transgression of the boundaries that separate the aesthetic from other cultural practices and from the social itself.

Peter Bürger (1984), a contemporary German analyst whose roots are critical-theoretical, proffers a similar, although this time Marxist-inflected, chronology. For Bürger (1984, p. 48) it is specifically 'bourgeois art' that sets itself up as an autonomous realm. Previously, art was intimately interwoven with the social. Primitive and mediaeval 'sacral art' fulfilled a cultic function, whereas its successor, 'courtly art' of the sixteenth and seventeenth centuries, functioned to promote 'sociability' among the courtier class. It is only from the eighteenth century that 'bourgeois art' sets itself up as a realm separate from the social with its own specific 'institutional' apparatus of production, distribution, and reception of aesthetic forms. Fredric Jameson (1984) has associated 'realist' culture with early or liberal capitalism and 'modernist' culture with organized capitalism or monopoly capitalism. Bürger in such a context would assimilate both 'realist' and 'modernist' art to autonomous and bourgeois art, the only distinction between them being that modernism with its inaccessibility and greater cult of the creator is even more autonomous, more 'auratic', than realism. Realism, as Wolin (1984-5, p. 11) has noted, in its accessibility, at least to the middle classes, was instrumental in identity-formation in the creation of a bourgeois public sphere in the nineteenth century. The more rarefied modernism played no such role. Yet both realism and modernism largely functioned as 'affirmative' culture in Marcuse's (1968) sense of the term. The very separation of the institutions of art from society neutralized the critical impulse of modernism, whereas realism functioned to centre, rather than to decentre, bourgeois identity.

The 'historical avant-garde' of the 1920s - especially Dada and surrealism, but also constructivism, De Stijl, the Bauhaus, and Neue Sachlichteit - was postmodern in the sense that it constituted a radical attack on the autonomy, on the aura, of the aesthetic. While I concur with much of Bürger's (1984, p. 57) analyses, I do not accept his claim that the 'failure' of this historical avant-garde came about because any radical attack on the institutions of art was impossible in bourgeois society. I do not agree that such a postmodern attack on autonomous and auratic culture is at all necessarily an offensive against 'bourgeois' art. The reason, I suspect, that the postmodern avant-garde of the 1920s did not have greater social effects was because of a delinkage or desynchronization of the cultural and the social. At this time ideological and economic conditions were unpropitious for a sizable *audience* for postmodernist culture. It is only from the 1960s that such an audience was created on a mass scale.

I take the avant-garde of the 1920s to be postmodernist. Because of this, and because of the particularly sharp way in which it set itself up as distinct from, and opposed to, modernist culture, this paper will devote a considerable amount of space to it. Now let us attempt to understand postmodernist culture - in the 1920s and today – through Walter Benjamin's notion of 'aura'. What Benjamin means by 'aura' or 'auratic art' is very much what Weber meant by the aesthetic in modernity constituting itself as a separate value sphere. But Benjamin also means a lot more. For Benjamin, natural objects as well as cultural objects can possess aura. He (1975b, p. 225) cites the example of a distant and majestic mountian range to be fully as auratic as a hypothetically existing never-photographed masterpiece by Picasso. 'Aura', Benjamin (1979a, pp. 250–1) writes, is 'a strange weave of space and time'. The auratic cultural (or natural) object is characterized thus by its 'unique appearance', its 'semblance of distance', and its 'duration'. The demise of aura, which Benjamin (1975b, p. 239) attributes not just to the incursion of mechanical reproduction, but also to the activities of the avant-garde of the 1920s and especially to surrealism, is correspondingly characterized by the overcoming of uniqueness, the need to bring things closer to people, and transience.

Let me systematically reconstruct the implications of Benjamin's analysis: (1) A cultural text can be auratic or nonauratic with respect to (a) the object depicted, (b) the means by which it is depicted, and (c) whether or not the text itself is mechanically (or electronically) reproduced. (2) The consumption or reception of a text may or may not be auratic, depending on whether it is individually or collectively consumed, or whether the audience views the cultural object in a state of immersion or distraction. (3) The very process of production may or may not be auratic, depending again on whether it is individualized or collective, and the extent to which it is expressive (auratic) or impersonal (nonauratic). (4) The *institutions* of art – that is, the ideas that animate art criticism, the museums, and the art schools – can foster either auratic or nonauratic art. (5) Nonauratic art fosters the interfertilization of high and popular culture. (6) Nonauratic art is for Benjamin somehow at the same time 'political', which is not true to auratic cultural forms. (7) The demise of aura entails the obliteration of the distinction between the cultural and the social. I shall address these points in this order.

(1a) In a cultural text the object depicted can either be auratic or nonauratic. In his 'Small History of Photography', Benjamin (1979a, p. 248) notes that in photography's early mid-nineteenth-century days, 'the client' who came to be photographed was 'the member of a rising class equipped with an aura that seeped into the very folds of the man's frock coat or floppy cravat', but that the later 'imperialist bourgeoisie' lost its aura in its 'deepening degeneration', its *Jugendstil* photos featuring a fashionable 'twilight' and a 'non-auratic pose'. Benjamin (1979a, pp. 248, 250, 256) writes that Eugene Atget's celebrated photographs 'initiate the emancipation of the object from aura', which worked 'against the exotic, romantically sonorous names of the cities'. The pictures of the like of empty courtyards and brothel addresses 'have been likened to the scene of crime' and 'pumped the aura out of reality like water from a sinking ship'.

(1b) The *means* by which an object is depicted in a cultural text can also be auratic or nonauratic. There are two variants of this. The first is in the use of increasingly technological means of production of cultural texts, in which the medium of construction is somehow reproducible and interchangeable. This was reflected in, for example, the Bauhaus's shift from an arts-and-crafts to a technological base in the course of the 1920s, and in the shift in cubism to the more geometric means of figuration of Léger after World War I (Willett 1978, pp. 13, 118–19). More important, however, in this break with high modernist aura is the postmodernist departure from the notion of the 'organic unity' of the 'integral work of art'. This was perhaps the most fundamental bone of contention between Adorno's high modernist aesthetic (Wellmer 1984–5) and what can be understood as Benjamin's postmodernist alternative. High modernist aura assumes the production of a *unique* work of art by (legitimation for this comes from Romanticism) the single creative individual producer. This singularity of the work of art, the idea of the *'work of art'* itself and the separation of the work of art, on the one hand, from the social, on the other, impute self-sufficiency, totality, and organic unity to the high-modernist text. Hence Adorno's demands on the use of a single stylistic principle – such as Picasso's cubism or Schoenberg's twelve-tone music – whose implications and permutations must be consistently worked through in order to achieve 'aesthetic rationality' (Bürger 1984–5, p. 127). Benjamin was sceptical of Adorno's enthusiastic embrace of the Weberian separation-of-spheres principle of modernity. Benjamin (1975a, pp. 83–4), like Weber, observed that the autonomy of the aesthetic and the separation of spheres more generally result in a 'shrinkage of experience', or what Weber called the creation of a class of 'specialists without heart'. Instead, Benjamin embraced the principle of collage and montage of Dada and surrealism, which so radically violated Adorno's principle of the organic unity of style. Benjamin used this avant-garde antiorganic use of the disparate and plural flotsam and jetsam of every-day life as artistic means in his own concept of 'allegory'. Postmodern collage and montage would function then for him as allegory in the most effective work of Dada, Russian constructivism, and surrealism.

(1c) Finally, and this was the central issue in Benjamin's 'The Work of Art in an Age of Mechanical Reproduction', aura is lost in so far as texts themselves are reproducible. This ranged from the reproducibility of the film which is now telescoped through television and video; to the opera or concert through the increased availability of gramophone recordings from the 1920s; and to the reproduction of paintings themselves through photographic means in books, magazines, and television. Rosalind Krauss has observed that this principle of textual reproducibility was prevalent, although at the same time given ideological denial, in modernism, itself. She notes the confusion of an audience sensitized to auratic art at the 1978 unveiling of the new cast of Rodin's *Gates of Hell*. Was it original? Was it authentic? Rodin in his will indeed bequeathed to the French nation the right to make bronze casts from his plaster models, a right that a National Assembly vote limited to 12 casts per model. The first bronze of the *Gates of Hell* was cast in 1921 well after Rodin's death. The original plaster lay scattered in pieces on his death, it not being clear just how Rodin would have wanted it pieced together. Was even the high modernist Rodin, the 'form-giver', the figure of the 'reflexively-intended hand-of-God imagery', also an instance of Benjamin's mechanical production, of the 'existence of multiples without an original'? Krauss notes that even in Rodin's *Three Nymphs*, it was the same plaster model that was realized for each of the three figures. Much the same can be said for the use of the 'grid' in countless high-modernist abstract paintings by Mondrian, Reinhardt, and many others. Does not the transparency, the reproducibility of the grid, contradict the modernist 'insistence on the opacity of the pictorial field', an insistence that is also a claim for its singularity and uniqueness? Krauss observes another case of mass reproduction in Manet's 'assembly line' style of the continued overpainting of a large number of canvases at the same time. Her point is that 'the discourse of the copy' existed also in high modernism, but it was repressed. In postmodernism, however, as in Rauschenberg's silk-screens, this discourse has entered fully into consciousness (Krauss 1981).

(2) In primitive, medieval, and courtly art, reception was collective. In autonomous and auratic art, reception by contrast is individualized and the audience is typically immersed in the work itself. In postauratic culture, Benjamin argues, reception is once again collective and now no longer occurs under conditions of 'immersion'. Rather, the consumption of culture takes place under conditions of 'distraction'. Benjamin's (1975a, pp. 241–2) paradigmatic example here is the cinema, in which the rapid succession of images makes contemplation impossible, and reception is collective. Reception under conditions of distraction is taken to its extreme in television, which is half watched in the course of pursuing other activities and in which very often, especially among children, entire programmes are not viewed at all; instead, fingers rarely leave the remote control device as there is a constant change of channels (Ellis 1982, p. 137). The same is true of our reception of postmodernist painting. No longer is there the immersion of contemplating the high modernist work of art. The intention instead is to shock the audience. When we view, for example, a Francis Bacon picture, the effect is immediate and often initially in the pit of the stomach (Deleuze 1981). Postmodern multimedia performances are an extreme example of consumption under distraction.

(3) The producer of the auratic work of art is characteristically the unique, gifted, and creative individual; the work of art is highly personalized. In the postmodern alternative the producer can be (and is) often collective and the production impersonal. On the first point, Erwin Piscator's Berlin theatre of the mid- and late 1920s recruited a dramaturgical collective, including Bertholt Brecht, to write and adapt plays. Ex-Bauhaus director Walter Gropius was to design a *Totaltheater* for Piscator's productions. George Grosz was set designer for Hasek's *Schweik*, which Piscator produced in 1928. In 1929 Piscator invited from the

Bauhaus first Oskar Schlemmer and then Laszlo Moholy-Nagy as scene designers. Brecht carried on this collective principle in the course of his later productions (Willett 1978). Also important was the *impersonality* of the new naturalism, which was seen, at least in Germany, as part of a critique of auratic, expressionist culture of the pre-war period. Piscator thus embraced the idea of a politically committed 'documentary theatre'. Influenced by Eisenstein, his epic theatre used naturalistic language, a technologically advanced yet nonornamental stage set, and was intended to make theatre into a mix of 'lecture hall and debating chamber' (Willett 1978, p. 151). Brecht later worked out of this mould in his different epic theatre. In his *Jungle of the Cities* he used contrived precise dates and times for each episode. His idea was to tell his story 'in a perfectly matter of fact and sober manner' (Willett 1978, p. 154). Eisenstein was probably the most influential pioneer of this impersonality and naturalism in his documentary style. His use of location shooting, natural lighting, and lay actors stood in total contrast to the older expressionist cinema. This new naturalism also stood in contradistinction to the straightforward narrative of classic realism; for example, Eisenstein's first film *Strike* was 'a montage of shocks, of images. . .' whose design was to turn disparate items into an artistic whole (Willett 1978, pp. 107–8). In Germany as well, directors such as G. W. Pabst turned away from the expressionist cinema that Fritz Lang had exemplified. In *The Love of Jeanne Ney*, Pabst used real-life detail such as broken mirrors and iron basins. Contemporaneous critics lauded this new cinema in which people were no longer made up to look like 'artificial dolls' (Willett 1978, p. 146). The impersonality of this naturalism constituted a postmodern challenge to the modernist cult of the singular and expressive creative artist.

(4) So far, in the characterization of postmodern as postauratic art we have spoken of the cultural text, of its reception and production, in terms of auratic and nonauratic. Perhaps even more important than these three elements are the 'institutions' of culture. 'Institutions' here should be understood in a sense consistent with Weber's sociology of religion, in which the institutions of the church mediate between the prophetic reactors of religious ideas and the 'laity' (Bourdieu 1987). The prophet would here be analogous to the producer of art, the religious

ideas to the cultural text, and the laity to the audience. Peter Bürger (1984, p. 22), in a rather similar vein, has defined the 'institution of art' in terms of (1) 'the production and distribution apparatus of art' and (2) 'the ideas which determine its reception'. Bürger's stress on the 'ideas' that are expressed in criticism is particularly important here. They influence not only the way the audience receives cultural texts, but also what gets exhibited in museums, the paintings we see in books and magazines and on television, and what gets taught in the art schools. The point here is that institutions define the discourses and narratives through which aesthetic experience is received. The concept of the integral work of art, of aura, in this sense is itself discursively created and, as already noted, can foster identity formation in the 'bourgeois public sphere'. Institutions in 'oppositional public spheres' can have a wholly different effect (Schulte-Sasse 1984). Discourses in the latter can produce nonauratic and political readings of cultural texts.

Roger Fry and Clement Greenberg, for example, played inordinate roles in shaping the sensibility of successive generations of a high modernist audience. For Greenberg who privileged the flatness of the modernist world of art, the masterpiece was 'a universal, transhistorical form'. Greenberg claimed that 'modernist art developed out of a past without gap or break, and wherever it ends up it will never stop being intelligible in terms of the continuity of art' (Krauss 1985a, pp. 1–8). If writers such as Greenberg had such effects on the generation of the 1960s, contemporary postmodernist artists and architects, as their critics have sorely lamented, have surely been similarly affected by the institutional mediation of poststructuralist theory. The problem is that much of this institutional intervention has quickly become part and parcel of the established academy. This stands in marked contrast to the antiauratic institutional role of the Bauhaus, the Russian Vkhutemas, and De Stijl in the 1920s which maintained their critical and oppositional thrust.

(5) The eclipse of aura creates partial and selective dissolution of the boundaries between high and popular culture. There are several variants of this new high/popular culture juxtaposition with different aesthetic and political implications. We may note initially the adoption by high culture of the objects of popular culture. An example from the 1920s is the almost universal

164

influence of Chaplin and jazz in the avant-garde. The musical sensibility of Stravinsky, Milhaud, Kurt Weill, and Hindemith was overwhelmingly influenced by jazz. The latter was partly formed in dissatisfaction with the expressionist and even symbolist affinities of Schönberg and his disciples' twelve-tone music. The newer music, which was 'dissonant, contrapuntal, rhythmically forceful' (Willett 1978, p. 162), instead downplayed the emotions. Otto Klemperer at the Kroll-Oper, for example, in this naturalist vein dispensed with crescendi, vibrato, and sentimentality. Opera featured jazz interludes. Weill's philosophy here was that songs should not blend with, but should deliberately interrupt, narrative in his contemporaneous documentary style operas (Willett 1978, p. 167).

(6) Willett (1978, p. 110) makes a distinction between two rather different uses of popular culture for high culture: the first is for political reasons, as in the case of the German avant-garde and particularly the Dada movement; the second is for formal reasons, and it is found in surrealism and more generally in the Parisian avant-garde of the 1920s. This distinction is useful in the consideration of contemporary postmodern culture. An example of such 'political' postmodernism in the fine arts is the work of Ed Kienholz, whom critics have labelled a neo dadaist. In an eminently Benjaminian vein, Kienholz has said that one can only understand a 'society by going through its junk stores and flea markets'. He explicitly confronted issues of racism in his 1960 commentary on the antisegregation struggles in Little Rock, Arkansas (*The Little Eagle Rock Incident*) and in his installation, *Five Car Stud*. The latter was set up in a tent and foregrounded five white bigots beating a black man in the glare of automobile headlights. He addressed the war in Vietnam in *The Eleventh Hour Final*, an installation of a living room in which a television screen broadcasts a fixed image of the evening news containing the week's death toll and the disembodied head of a Vietnamese child. He and Nancy Reddin Kienholz have more recently addressed issues of gender inequality in their *Berlin Women* (1982). Early on and independently, although contemporaneous with the beginnings of the Pop movement, Kienholz began making use of junk material in the late 1950s. His installations, such as *Roxy's*, which features decapitated whores with mechanical pelvic movements in a brothel, and *The Back*

Seat Dodge—'38, which puts its viewers in the place of voyeurs of a necking couple whose heads are melted into one, deal naturalistically with the seamy and discarded side of social life. At times his work has been cast in a Tzara-like parody of high modernist art. Whereas Robert Rauschenberg already had produced an erasure of a De Kooning drawing in the early 1950s, Kienholz assembled his *Odious to Rauschenberg* in 1960. The latter was to be posted in a box, to which was attached an electric cord. When plugged in, a tongue would stick out of the apparatus; additionally it contained an electric device that was intended to block television reception in the immediate area. Nearly two decades later his installation *Art Show* at the Centre Pompidou foregrounded figures with tape decks for hearts, which gave out phoney art jargon, with hot air literally coming out of the figures' vents (Rickey 1983).

The political significance of the vulgarization of high culture is exemplified in the more complicated case of Andy Warhol. Considerable controversy has been generated as to whether his work undermines or reproduces contemporary power relations (Lyotard 1980; Jameson 1984, p. 63). In Warhol's postmodernism there is an overproduction of cultural goods in relation to the quantity of meanings that consumers bring to the cultural marketplace. There is an overload of sounds, of images, of words to the point at which a number of these cultural goods cannot be found meanings that can be attached to them (Ratcliff 1985). In Warhol's 1965 film, *Kitchen,* there is no plot, no character development, and indeed the characters have interchangeable names. What these characters are engaged in, however, is a competition for the attention of the camera, for which during the course of the film they posture and scheme. The same overproduction ethos, that of turning out in principle reproducible cultural goods based on unskilled labour, and to which meaning can only be implausibly attached, underscores his 1978 'Oxidation' series, in which aleatory colour schemes are created through Warhol urinating on bronze- or copper-covered canvases. As does his 1984 'collaborative' work with Jean-Michel Basquiat and Francesco Clemente, in which he silk-screened the paintings of the two young artists (Ratcliff 1985, p. 70). The scarcity of meanings in the cultural marketplace, as Carter Ratcliff (1985, p. 74) observes, is also a 'scarcity of self'. Warhol drove this point home and develops this thematic oversupply of signifiers in his ploy in the 1980s of sending someone else (with silver-sprayed hair) out on the lecture circuit in his place. Although Warhol's images so perfectly captured the essence of postmodern cultural overproduction, he was too much the cultural entrepreneur to be fully taken in by it. He clearly understood that the postmodern audience is radically different from previous audiences in that it brings to the marketplace a set of ideal interests that are no longer connected with meanings, but in which demand has become increasingly oriented to detached, shallow, and meaningless signifiers that he obligingly produced.

(7) Postauratic art entails the destruction of the distinction between the cultural and the social. Although Sontag (1979) may have been guilty of exaggeration in her claim that Benjamin's most important influence came from surrealism, it is certain that he was enthusiastic about surrealism both as a movement in the arts and as often explicit politics. Benjamin, who was particularly impressed by Aragon and Breton, shares this influence with poststructuralists Foucault, Derrida, and Deleuze, although, to the latter, surrealists such as Bataille, Artaud, and Magritte have been most significant. Both Benjamin and the poststructuralists understood the surrealist lineage as running through Rimbaud, Lautréamont, Mallarmé, and Nietzsche. My point here is that the surrealists and Benjamin spoke of the destruction of the (modernist and auratic) distinction between art and life. Benjamin's concept of 'allegory' which, Sontag (1979, p. 17) argues, is the governing concept in his two most substantial works on Baudelaire's *Paris* and *The Origins of German Tragic Drama*, does have roots in surrealism.

Semiotics has conventionally spoken in terms of a tripartite model of signifier, signfied, and referent, in which the signifier is commonly a word or statement, the signified is a concept or thought, and the referent is the object in the real (and social) world to which both signifier and signified connect. In the language of semiotics, high modernism would be characterized by the radical separation of the signifier from the real (and social) and by a formalism of the signifying material. In postmodernism and in surrealism it is the *referent*, the real itself, that becomes the signifier. Thus, it has been argued that photography is the quintessential surrealist art form, that photographs are like 'death masks', like footprints in the sense of being 'imprints of the real' (Krauss 1985b, p. 110). Surrealist spokesperson André Breton compared the camera with psychic automatism in that both for him were processes of mechanical recording. Surrealist photography indeed developed techniques that self-consciously played upon this juxtaposition of the real as signifier and the signifier as real. This was the case in their technique of writing or drawing on photos, or photographing bits of reality, like J.A. Boiffard's telescopically enlarged shot of a big toe (*Le Gros Orteuil*), which seem primarily to be (in this case phallic) signifiers. It is also illustrated in the 'doubling' technique of using double exposures in which the first shot is read, not photographically, but as a signifying element whose referent is the second shot (Krauss 1985b, p. 109). Surrealists not only saw art as being composed of signifying elements drawn from the real, but also understood reality to be composed of signifying elements. Pierre Naville, for instance, enthused that we should get pleasure from the streets of the city in which kiosks, autos, and lights were in a sense already representations, and Breton spoke of the *world* as 'automatic writing' (Krauss 1985b, p. 99).

This thematic of the real, or the referent, as signifier is essential to the surrealist strategy that Walter Benjamin understood in terms of 'allegory'. Surrealist allegory, in Breton's words, would be based on 'the bringing together of two more or less distant realities', these realities forming 'an aggregation based on elective affinities' (Kuspit 1983, p. 58). The point here is that these surrealist signifiers in 'allegory' are real, already referents. Further, surrealist allegory for Benjamin is a method in which these figural signifiers are taken from 'the petrified and insignificant', from Breton's 'dresses of five years ago' (Sontag 1979, p. 26). This bringing together of 'two more or less distant realities' creates the surreal *point sublime*. This 'profane illumination', this 'poeticization of the banal' was a matter, for Breton, not just of painting, literature, and photography, but also of life and love, the latter arising in no small portion from an intoxication in connection with the things of the beloved.[2]

Benjamin (1979b, p. 226) wrote of the surrealist movement that 'life only seemed worth living where the threshold between waking and sleeping was worn away in everyone as by the steps

168

of multitudinous images flooding back and forth, language only seemed itself where sound and image, image and sound inter-penetrated with such felicity that no chink was left for the penny-in-the-slot called "meaning" '. Benjamin's allusions in this passage are not just to the dominance of image and sensation and the devaluation of meaning in surrealism, not just to its char-acteristic patterning by eruptions of the primary process into consciousness, but also and especially to surrealism's uncon-ditional refusal to consider art as of a different order than life.

CONCLUDING REMARKS

I have tried to show how Walter Benjamin's notions of 'aura' (and also of 'allegory') can be used in the analysis of postmodernist culture. I have at the same time suggested that Benjamin's own aesthetics were very much a postmodernist aesthetics. Benjamin's own optimism regarding mechanical reproduction in culture, his advocacy of collective reception, his devaluation of meaning, his advocacy of pastiche-like allegory as distinct from the 'organic work of art' are, we have seen, all part and parcel of his break with a high modernist and auratic aesthetics. His sympathy with the antiauratic surrealists, his proclivity for finding aesthetic signifiers among the flotsam and jetsam of every-day life, his refusal to consider art as of another order of life, and his affirmation of the political nature of the aesthetic are again also integral to the postmodernist pro-gramme.

One important assumption of the modernity/postmodernity controversies is that the political left of Marxists and Critical Theorists is aligned with the modernists, whereas those (especially French-influenced poststructuralists) who connect somehow to postmodernism are apolitical and have little concern with contemporaneous social struggles. Benjamin's fully politi-cal postmodernism throws this assumption into question. Benjamin may never have convincingly reconciled his commit-ment to such an aesthetic project with his Marxist convictions. Yet he wrote:

The collective is a body, too. And the *physis* that is being organized for it in technology can, through all its political and factual reality, only be produced in that image sphere to which [surrealist] profane illumination initiates us. Only when in technology body and image so interpenetrate that all revolutionary tension becomes bodily collective innervation, and all the bodily innervation of the collective becomes revolutionary discharge, has reality transcended itself to the extent demanded by the *Communist Manifesto*. For the moment, only the Surrealists have understood its present commands.

(Benjamin 1979b, p. 239)

Althusser (1972, pp. 23-4) once asserted that scientific and social-scientific revolutions were made possible by preceding revolutions in philosophy. Today some analysts (Frisby 1985; see Chapter Five above) are beginnng to suggest that the place to look for formative conditions of paradigm change in the human sciences is instead in the aesthetic sphere. Thus, it has been argued that a set of at least tacit beliefs that underlay aesthetic modernism also underlay the birth of classical sociological theory in the work of Weber, Simmel, and Durkheim. It has equally been mooted that *post*modernism in the aesthetic realm – and I have argued that such postmodernism first surfaced in the Surrealism and more generally in the historical avant-garde of the 1920s – has been an important condition of formation of poststructuralism in the human sciences (Huyssen 1984; see above, Chapter Three). Benjamin's contribution to the human sciences, which converges remarkably with poststructuralism, also bears the stamp of the postmodern aesthetic programme, only some 40 years *avant la lettre*. Thus, the relationship of critical theory to postmodernism and poststructuralism is indeed a far more complex matter than is commonly assumed. If Habermas has relegated the aesthetic realm to foreground the place of practical and theoretical reason, and if Adorno has attributed priority to the aesthetic, albeit a rationalized and formalized aesthetics from which connections to the social-political are at best obscure, then Benjamin, probably critical theory's foremost *sociologist* of culture, has – much like French poststructuralism – promulgated an aesthetics and politicized understanding of art and culture that on a range of essential points are effectively postmodernist.

Acknowledgement

This chapter first appeared as an article in *Current Perspectives in Social Theory*, Volume 8, pages 197–213, 1987, and is reproduced by permission of JAI Press Inc, USA.

Chapter Seven

DISCOURSE OR FIGURE?
POSTMODERNISM AS A
'REGIME OF SIGNIFICATION'

Some of the very best and sharpest critics of postmodernism have put forward a strikingly similar, yet quite powerful, argument against the claim that we live in some important sense in a postmodern era.[1] Analysts such as Anderson (1984), Frisby (1985) and Callinicos (1985) have thus aggressively disputed Lyotard's famous pronouncement that the contemporary scepticism before 'metanarratives' has been midwife to the birth of the postmodern condition. Such analysts point out such a refusal of the 'great narratives' and the 'foundationalisms' took place, not in the past decade or two, but were integral to the very rise of modernism itself. Thus Baudelaire, arguably the godfather of aesthetic modernism, broke with the foundationalist assumptions of realism to celebrate the transitory, the fleeting, the contingent. And Nietzsche, well before the turn of the century, castigated foundationalisms not just in the aesthetic realms, but similarly refused the certainties of notions of unconditional ethics and realist, mirror-of-nature epistemologies. Indeed a recent collection of essays shows a remarkable convergence of opinion among contributors supporting the propositions that Max Weber himself had an eminently post-Enlightenment and 'post-metanarrative' idea of modernity (Whimster and Lash 1987).

It is helpful in the understanding of the modernist, late nineteenth-century departure from foundationalism, if we think in terms of the traditional sociological, structural–functional model which features the process of differentiation. Let us however confine this process of differentiation to only the cultural realm. In this sense the non-referential and anti-realist nature of, for example, modernist painting and literature can be seen in terms of the differentiation of aesthetic forms from the real world. And the modernist critique of realist epistemologies (present, for example, in Durkheim's 'sociologistic epistemology') is a matter of the differentiation of the 'theoretical realm' from the real world. The differentiation of fact from value, of the ethical from theoretical spheres, is similarly evidenced in Weber's work, and in the work of English philosophers such as Moore and Stevenson (MacIntyre 1981).

This process of differentiation is integral to the process of 'modernization'. Modernization conceived as differentiation is of course the linchpin of Parsonian sociology, but can be traced back through the work of Weber and even of Lukács to the aesthetic writings of the mature Hegel (Kätz 1982). And if modern*ism* is the result of a stage of differentiation whose onset is proper to the late nineteenth and early twentieth centuries, then modern*ity* is the product of a much earlier stage of this differentiation process. On this account the Renaissance would document the differentiation of cultural from religious realism, and, as Hegel underscored, the differentiation of the aesthetic realm from the social. It makes sense perhaps, then, to speak in terms of an 'early' modernity of the Renaissance and the Enlightenment, and a 'late' or at least later modernity co-extensive with the much later rise of aesthetic modernism. Both of these would be products of a continued modernization process based on a principle of cultural differentiation.

The critics of postmodernism are thus correct in their contention that what Lyotard takes to be postmodernity is in fact part and parcel of modernism. This however does not entail that postmodern culture does not exist. Indeed I think it does exist, but that Lyotard has not got it quite right. I think that if modernism and modernity result from a process of differentiation, or what German social scientists call *Ausdifferenzierung*, then postmodernism results from a much more recent process of *de*-differentiation or *Entdifferenzierung*. There has been in this sense de-differentiation in the postmodernist attempt to drain the aura from the work of art. De-differentiation is also present in the postmodernist refusal to separate the author from his or her oeuvre or the audience from the performance; in the postmodernist transgression of the boundary (with no doubt greater or lesser success) between literature and theory, between high and popular culture, between what is properly cultural and what is properly social.

In Chapter Three I illustrated this characteristic de-differentiation in conceiving of postmodernity in terms of the notion of 'desire'. Here, 'modernist' Freudian theory would conceive of the psyche as differentiated into two spheres – of desire, on the one hand, and the conscious mind on the other. Postmodern psychotherapy, in contradistinction, could no longer speak in terms of such differentiation. Desire instead would have to be on the very 'surface' of a now largely de-differentiated psychic apparatus. Similarly, the no longer representational, modernist painting would correspond to the formal principles of rationality of the secondary process, while the postmodernist painting of, say, Francis Bacon, would break with such principles of formal rationality and show again desire on the canvas's surface (Deleuze 1981).

In what follows I should like further to work through the implications of conceiving of postmodernism in terms of de-differentiation. This time I want to concentrate on what might be called the postmodern mode of signification, or a postmodern 'semiotics'. In Chapter Three I argued that a postmodernist culture that foregrounded 'desire' signalled somehow a renunciation of signification. This resulted in a sort of 'naturalism', which relegated signification and semiotics to the ranks of the merely modern, with whose possible political implications I am not entirely happy. In what follows I shall claim that postmodern cultural forms do indeed signify, only that they signify differently. I shall argue that modernist culture signifies in a largely 'discursive' way, while postmodernist signification is importantly 'figural'. The terms 'discourse' and 'figure' of course are taken from Lyotard. My conception of postmodernist de-differentiation via an aesthetics of desire was also in large part dependent on Lyotard's work. Little of this work draws on Lyotard's *Postmodern Condition* (1979), on which so much ink of secondary analysis has been spilt, and which, as indicated above, I think is largely misconceived. The work in which Lyotard is the most valuable about post-modernism is, I think, his earlier work, in which he does not directly address the topic at all. In Chapter Three I contrasted desire with discursive signification. The notion of figural signification developed in this chapter is fully consistent with the notion of desire in Chapter Three.

The body of this chapter will then attempt to construct as contrasting ideal-types a 'discursive' modernist sensibility with a 'figural' and postmodernist sensibility. In this context the discursive (1) gives priority to words over images; (2) valuates the formal qualities of cultural objects; (3) promulgates a rationalist view of culture; (4) attributes crucial importance to the *meanings* of cultural texts; (5) is a sensibility of the ego rather than of the id; (6) operates through a distancing of the spectator from the cultural object. The 'figural' in contradistinction: (1) is a visual rather than a literary sensibility; (2) devalues formalisms and juxtaposes signifiers taken from the banalities of everyday life; (3) contests rationalist and/or 'didactic' views of culture; (4) asks not what a cultural text 'means', but what it 'does'; (5) in Freudian terms, advocates the extension of the primary process into the cultural realm; (6) operates through the spectator's immersion, the relatively unmediated investment of his/her desire in the cultural object.

This contrast of the two, discursive and figural, 'regimes of signification', will be addressed via rather theoretical considerations first, of Susan Sontag's contrast of an (I think, postmodernist) aesthetics of sensation with a (modernist) aesthetics of interpretation, and second, briefly, through Lyotard's more systematic distinction of 'discourse' and 'figure'. Then I turn to the (in large measure postmodern) avant-garde of the 1920s and examine how surrealism worked through the opposition between an image-centred culture, associated with the unconscious, and a formalist, word-centred culture, associated with the conscious mind. Finally cinema, and the cinematic experience, is addressed in a similar vein. Here it is noted that even in mainstream cinema, narrative content is increasingly losing centrality and giving way to a more image-centred 'spectacular' cinema. It is then argued further that in non-mainstream, critical cinema, a new image-centred mode of signification, based on an alternative 'regime of pleasure', may come increasingly to displace the most pervasive type of critical cinema which is modernist, discursive, and intellectualist.

SENSATION VERSUS INTERPRETATION

The new postmodern sensibility was perhaps first given systematic articulation by the critic Susan Sontag in the middle 1960s. Sontag counterposed an aesthetics of sensation to what she described as an aesthetics of 'interpretation'. She claimed that, 'in a culture whose already classical dilemma is the hypertrophy of the intellect at the expense of energy and sensual capability, interpretation is the revenge of the intellect upon art'. 'It is simultaneously,' she (Sontag 1967, p. 7) continued, 'the revenge of the intellect upon the world. To interpret is to impoverish, to deplete the world – in order to set up a shadow of "meanings" '. Sontag's attack on interpretation was two-pronged and aimed at both works of art and art criticism. Her attack on any notion of art as 'expressive' was generalized into an opposition to works of art whose main effect on an audience lies in their 'meaning'. She thus had little use for cinema which gave great weight to symbolism, and unfavourably contrasted symbolist poetry to the work of poets like Ezra Pound whose world operated, not through meaning, but through the 'direct impact of words'. For Sontag, who contrasted an 'erotics of art' with 'hermeneutics of art', a work of art should be, not a 'text', but another 'sensory' thing in the world (Sontag 1967, pp. 165–7).

What Sontag saw as the 'new sensibility' was clearly not a literary sensibility, but foregrounded a 'cooler art' with 'less content'; it favoured not the novel, but music, dance, architecture, painting, sculpture. She discussed in this context who she saw as the twentieth century's two most influential analysts of theatre: Brecht and Antonin Artaud. Sontag (1967, p. 21) advocated, against Brecht's 'theatre of dialogue', an Artaudian 'theatre of the senses', whose driving force would be, not the playwright, but the director. This sort of theatre was not literature but was visual, its effects created through sounds and images. To the Brechtian 'didactic theatre' or 'theatre of the intelligence' was opposed the 'theatre of magic, of gesture, of "cruelty" ' (Sontag 1967, p. 173).

Sontag's postmodernist aesthetic was formed in opposition to contemporaneous 'hermeneutic' criticism, which for her foisted Marxian and/or Freudian interpretations onto the meanings of literature. However, her main opponent here was what has come to be known as the cultural conservatism among New York's intelligentsia, purveyed today by writers such as Daniel Bell and Irving Howe, but whose perhaps most influential figures were Lionel Trilling and Clement Greenberg. Cultural conservatives privileged the auratic work of art, whether realist or high modernist, either on grounds of the significance of its meaning, or on Apollonian grounds of its formal qualities. By contrast Sontag's postmodern criticism aggressively disputed such a separation of text and life. She (1967, p. 300) broke with such an implicitly Arnoldian view of art as a 'criticism of life' and instead endorsed a Nietzschean aesthetic in which even ideas should function as 'sensory stimulants' and in which art is an extension of or a 'supplement' to life.

Jean-François Lyotard provides a theoretical grounding to Sontag's distinction between a modernist hermeneutics and a postmodern aesthetics of sensation in his counterposition of 'discourse' and 'figure'. Lyotard's 'discursive' is the Freudian secondary process, the ego operating in terms of the reality principle. The figural, by contrast, is the primary process of the unconscious which operates according to the pleasure principle (Lyotard 1971; 1973; 1984). Lyotard's notion of the figural is formulated partly as a critique of Lacan's dictum that the unconscious is structured like a language. Lyotard holds that we can best understand the nature of the unconscious through examining precisely how it is *not* structured like a language, that the most important criterion of demarcation of the unconscious from the ego lies in the ways that the former does not operate as does language. This has crucial implications for Anglo-American and Continental Culture Studies, whose Lacanian impulse has arguably prevented the establishment of important distinctions between cultural forms. We should note here that Lyotard does not maintain that the unconscious does not *signify* but only that it does not signify like a language.

Lyotard's (1984, p. 69) understanding of 'the discursive' is rooted in his understanding of language as a means by which the ego discharges energy according to the reality principle. That is, in the secondary process energy is discharged 'through activities of transformation and verbalization'. In the primary process, by contrast, energy is discharged (and desire is fulfilled) through cathexis; through investment in 'perceptual memories'. Lyotard further clarifies this distinction in discussion of fantasies and hallucination. He observes that fantasies operate like the primary process in that they 'fulfil desire' without the transformation of external reality but instead through the cathexis of, for example, the perceptual memory (image) of an organ. And hallucinations resemble the primary process in that again energy is discharged through investment in perceptual memories, through the displacement of energy from what Lyotard (1984, pp. 57–68) calls the 'verbal-motor' end of the psychic apparatus to the 'perceptual' end. Lyotard then has initially defined 'discourse' and 'figure' as two alternative means for the discharge of psychic energy. Discourse discharges energy through the transformation of the external world, while 'figures' are perceptual memories through which psychic energy is straightaway discharged by investment in them.

There is another important way secondary and primary processes are for Lyotard characterized through the language/ image opposition. This again relates to Lyotard's focus on *perception* in the unconscious, which derives from the influence of Merleau-Ponty's phenomenology of perception on his work. Here the secondary process does not just operate through discourse, but is structured like discourse, while the primary process does not only discharge energy through the use of perceptual memories, but is structured like a 'perceptual field'. That is, the unhindered mobility of the eye in the 'continuous and asymmetrical visual field' resembles the 'unhindered mobility of cathexis' in the primary process. Discourse, on the other hand, does not have the same unhindered mobility. It must proceed according to a set of obstacles, a set of rules, that is, through a 'process of selection and combination of language', which itself is more bound than mobile in language's articulated and differential nature. Similarly, in the secondary process the investment of energy is canalized by rules, by obstacles, that the defence mechanisms of the ego construct, which subordinate the possibility of energy discharge to the 'transformation of the relationship between the psychic apparatus and the external world' (Lyotard 1984, p. 58; Dews 1984).

Lyotard has thus asserted the existence of two alternative economies of desire. In the first, the discursive, the secondary process makes inroads into the primary process. For example

Lyotard considers Freud's 'talking cure' itself to promote a discursive economy of desire through the colonization of the unconscious by discourse; through the subversion of the primary process by language and the transference (Lyotard 1984, p. 106). What he prefers of course is a figural economy of desire; he wants a sensibility, a culture and a politics in which the primary process 'erupts' into the secondary process like 'the application of a force to text' (Dews 1984, p. 47). Lyotard's (1984, pp. 60–1) aesthetics is an aesthetics of Freudian 'unconscious space', which (i) permits condensation and other contradictions; (ii) permits the mobility of cathectic energies and hence displacement; and which (iii) severs temporality from rule-boundedness. This figural aesthetics is a doctrine which opposes the subordination of the image to the dictates of narrative meaning or represent-ation; to language like rule-bound formalisms (hence his preference for Cage over Schoenberg); or (in his (1984, p. 80) example of advertising images) to the dictates of capitalism and the law of value.

What both Sontag and Lyotard have endorsed is an effectively postmodernist aesthetics based on paradigm of cultural de-differentiation. Sontag was arguing in the context of intellectual New York of the early 1960s. Then, as arguably now, the terrain of debate was partly structured by the polarization of a serious and moral 'uptown' high modernist culture versus a more self-consciously populist and 'funky' yet equally elite, 'downtown' culture. Sontag argued against what was in effect the differentiated mode of signification implicit in the assumptions of uptown culture. This was the thrust of her attack on 'hermeneutics', whether the latter be of Arnoldian, Freudian, or (reformist) Marxist complexion. Her attack on hermeneutics was an advocacy of de-differentiation in three important senses. First her challenge to the primacy of 'meaning' and support of 'cool' rather than 'expressive' aesthetic assumptions was at the same time an advocacy of the collapse of some sort of deep level of signified into the signifier. Second, her refusal of the counterposition of text and reality and determination to see the work of art as a 'sensory thing', was simultaneously an insistence that this already overloaded signifier was in fact not very different from a referent. Third, her dispute with 'interpretation', which is for her also a dispute with any kind of critical theory, is due to

the assumptions of cultural differentiation built into the former
and latter. In both there is a differentiated level of criticism
standing over and above both art and life. Sontag counterposes to
critical theory, casting adrift from both Marx and Freud, a de-
differentiated Nietzschean aesthetics of affirmation, in which
aesthetic analysis would be a supplement to art and art a
supplement to life.

Lyotard similarly has proposed a de-differentiated semiotics.
Arguing in the very different Parisian intellectual climate of the
early 1970s, he assimilates assumptions of differentiated
signification to Lacanian and orthodox Freudian
psychoanalysis, to the commodity form in capitalism, to the
ordered temporality of narrative realism and to the formalism of
Adornian aesthetic rationality. Unlike Lacan, Lyotard very
rigorously distinguishes between the image-based (in perceptual
memories) signification of the unconscious and the discursive
signification of the ego. His subsequent endorsement of the
former, figural signification is an endorsement of cultural de-
differentiation in two important senses. First, in the sense that
unlike words or utterances, images signify iconically, i.e.
through resemblance, and hence are less different from referents
than properly linguistic signifiers. And second his promotion of
the colonization of the secondary process by primary process in
art and in psychoanalysis is also a rejection of the psyche rigidly
hierarchized into levels for one in which desire is no longer an
underlying 'essence'. Instead desire is present on the very surface
of social and cultural practices.

Let us move now from the level of cultural theory to cultural
'practice'. We will find here, in the case of surrealism, a not
dissimilar state of affairs. In arguing, in what follows, that
surrealism also exemplifies de-differentiated signification I will
be *eo ipso* arguing that surrealism exemplifies postmodernism.

SURREALISM: THE REAL BECOME SIGNIFIER

Surrealism was self-consciously 'figural' in its foregrounding of
the visual. André Breton, self-styled 'pope' of the surrealist
movement, contrasted a high modernist aesthetic in which all art
would be based on a musical model with the surrealist (and, in
the present context, postmodern) idea that all art should partake

of a visual mode. And indeed the reflections on art by modernists such as Flaubert, Klee, and Auguste Macke did hold that literature and painting should be like music in a quest for the attainment of formal qualities and in a departure from realist notions of representation. Breton, on the other hand, juxtaposed the 'savage eye' with the 'educated ear' and celebrated the immediacy of the visual (Krauss 1985, p. 93). Surrealist écriture automatique, grounded in a Freudian unconscious structured through free association and perceptual memories, presented vision itself as a written form, a 'cursive' rather than a discursive flow, which Breton understood to be, not representational, but immediate.

Semiotics has conventionally spoken in terms of a tripartite model of signifier, signified, and referent, in which the signifier is often a word or statement, the signified is a concept or a thought, and the referent an object in the real world to which both signifier and signified connect. In the postmodern and figural aesthetic suggested by Lyotard, we saw above, that the image took the place of the word as signifier. In the surrealist movement, by contrast, it was the, equally figural, *referent*, the real itself, which becomes the signifier. Thus Rosalind Krauss can argue that photography is the quintessential surrealist art form. Photographs, she (1985, p. 110) observes, are like death masks, like footprints in the sense of being 'imprints of the real'. Breton compared the camera with psychic automatism in that both for him were processes of mechanical recording. Surrealist photographers indeed developed techniques which self-consciously addressed this juxtaposition of the real as signifier and the signifier as real. This was the case in their technique of writing or drawing on photos, or photographing bits of reality – like J. A. Boiffard's telescopically enlarged shot of a big toe (*Le Gros Orteil*) – which seem primarily to be (in this case phallic) signifiers. It is also illustrated in the 'doubling' technique of using exposures in which the first shot is read, not photographically, but as a signifying element whose referent is the second shot. The point here is that not only did surrealists see art as being composed of signifying elements drawn from the real, but understood reality to be composed of signifying elements. Thus Naville enthused that we should get pleasure from the streets of the city in which kiosks, autos, and lights were in a sense already representations, and Breton spoke of the world itself as 'automatic writing'.

This thematic of the real, or the referent, as signifier is essential to the surrealist strategy which Walter Benjamin understood in terms of 'allegory'. Surrealist allegory would be based on, in Breton's words, 'the bringing together of two more or less distant realities', these realities forming 'an aggregation based on elective affinities' (Kuspit 1983, p.58). The point here is that the surrealist signifiers in 'allegory' are real, are *already* referents. Further, surrealist allegory for Benjamin is a method in which these figural signifiers are taken from 'the petrified and insignificant', from what Breton spoke of as the 'dresses of five years ago' (Sontag 1979, p. 26). This bringing together of 'two more or less distant realities' creates the surreal *point sublime*. The latter is a 'profane illumination', a 'poeticization of the banal' and was a matter for Breton, not just of painting, literature, and photography, but also of life and love, the latter arising in no small portion from an 'intoxication' in connection with the things of the beloved. There is surely a significant thematic of Benjaminian allegory in surrealist painting, in the young De Chirico's and Ernst's, not to mention Dali's, poeticization of petrified figures, or even in De Chirico's later, more kitsch method of juxtaposing scenes from Antiquity with the banal present (Dell'Arco 1984, p. 82). De Chirico himself, upon arriving in New York in the mid-1930s, compared its architecture with his metaphysical paintings as a 'homogeneity and harmonic monumentality formed by disparate and heterogeneous elements'. Such surrealist allegory mirrors the process of displacement and condensation in dreams and in the primary process more generally.

Benjamin (1979b, p. 226) wrote of the surrealist movement that 'life only seemed worth living where the threshold between waking and sleeping was worn away in everyone as by the steps of multitudinous images flooding back and forth, language only seemed itself where sound image, image and sound interpenetrated with such felicity that no chink was left for the penny-in-the-slot called "meaning" '. Benjamin's allusions in this passage are, not just to the dominance of the figural and the devaluation of meaning in surrealism, not just to its characteristic patterning by eruptions of the primary process into consciousness, but also and especially to surrealism's unconditional refusal to consider art as of a different order than life. Perhaps the exemplar of this surrealist categorical imperative was Antonin Artaud. Artaud's initial public appearance before literary France came in the form of 'life' and not art, in the publication of his personal correspondence with *Nouvelle revue française* editor Jacques Rivière, after the latter had refused his poems due to their failure to live up to certain formal canons. As Derrida (1978b, p. 234) noted, Artaudian theatre was not to refer to life or represent life but instead to be life. Theatre was to be a 'genuine reality', an 'event' like, Artaud proposed, a police raid on a brothel. He wrote in a theoretical essay published in the collection *The Theatre and Its Doubles*, 'For if theatre is a double of life, life is a double of true theatre . . . The double of theatre is *reality* which today's mankind leaves unused' (Esslin 1976).

Artaudian theatre is profoundly figural theatre. Key here was the influence of non-western cultural forms on Artaud – first the foregrounding of actors' movements and the absence of props in Japanese theatre; then his exposure to Cambodian dance in 1922; but most importantly the Balinese Dance Theatre which Artaud witnessed at the Colonial Exhibition in Paris in 1931, after which he wrote a succession of now canonical theoretical essays on theatre. In Balinese dance, as Esslin (1976, p.35 passim) notes, all of Artaud's 'ideas of a non-verbal, magical theatre of light, colour and costume seemed realized'. Several aspects of Balinese dance as interpreted by Artaud have important implications for the understanding of postmodern culture in that they illustrate cultural de-differentiation. First such theatre, in a sense reminiscent of premodern art, takes on important ritualistic functions; the implication is that, in contradistinction to autonomous, modernist theatre, (postmodern) theatre itself should double as cultural ritual. Second, the absence of clarity as to whether Balinese dance is, on the one hand, art, or on the other, life, underscored for Artaud the importance of cancelling the separation of the two realms. Third, the centrality of body movements in such theatre helped Artaud to develop his own aesthetics 'of the body'. Fourth, the cries in Balinese dance seemed to Artaud to have a cosmic power and communicated not through the differentiated and 'shadow' realm of meaning, but, directly, through impact.

What struck Artaud perhaps most of all about Balinese dance was the centrality of actors' bodily movements. He wanted actors, through for example exaggerated breathing, to establish an identity between their bodies and the bodies of spectators. Artaud had in some ways a curiously desexualized view of the body and spoke of a 'body without organs', which was for him a body deprived mainly of functions of reproduction and defecation, that was mainly a locus of feeling and sensation. Yet his idea of theatre was, unlike poetry or the novel, intended 'to reach the organism directly, and in the period of neurosis and low sensation into which we are about to plunge, to attack that low sensuality by physical means which it will not resist' (Esslin 1976, p. 70; Deleuze and Guattari 1984, pp. 9–15).

Theatre, then, in Artaud's sense is not about life, but is a *supplement to life*. Theatre's task is 'to smash language in order to touch life'; it is to show that the force of the aural lies in sound (reduplicating for Artaud the significance that dreams give to the sounds in speech) and not words (Sellin 1968, pp. 49–52). Speech on this account functions primarily not as a conveyor of meanings, but as incantation – in which voices have, so to speak, a magical effect independent of the meanings of words. Incantatory speech is paradigmatic in contemporary Artaudian theatre and in surrealism and postmodernism more generally, are I think a sort of bodily aesthetics. This would contrast with both a 'realist' aesthetics of meaning and modernist formalism. Walter Benjamin (1979b, p. 239), in a rather similar context, called for a politics in which 'technology, body and image so interpenetrate that all revolutionary tension becomes bodily collective innervation, and all the bodily innervations of the collective become revolutionary discharge'. Artaud, the least political of the surrealists, promulgated an aesthetics in which 'the bodily' applies both to means of production and conditions of reception. He understood literature not to be formal craft, but instead viewed writing as a bodily process, a process which he experienced as wreaking pain, suffering, and destruction on his own body (Sellin 1968, p. 83).

In its usage of the real or referent as signifier, surrealism eminently illustrated de-differentiated signification. The surrealist aesthetic advocates signification, not through meaning, but through impact. And this impact is to be achieved in a particular way, i.e. through a 'profane illumination' brought about through the juxtaposition of two or more seemingly incongruous figures. The surrealist innovation thus is a problematization not just of the nature of high modernist painting and of the signifier, but also a problematization of what constitutes the real. It is thus similar to Warhol's silk-screens, which problematizes, not just high art, but also the real in that it reveals reality itself to be composed of images. The source of the surrealist and pop art's problematization of both signifier and referent are different, however. For Pop Art the source is the Baudrillardian society of the image. For surrealism it is the Freudian unconscious. Surrealist allegory, which attains its 'point sublime' and impact through the juxtaposition of 'two more or less distant realities', proceeds on three levels. First as signification in the unconscious through displacement and condensation. Second, in the work of art. And third, in every-day reality. In each case the result is not only a problematization of the real, but a problematization of the positioning of the subject. The eruption of the primary process and its analogues in art and reality foster an ambivalent positioning of the subject. They foster the development of, in contradistinction to any type of fixed positioning, what Deleuze and Guattari (1984) have called the 'nomadic subject'. This mobile positioning of subjectivity is in itself political in that it leaves space for alternative forms of identity construction as well as the toleration of 'difference' in identity construction.

The second major aspect of cultural de-differentiation addressed by surrealism is the issue of avant-gardes. Although surrealism (unlike contemporary postmodernism) was rather self-consciously an avant-garde, the logic of the surrealist ethic involved a dispute of the very nature of avant-gardes. The Artaudian break with the 'double' and embrace instead of the 'supplement' entails the rejection of avant-gardism in aesthetics, politics, and theory. If art is no longer to be considered as of a different order than life, then the idea of aesthetic avant-gardes is questioned. If theory itself is to be no longer the 'double' of art or life then Nietzschean affirmation, and not critical theory, would be on the intellectual agenda. It is in this context that Benjamin's work qualitatively differs from Adorno's and Habermas's. Benjaminian allegory functions perhaps as crucially as supplement as it does as 'criticism'. Finally, the challenge to political avant-gardism, exemplified in Benjamin's effective call for a politics of the supplement, quoted just above, is a shift towards de-differentiation in political culture. It is a condemnation of the strong state as well as of the centralized Marxist vanguard party, and move towards the implicit embrace of anarchist doctrines. Such a rejection of state and vanguard party with its accompanied space opened up for pluralism and difference is of potential significance for left political culture today.

CINEMA: FROM THE REPRESENTATION TO THE REALITY

Cinema, taken generically, signifies in a de-differentiated manner. No other form of cultural representation – not painting, nor literature nor music nor even television – can signify quite as figurally as can cinema. That is, cinematic signification, especially in the age of high technology and 30-million-dollar film, comes closer than other forms of signification to resemblance of reality.

Cinematic signification again taken generically is further de-differentiated in that it portrays the primary process and sexuality, not as a deep otherness, but as erupting on the very surface of representations. This is true on four counts:

(1) The experience of cinematic viewing – the dark, the succession of images ('perceptual memories'), the wonder, the wish fulfilment – has, as Metz (1982, pp. 106–9) observed, a very great deal in common with the experience of dreaming and of unconscious processes.

(2) As Benjamin (1973) noted, cinematic reception, unlike reception of the painting or the novel, takes place, not in a state of 'contemplation', but of 'distraction'. Cinema consists of a set of mechanically reproduced images which can be presented along the lines of the temporal causality of narrative realism. But as a literal succession of images they come closer to the disconnected temporality of the succession of perceptual memories in the unconscious.

(3) Film itself, is, as De Lauretis (1984, pp. 85–6) observes, a discourse (in the Foucauldian sense) of sexuality. Cinema was born virtually contemporaneously with the other great discourse

of sexuality, psychoanalysis. Cinema, further, more than any other cultural product, has been structured around sexuality, or rather around the objectification of male desire in screen images of women – that is, film narratives themselves have been structured by such a patriarchal economy of desire. These origins continue characteristically to put their imprint even on contemporary cinematic productions.

(4) Cinema has always given primacy of place to *images*. Cinema is always an 'imaging machine'. This is a point not to be neglected in the context of the film criticism which has become dominant in Anglo-American culture studies. Grounded in the work of Barthes and Lacan, such criticism has looked instead at how cinema operates like a *language*. In doing so it has often tended to neglect crucial distinctions between the nature of language and the nature of images. In contrast to such 'an increasing grammatization of discursive and textual operations', analysts such as De Lauretis (1984, p. 45) want instead to examine how cinema produces its specific effects on spectators through what is specific to *images*. Images, she notes, are signifiers of a different order than language. The elements of language are relatively arbitrary in regard to their referents in the real world, whereas images signify through their 'iconicity', through their resemblance to referents in the real world (Eco 1976, pp. 191ff). Moreover, 'images articulate meaning *and* desire' in a way that words or 'utterances' do not. That is, more than to words, 'not only semantic and social values but affect and fantasy as well, are bound to images' (De Lauretis 1984, pp. 8, 38).

Given this figural 'bias' built into the cinematic apparatus, it still makes sense to speak in terms of realist, modernist, and postmodernist films. One way to make sense of these different paradigms in cinematic signification is through Laura Mulvey's (1981) distinction between 'narrative' and 'spectacle'. Mulvey argued that mass-market cinema has been structured around the 'spectacle' of women's images. Here she identified film 'narrative' with Freud's ego and spectacle with the sexual instincts of the id. In her account of realist cinema, the beginning of a film would centre on the spectacle of the free, desirable, perhaps somehow dangerous female lead. As the film progressed, however, and as the male star tamed, captured, and finally possessed his female counterpart, the place of spectacle would be increasingly subordinated to that of narrative. My point in this context is that in films of recent years 'spectacle' – especially if we expand the definition of spectacle to include also images marked by the aggressive instinct – does *not* any longer become subordinated to narrative. That is, there has been a shift from realist to postmodernist cinema, in which spectacle comes heavily to dominate narrative.

A number of analysts have noted this. Coates (1985, pp. 27, 77), for example, argues that in recent decades narrative has broken down to be replaced by a cinema of 'isolated heterogeneous events held together by the ramshackle constructions of Victorian melodrama', and that from the mid-1960s we have seen the dissolution of the distinction between realist and nonrealist film. Heath has noted a new presence of the body in contemporary films; in, for example, films like *Jaws* which feature mutilations of the body. He (1981, pp. 185–8) points to the pervasion of pornographic films in popular cinema in which 'the compulsive repetition of sexuality' takes the place of narrative. He (1981, p. 190) observes the 'suppression of voice' in pornographic cinema, a phenomenon which has extended to commercial cinema in general, in which voice is increasingly 'a support for a certain visible presence of the body'. This shift from a narrative cinema to a postmodern cinema of spectacle can be detected in some of the biggest moneyspinning films from the mid-1960s, such as Spaghetti Westerns (Frayling 1981, pp. 39f), in which realist narrative structure is violated by the presence of events which are interchangeable or gratuitous, by films like Scorsese's *Mean Streets* which resolutely refuse to end. This tendency was reinforced in the mid and late 1980s in which the blockbuster box office hits have been, for example, the Indiana Jones films and *Ghostbusters* and the Stallone and Schwarznegger films which have catered especially to an audience in their early teens, and use plot as an excuse for a succession of spectacular events.

This shift to figural and postmodern films has also taken place in art cinema. Only, whereas in mass-market films postmodernism has partly displaced narrative realist films, in specialist cinema it has come to challenge 'high modernism'. Modernist cinema is cast in a Brechtian mould of distantiation and bears formalist characteristics. Pivotal to such a 'discursive' cinema is Jean-Luc Godard. He has pursued this goal via techniques which lay bare the cinematic convention. In this context MacCabe (1980, p. 44) comments on the use of 'montage', which Godard counterposes to 'image'. Montage is a 'juxtaposition of images and sounds' without 'a unity imposed by the director'. Montage always 'places the spectator's look in question, (it) poses the question of its constitution, and makes the institution of cinema the question of every film'. Distancing and the critique of spontaneity and freedom motivate such practices as the use of tableaux to break narrative continuity and let the spectator stand back, and characteristically Godardian elucidation of the relations of production in the film production process (Cook 1985, pp. 137, 166).

There are several techniques that Godard uses to produce distancing and consequently the disinvestment of desire in images. First is his extraordinary valuation of words themselves. Godard has used the voice-over in a documentary type style, adopted for the Soviet director Vertov. This is true particularly in his political films, in which the relationship of language and image is questioned through the juxtaposition of political discussion, on the one hand, with prima facie unrelated images, on the other. Films such as *British Sounds* were conceived in order to 'portray the struggle between images and sounds', and were especially concerned with 'how sounds can be used against the image'. Similarly in *Deux ou trois choses*, released in 1966, the voice-over misdescribes the hair colour and actions of a part-time prostitute. Likewise, *Le Gai Savoir*, made in 1968, was a gloss on Rousseau's *Emile ou l'éducation* and propounded that 'the central problem of education is to provide some understanding of the sounds and images that bombard us in our everyday lives' (MacCabe 1980, p. 20).

If Godard's post-1968 films deliberately gave primacy to sounds over images, his earlier, less didactic films were themselves critiques of an image-centred politics, and in particular of the very political use of images in advertising. Thus in *Une Femme mariée* (1964) he, conscious that 'the image is a cultural product', was 'interested in advertising, the body, the commodities produced for women and the image which sells the commodities' (Mulvey and MacCabe 1980, p. 92). In the film the protagonist, Charlotte, works in an ad agency; she has an affair

and lies to both husband and lover. Her gaze is constantly
directed at advertising images which then become *her* image. In
Deux ou trois choses, the prostitute-protagonist's 'position is
also determined by the advertisements which constantly produce
images for her'. Godard has revealingly said that cinema is
dependent on capitalism in two senses: first in the making of the
film and second that 'in film the money comes back in the image'
(MacCabe 1980, p. 27). Thus the Godardian question – 'who
speaks in the image?' – is given answer in Adornian tones: it is
the 'system which decrees that the order of money determines the
order of the image' (MacCabe 1980, p. 45). Godard had instead
proposed a critical cinema which gives an activist role to the
spectator. By posing a challenge to the spectator's libidinal
investment in the image, he returns the question of desire to the
eye of the spectator him- or herself. In questioning both narrative
and pictorial realism and creating an effect of distancing, he
poses for the spectator the issue of actively transforming reality
(Heath 1981, p. 63).

Despite the sharply effective critique of patriarchal and
capitalist economic of desire, Godardian modernist 'counter-
cinema' does have certain limits (Wollen 1982). The substitution
of a regime of 'intellectualist displeasure' for one of visual
pleasure limits accessibility even for the art cinema audience. By
contrast, as De Lauretis has noted, a different and more recent set
of developments seems to be taking shape. She (1984, p. 46)
writes,

> what matters is once again spectacle, as in the earliest days of
> cinema. Contradiction, paradox, ambiguity in the image as
> well as the textualized overlay of sound, language and image
> no longer produce distancing effects by baring the device of
> cinema and thus inducing rationality and consciousness. *They
> are the spectacle*, the no longer simple but excessive, 'perverse'
> pleasure of current cinema.

Surely this contemporary trend towards a figural cinema of
spectacle in today's avant-garde often results in a repetition for
the highly educated middle classes of patriarchal and capitalist
economies of desire. Yet, De Lauretis argues, this new figural
cinema at least poses the question of 'how to reconstruct and
organize vision from the impossible place of female desire'. She

(1984, pp. 69, 87) calls for the production of films structured by an alternative economy of desire, for a 'microanalytics' of cinema with 'effects of resistance and counterinvestment'.

It is possible then to speak of four ideal-types of cinematic signification.

(1) *Realist or narrative cinema*, whose roots are (a) pictorially, in Quattrocento perspective, and (b) narratively, in the non-teleological causal temporality, with beginning, middle, and end, of the nineteenth-century novel (Heath 1981, pp. 28–37).

(2) *Mainstream postmodern cinema*. Here we find basically 'figural' films, which foreground spectacle over narrative, for example, several of the Spielberg films and many of the late 1980s horror and gothic films, and the Rambo and Schwarzenegger films. Like mainstream narrative cinema, these postmodernist films position the spectator in a fixed and rigid space. Analysts like Mulvey and De Lauretis assume that all forms of cinema position the spectator through his/her investment of psychic energy in films. In narrative or realist cinema this mainly takes place through the identification of the spectator's ego with the hero of the narrative who serves as a sort of model or 'ego-ideal'. In mainstream figural cinema, which foregrounds spectacle, the investment of psychic energy and hence positioning of the subject would be, not via ego and secondary process, but via primary process. The point is, in cases both of realist and mainstream postmodernist cinema, that the subject is placed in a fixed, rigid, and stereotyped position.

(3) *Modernist or 'discursive' cinema*. In this there is a much more ambiguous and open positioning of the subject. This takes place through the problematization of cinematic representation. This is integral to cultural differentiation because is separates the process of signification from reality. It is 'discursive' in Foucault's sense of 'discourse' (in *The Archaeology of Knowledge*) in that it draws attention to the rules, the norms, and conventions of cinematic signification itself. It is further discursive in the Foucauldian sense (and exemplifies cultural differentiation) in that primacy in modernist cinema is given to this separate cultural and discursive level.

(4) *'Transgressive' postmodernist cinema*. This, like mainstream postmodernist cinema, is figural and privileges spectacle. The difference is that it, like modernist cinema, positions the

spectator in a 'nomadic', rather than a sedentary, manner. It does so, however, not like modernist cinema through the problematization of representation, but instead through the problematization of the real. The parallels with painting are immediately apparent. Modernist painting, as theorists as diverse as Adorno, Greenberg (1983), and Wollheim (1980) have observed, draws the attention away from reality and to the picture surface itself, to the systematic development of possibilities in the aesthetic material. In brief, to the signifying process. Much the opposite with postmodernist surrealism and pop art. Here not the signifying process but the fixed nature of *reality* is questioned. Consider, say, a recent cult modernist film, Jim Jarmusch's *Stranger than Paradise*. In this Jarmusch does not follow the cinematic norm of letting a sequence develop to a climax and then cutting to another sequence. Instead he lets the sequence continue until long past its climax, after which the camera unduly lingers on the characters sitting around, being bored. Jarmusch here is experimenting with and calling the spectator's attention to cinematic conventions. He thus calls the audience's attention to the signifying practice.

In comparison a postmodernist film like Beneix's *Diva* or David Lynch's *Blue Velvet* will not distance the spectator or call his/her attention to the 'picture surface'. These films instead bring the viewer right into the film with a rather startling immediacy, but having done so, the 'real' that the spectator has been drawn into is revealed as artifice. Thus at the end of *Blue Velvet* the camera focuses on a flower, which then turns out to be made of papier mâché. It shows a return to 'normalcy' in its ending which is in fact a send-up and suggests an integral flimsiness and instability to reality itself. In *Diva* much of the shooting highlights the interiors of the domiciles of the two main protagonists, Jules and Borodin. But the reality of Jules's living quarters turns out already to be a set of images, i.e. a disused garage, in which pop art rubs shoulders with wrecked 1950s autos on the model of those in Nicholas Ray's *Rebel Without a Cause*.

The contrast of such transgressive, figural films with their mainstream counterparts should also be clear. All figural cinema, or cinema which privileges spectacle over narrative or discourse, operates – as Mulvey suggests – largely on the model of and through the primary process. Consider, for example, a mainstream figural film, like the politically objectionable *Fatal Attraction*. This – which several British critics have seen as a post-AIDS film – is postmodernist in its mixture of genres: it starts out as a straightforward melodrama and shifts into a horror or 'stalk and slash' genre. Equally, instead of the narrative coming progressively to dominate the spectacle (as in realist cinema), the spectacle instead comes to dominate the narrative. But its treatment of sexuality and violence, its treatment of the single working woman as if she were a virus (which is then set as polar opposite against the 'healthy' family unit) tends to position rigidly the spectator (Williamson 1988). Compare, on the other hand, some of David Cronenberg's work. Cronenberg himself has commented that *The Fly* and others of his films are about how viruses deform bodies, and that his originality lies in that he is 'on the side of the virus'. In this sense *The Fly* is also a post-AIDS movie. Yet the director contrives to evoke sympathy in the spectator towards the half-human protagonist played by Jeff Goldblum, and, by implication, ambiguity towards the virus and death itself. Here the spectator is much more ambiguously positioned, as he/she is by the problematization of representation and reality in Cronenberg's *Videodrome*. The same might be said for the mix of sexuality and violence in *Blue Velvet*. Some feminist critics have condemned this film for itself not roundly condemning violence towards women. Yet is not David Lynch pushing back boundaries and underlining the instability of subjectivity when he shows, not just the villain played by Dennis Hopper, but the hero, engaging in sadistic behaviour? Is not the whole notion of hero (or even anti-hero) of a narrative thus problematized? Is not the problem of sadistic behaviour towards women made deeper and more urgent through this sort of portrayal than through, say, the simple moral condemnation of a villain who beats a woman?

CONCLUSIONS

I hope that my enthusiasm for the subject material in the above discussion will not be mistaken for any wholehearted support of some sort of postmodern aesthetics or politics. In the visual arts, for example, I believe that the work of Barnet Newman is of immeasurably more value than that of Andy Warhol. In politics, it is true that the world of such postmodernist critics as Susan Sontag and Rosalind Krauss is marked by a notable absence of a vision of a better world. Such a vision was present in the preceding generation of modernists; in Lionel Trilling, Irving Howe, Greenberg and Daniel Bell and others, many of whose political origins were Marxist.[2] It is, however, likely we do live in a culture that is in important ways undergoing a process of de-differentiation and hence 'post-modernization'.[3] It would then be folly for the political and cultural left to ignore this process because they find it unpleasant. A lot of future conflicts are going to be fought out on this new cultural terrain and the left needs a better understanding of it. Such conflicts can be fought out with a vision of a better world as I hope some of the above discussion has suggested.

What I have tried to do in the body of this paper is to further the understanding of postmodern culture in consideration of the latter as a figural and de-differentiated mode of signification. I have no pretensions to the type of expert knowledge of semiotics that students of linguistics will have. I do want to claim, however, that the sociological analysis above shows that postmodern cultural objects signify differently than do modernist cultural objects. I have suggested then that postmodern signification is a de-differentiated 'regime of signification' on a number of counts:

(1) It is a figural, as distinct from discursive, regime of signification. To signify via figures rather than words is to signify iconically. Images or other figures which signify iconically do so through their resemblance to the referent. And signifiers (figures) which resemble referents are less fully differentiated from them than signifiers (words, discourse) which do not.

(2) The devaluation of meaning in postmodern signification is simultaneously the de-differentiation of signifier and signified. In this sense the recent popularity of pragmatics in academic linguistics is a postmodern phenomenon, as is the importance of speech act theory in the social sciences in the past decade or two. The study in these of the use or effectiveness of language devalues the signified and meaning. Further, in speech act theory the representation (speech) is collapsed into the real (action). Such a

de-differentiation of signifier and referent has also been present in the claims of the followers of Althusser in the 1970s that ideological practices were material practices and of the followers of Derrida in the 1980s about the 'materiality' of language. In all of these renderings, signifiers function as referents or *les mots* as *les choses*.

(3) If in contemporary pragmatics, the signified begins to wither away and the signifier to function as a referent, in surrealism (and to this extent surrealism is postmodern) the referent functions as a signifier. If for Althusserians and post-structuralists the signifier has become material (a referent), then for the surrealists and for Walter Benjamin the material (referent) became signifier. In both cases there is a de-differentiation, arguably a confusion, and surely the problematization, of the relationship between signifier and referent. Thus the surrealists suggested that we experience every-day life as if its materiality were a network of signifiers. In this sense the claims of post-structuralists about the materiality of language is only the flipside of their claims about life being a 'text'.

(4) This de-differentiation of signifier and referent is not just a matter of every-day life being experienced as a spatio-temporal configuration of signifiers, it is also a matter of the content of properly cultural objects themselves. Thus photorealism is unlike realist renderings of the referent and unlike modernist devaluation of the referent. Photorealism indeed attributes substantial value to the referent, but understands the referent to be itself a signifier. Much the same can be said for Lichtenstein's comic-strip pop art or Alex Cox's use of Lichtenstein-type devices in his film *Repo Man*. In neither case, as in modernism, is attention to be drawn to the aesthetic material itself, or to Greenberg's 'surface of the canvas'; the spectator's attention is drawn instead to the referent, to the real world. But the referent again becomes signifier to the extent that the viewer is reminded how like a comic strip the real world has become, or to what extent the real world now comprises comic strips. This is patent as well in cult films of the 1980s such as Luc Besson's *Metro (Subway)* as well as others mentioned above. Like realist cinema and unlike modernist cinema, these films do not 'lay bare the device' or call the viewer's attention to cinematic conventions. Attention in these films, like in realist films, is called to the

referent, only the referent turns out to be, like the ear or the flowers in *Blue Velvet* and the imaged and real automobiles in Jules's living quarters in *Diva*, a set of false, glossy, or monstrous signifiers.

Let me finally end, both theoretically and politically, on a speculative note. To say, following Habermas, that cultural modernization is a process of differentiation and autonomization and that postmodernization is a process of de-differentiation and implosion is to be content with a purely descriptive analysis of cultural change. What, one wonders, is the 'motor' of all this? Even if one were to, as I do, empathize with sophisticated functional Marxism of, say, G. A. Cohen and speak of the compatibility or incompatibility of certain sets of cultural forms with certain other sets of production relations, one would still be looking for an explanation of the specific properties of those cultural forms. Perhaps the key to this lies in the realm of culture itself. Suppose we were to begin with a crude distinction of 'social nature' and 'social culture', in which the latter were conceived in its narrow sense as representation rather than in the broad sense as symbol. Given this, the cultural history of the West (and not only the West) could be captured by a process in which the totality of 'social facts' comes to comprise an increasingly greater proportion of 'cultural' facts and an increasingly smaller proportion of 'natural' facts. At a certain juncture (the onset of modernism?) in such a chronology, cultural facts would accumulate to a point at which they could no longer be considered solely as representations, and the whole problem of their proper materiality and hence character as representations would have to be taken seriously. This would be the time also of the fullest differentiation and autonomization of cultural facts. At some later point in time in this scenario (especially with the mechanical and then electronic production and reproduction of representations), cultural facts would become so pervasive that they would come to challenge 'natural facts' for hegemony, and would even to some extent constitute the norm. What would now be problematized is, not as in modernism, the character of representations, but the character of reality itself.

What then are some political implications of postmodernism conceived *per se* as cultural de-differentiation? The answer may be that some sorts of postmodernist de-differentiation are implicitly 'reactionary', and other sorts potentially integral to a reconstructed left political culture, and still other sorts can politically cut either way. I suggested above that the postmodernist rejection of avant-gardes and criticism, and embrace instead of 'affirmation' and the supplement, is not at all necessarily conservative. Its consequences are hostility to the strong state and vanguard party and sympathy with pluralism and perhaps forms of anarchism. The postmodernist reaction to commodification is of different colour. Modernist differentiation, whether in Adornian, Brechtian, or Godardian guise, has provided the distance for the unambiguous critique (the 'disinvestment of desire') of the commodity form and the commodification of culture. The prophets of the mid-1960s, Venturi and Warhol, on the other hand rejoiced at the interpretation of culture and commodity. The process of de-differentiation that they celebrated has arguably increased exponentially in the past two decades. Only its mechanism seems to have changed. Recently there has been, not so much the colonization of representations by the commodity form (though this has happened too), but the colonization of the commodity by culture. Hence advertisements began as bits of information to help market commodities. Then, with the advent of ad agencies, the adverts themselves became commodities. Not long after, images rather than information became the content of these new commodities (Leiss 1983). The final step in very recent years is that already existent cultural representations, in pop music, have come to accompany the images. Finally the new adverts themselves were partly responsible for the revival of early 1960s soul music in the late 1980s. A similar story of the colonization of the commodity by culture could surely be told about pop videos (Frith and Horne 1987). Thus postmodernist cultural de-differentiation of representations and commodities seems unambiguously to have reactionary political-cultural consequences.

The main argument of postmodernists who have sympathies with the political left seems to have been that postmodernism can be supportive of a left politics rooted in principles of pluralism and 'difference'. This seems a contradiction on the face of it. How can a cultural paradigm whose main principle is *de*-differentiation contribute to a political culture grounded in the apparently opposite principle of difference? Perhaps the example of 'gender bending' in contemporary adverts and popular culture in general can provide a clue here. The deliberate ambiguity in gender and sexual preference built into images problematizes reality and the normative in a sense not dissimilar to the way that surrealism and pop art (discussed above) operate. The effect is a much more ambivalent and less fixed positioning of subjectivity. If subjectivity is less fixed, then space is left for the construction of identities, and collective identities, which deviate from the norm (Lury 1987). That is, space is left for difference. The other precondition of difference and left pluralism is tolerance. And it would seem to follow that political-cultural tolerance is also furthered by the 'relatively autonomous' subject positioning fostered by de-differentiated representation.

Acknowledgement

This chapter first appeared as an article in *Theory, Culture and Society*, Volume 7, Numbers 2–3, pages 311–36, 1988, and is reproduced by permission of Sage Publications, London.

Part Three

MODERNISM AND POSTMODERNISM: SOCIAL CORRELATES

Chapter Eight

MODERNISM AND BOURGEOIS IDENTITY: PARIS/VIENNA/BERLIN

In the decades around the turn of the twentieth century, the cultural life of major western cities changed. The nature and import of those changes is one of the questions at the heart of the current debates about 'modernity' and 'modernism'. Did this modernism, in Jürgen Habermas's terms, deepen and extend the rationalist Enlightenment project,[1] or did it undermine that project?[2] Here, focusing primarily on changes in art and architecture in Paris, Vienna, and Berlin during this period, I shall try to show that there is no single 'modern' but rather a plurality of modernisms each with its own specific national characteristics and significance. I shall argue that Viennese modernism can be seen as in some sense a 'Baroque' modernism which seems largely to have run counter to the Enlightenment project. And that Parisian modernism did indeed represent a deepening Enlightenment rationality. Berlin modernism, meanwhile, was an altogether different and surely stranger brew. Sometimes it thematized a heightened irrationality, at others it slid into hyperrationality, while at still others it seems to escape the logic of these categories altogether.

To draw out these differences and peculiarities, I shall look particularly at the place of the different national bourgeoisies in these three cities. In each case, the form of the bourgeoisie - and the nature of the city's modernity - was determined by its relationship to other collective agents, to its own 'significant other'. Viennese modernism, I shall argue, must be understood primarily in terms of the bourgeoisie's relationship to the aristocracy. In Paris, it was the relationship to the petite bourgeoisie that was crucial; and in Berlin, the relationship to the state.

The now voluminous literature on modernism and postmodernism has been dominated by philosophers and modern language theorists and historians of architecture. This has contributed to an unusual neglect of the social dimension and in particular the importance of social class. Two of the most important exceptions to this have been works by the cultural historians, T. J. Clark and Carl Schorske. Their books, *The Painting of Modern Life* and *Fin-de-siècle Vienna*, though receiving recognition in specialist circles, have not had any sort of widespread resonance in the more general debates. The reason for this I think is, not in spite of, but *because* their work is so, ultimately, *sociological*. One of the aims of this essay is to tap the full sociological richness of Clark's and Schorske's work, both in understanding of what modernism is and in the explanation of modernism via class and bourgeois identity in Paris and Vienna.

This chapter proffers two theses: a general and a comparative thesis. The general thesis is that the disruption of stable bourgeois identity makes possible the rise of modernism, which in turn further destabilizes bourgeois identity in a sort of virtuous circle. The chapter's main focus, however, is the *comparative* thesis which is that clues to the contours of various modernisms can be found in examining various types of (disrupted) bourgeois identities. And, further, that such variation in bourgeois identity, and hence in national modernisms, is largely determined by the place of different classes and class fractions in (1) the power bloc and (2) those challenging the power bloc.

This said, the chapter is divided into four parts. The first of these is devoted to systematic consideration of what modernism is. The central claim here is that modern*ization* is a process of differentiation (a) of cultural spheres and (b) of the cultural realm from the social realm. Modern*ism*, the tip of whose iceberg is visible by the mid-nineteenth century, but whose social conditions of existence are pervasive only from the end of that century, is an end point of this differentiation, a point at which spheres take on full autonomy. The full autonomy, and self-referentiality of the aesthetic sphere, on this account, is matched by the full autonomization of the social itself. Both spheres – the aesthetic and the social – then co-exist, each on the terms of its own 'facticity'. The rendering of the 'facticity' of the social by that of the aesthetic is a crucial, first realist and then naturalist, moment of this modernization process, after which aesthetic modern*ism* moves into full self-referentiality.

The second section looks at Paris and Vienna, and largely drawing on Clark and Schorske, respectively, at the visual arts and the social structuring of urban space. In both these arenas, a distinctly 'popular' Parisian modernism is contrasted with its 'baroque' Viennese counterpart, and the social class basis of this contrast is elucidated.

I then turn to draw on a variety of sources to investigate Berlin modernism in greater detail and depth. And in this a second theme arises to join the social class explanation of modernism. This theme is that of civil society versus the state. The point argued here is that characteristically German bourgeois identity was fundamentally bound up with statist ideology. And cultural modernism, in challenging such identity, at the same time challenged the very structure of the German state. The third section of the essay, then, examines the role of the state – first, in the restructuring of Berlin's modernizing urban fabric and then as the central antagonist to the city's 'Secession' movement in the visual arts.

The fourth and final section of the chapter looks at the role of the Jews in modernist Berlin. The Jews here are crucial in their importance as part of a new class fraction in the German bourgeoisie. In this role they featured centrally as producers, as a reception class, and in the institutions of aesthetic modernism. Excluded, effectively, from the state, and hence symbolically excluded from the bourgeoisie, Berlin Jews as allies of modernism were simultaneously partisans of civil society against the German state.

MODERNISM: CULTURAL AND SOCIAL 'FACTICITY'

The problem of aesthetic modernism can perhaps be best approached via the time-tested framework of the sociology of modernized. What I am referring to is elementary structural-functionalist sociology, in which modernization is seen as a process of structural differentiation (*Ausdifferenzierung*). In this, modernized societies quite straightforwardly have more highly differentiated social structures than do traditional societies.

Jürgen Habermas in *Theorie des kommunikativen Handels*³ has used this framework specifically to analyse the cultural realm, and the sketch below follows partly from Habermas. In crudest outline, the schema goes something like this: The early steps of cultural modernization through differentiation can be seen in the comparison of the more modern 'world religions' with the culture of primitive societies. The world religions constitute an 'advance' from primitive societies in that individuals learn to differentiate representations, in the form of words, concepts, and categories from real tangible objects and processes. Further, in the world religions the sacred is differentiated from the social; that is, that primitive religions are 'immanentist', as Talcott Parsons underscored, while world religions are 'transcendentalist'.⁴ Secularization in the so-called 'Early Modern' period, in which symbolic entities are progressively differentiated from real entities, inaugurates a further advance. And it is possible to note, as Max Weber does, a sort of transitional phase in the movement towards a fully-fledged modernity that comes into being in the seventeenth and eighteenth centuries. Now one can speak of the development of autonomous 'life-orders' or 'value-spheres', and in particular of the eighteenth-century autonomization of theoretical, ethical, and aesthetic spheres.⁵ But full autonomization and thus full cultural differentiation had not yet come to pass. In, for example, Enlightenment natural law, theoretical and ethical spheres are not yet separate, to the extent that moral practical or normative validity is still often grounded in (theoretical) fact. Moreover, the cultural spheres have not yet fully been separated from external reality as unproblematic assumptions of epistemological and aesthetic realism continue to predominate.

It is only with the development of more radical differentiation in the decades around the turn of the twentieth century that it is possible to speak of a fully-fledged and optimally differentiated cultural modernity. This radical autonomization of cultural spheres entails a sharp departure from what is known as 'foundationalism'.⁶ 'Foundationalism' means that an external set of phenomena imposes an order on, or serves as a 'foundation' for, a given cultural practice. For example in the theoretical or epistemological sphere, foundationalism would entail the belief that concepts or statements somehow correspond to the real world; in ethics, foundationalists might propound the belief in an unconditional ethics. In aesthetics, foundationalists would valuate realist canons which privilege Quattrocento perspective in the visual arts and an externally ordered narrative structure in literature. All of these foundationalisms are subjected to thoroughgoing challenges, as perhaps given voice to with greatest immediacy and impact in Nietzsche's radical epistemological, ethical, and aesthetic scepticism, in turn-of-the-century cultural modernism.

What are the implications of this radical break with foundations, this radical automization of cultural spheres? Put simply, the implications are contingency, facticity, what Weber called '*Eigengesetzlichkeit*'.[7] That is that practices in theoretical, moral-practical, and aesthetic spheres become 'contingent' in their independence from externally imposed order. In their very independence, these cultural practices take on a certain 'facticity' or 'materiality', very much like the profane materiality of the practices of every-day life. '*Eigengesetzlichkeit*' means self-legislation. This implies, in the absence of foundationalist or externally imposed 'legislation', that cultural practices – e.g. in the various scientific disciplines, in the arts – must develop their own rule-boundedness and their own conditions of validity.

Modernism then can be defined as the absence of externally imposed order on aesthetic practices. This leaves open two ideal-typical possibilities. Aesthetic practices can either celebrate this absence of external ordering and accentuate disorder, randomness, the irrational in cultural objects. Or they can develop their own autonomous ordering. This second possibility for modernism was partly what Adorno was referring to when he spoke of 'aesthetic rationality'. Both of these types of modernist autonomy can be seen in the development of the work of Arnold Schoenberg. In Western music the established framework for stability and order has been the diatonic harmonic system which was developed in the Renaissance. Movement, in Western music, even as early as the seventeenth and eighteenth centuries, has always been in a direction away from the diatonic and through dissonance. In the end, however, this movement always falls back into order or into 'cadence'; back into the framework of the triad, the element of 'authority, stability, consonance and repose'.[8] In the nineteenth century, Beethoven and especially Wagner moved in the direction of the expansion of dissonance. In his earlier work, Schoenberg reached for an almost total emancipation of dissonance in 'atonality'. At this point Schoenberg was close to the first ideal-type of modernist practice in his accentuation of contingency. In his later development of the 12-tone system Schoenberg illustrates the second, rationalist modernist ideal-type, in a sense that it is quite clear that the new order is a created and posited ordering. In his 12-tone music, as Schorske observes, Schoenberg confirms a 'faith in a hard vision of the world that could both accept a pulverised reality and posit it in an order that was not inherent in it'.[9]

The very radical autonomy of modernist cultural forms makes their social or social-historical explanation an extremely difficult pursuit. How can one possibly advance a social explanation for practices whose very constitutive principle is their *independence* from society? Several analysts in recent years, most notably Schorske, Bell, Marshall Berman, and T. J. Clark,[10] have attempted to tackle this issue, though they have, I think, enjoyed only partial success. What is clear, as these and other scholars have abundantly shown, is that parallel changes are proceeding roughly concomitantly in the aesthetic sphere and in society. In the aesthetic sphere, as I mentioned, fundamental is a pronounced break away from an anchoring by an externally imposed order. In the social sphere four parallel phenomena, all entailing a disruption of foundations, order, and stability, can be identified, as follows.

(1) *A rejection of history.* In Paris, Vienna and Berlin, modernism meant a break with a preceding historical or historicist style that predominated especially in painting and architecture. In painting, historical figures were typically portrayed and the paintings executed in a classical style enshrined as 'official' by national academies of art. In architecture, previous great historical styles were imitated. This pre-modernist embrace of history was surely not an embrace of change or of movement. History was on the other hand associated with stability, with coherent and fixed national and individual identities. Such stability was also inherent in the Whiggish assumptions of historical progress. The modernist rejection of the historical style and history was itself an embrace of movement and change. It entailed the rejection of historical generations and hence the 'de-

centring' of national and individual identities. The modernist and Nietzschean devastation of the idea of historical progress was at the same time a devastation of assumptions of order, authority, stability, consonance, and repose.

(2) *Urbanization and the disruption of a stable sense of time and space.* Urbanization was accompanied by the building of national and municipal railways. The use of such transport meant an enormous change in the experience of temporality, among other things a sharp increase in the quantity of stimuli perceived in a given unit of time. It could imply a disordered experience of time, or, to the contrary, a re-ordered temporality as was the case in the experience of new recruits to factory work. In comparison with the village or the 'pre-modernist' city, not just the sense of time but the experience of space was altered. The new variegated urban space meant the experience at any one time of a greater number and a greater variety of impressions.[10] It entailed the creation of open and impersonal public spaces. In a very important sense Vienna and Berlin were much more typically 'modernist' cities, almost along the lines of American cities like Chicago, than were cities like London and Paris which underwent slower and more organic growth. The population of both Vienna and Berlin at least quadrupled in the half-century from 1860 to 1910. This disruption of spatio-temporal assumptions was not only paralleled in the world of art but also in philosophy, from the incorporation of time and space into the subject in Kant's 'transcendental aesthetic' to Bergmann's writings.

(3) *The Id and the Ego.* At this juncture a number of assumptions regarding man's rationally-ordered consciousness were being of course challenged. This 'explosion of the instincts' was at the same time an explosion of contingency into the world of order. This libidinal energy, once let loose, could itself be exposed to an ordering, as in the theory of Freud and the practice of psychoanalysis. Or it could revel in its very contingency, as in Nietzsche's will-to-power. That this experience was not confined to the realm of theory, and was rather widespread in bourgeois strata, is immediately clear to the reader of Proust, Mann, or Musil.

(4) *The challenge to the bourgeoisie's hegemony.* Aesthetic modernism was born contemporaneously with the transition from 'liberal' to 'organized' capitalism.[11] This transition was

characterized, *inter alia*, by the explosion of the popular classes onto the political and social scene. The previous social and political hegemony of the bourgeoisie was, in a sense, perhaps not largely dissimilar to the above-mentioned phenomena, experienced as order and stability. For many social scientists indeed the hegemony of the bourgeoisie would be seen as the basis of the other just-mentioned types of stability. The bursting upon the scene of an organized working class carrying out industrial action on a substantial level, or not just working-class suffrage but, for the first time, mass political parties, and especially working-class parties must have been at least partly experienced as an eruption of contingency and chaos into a world of order. So must have the entry into politics of growing petit-bourgeois anti-semitic political forces. Socially too, with the creation of boulevards, department stores, and railway stations, the popular classes were more visible to the bourgeois, and no longer hidden away in their traditionally invisible ghettos.

Each of these social factors runs parallel to characteristically modernist phenomena in the aesthetic realm. Each of them is part and parcel of the turn-of-the-century crisis in the hegemony of the bourgeoisie. Taken together they go a long way in explaining the birth and persistence of aesthetic modernism.

But to speak of parallel processes co-existing in the social and aesthetic spheres is not a very satisfying explanation because the causal mechanisms which connect the two spheres are not properly elaborated. A place to look for such mechanisms, as T. J. Clark has suggested, might be in the *content* of modernist and proto-modernist works of art. The modernist revolution in art is largely a formalist revolution, or a revolution in which art becomes judged not as much by its content as by its form. The modernist revolution means of course a break with the traditional aesthetics of beauty which is also a foundationalist aesthetics of order. So it entails a break with not just the importance of content, but also with traditional and established aesthetic form. For modernists, and here critics as far apart as Adorno and Clement Greenberg have a large area of common ground, most important in determining aesthetic value is the systematic working through of the possibilities of a given aesthetic material.[12] Nonetheless the key to understanding this formalist revolution might lie in looking at the content of proto- and early modernist works.

The basic argument, as Clark puts it, is the following. Proto-modernist painting, for example naturalist and impressionist pictures, are 'paintings of modern life'. That is, the content of such paintings, unlike historicist painting, is modern life. For such content to exist in the aesthetic realm, modern life must exist in the social realm. This is the beginning of an explanatory mechanism which elucidates the relationship between social and aesthetic spheres. Now such a mechanism must be identified which connects content and form inside the aesthetic realm. The challenge to academic painting that impressionism posed was a challenge both in form and in content. In both content and form there was a parallel shift from the classical and idealized to the every-day and contingent. In painting public outings in parks, café-concerts, and common prostitutes instead of great and idealized historical figures, Manet, Seurat, and others were painting, no longer the ordered, but the contingent. In departing from the tenets of classical execution, they were moving towards contingency in form. It is but a short step, and it logically follows, from the consideration of social reality as contingency and facticity to the consideration of the painting process itself in terms of such contingency and facticity.[13] If social life is seen as no longer ideally ordered but as made up of every-day material practices, and painting is part and parcel of social life, then painting should be made up of similar practices. Focus would then be on the painting process itself, as in modernism, rather than on what is being painted. Hence we have moved from modernism in content to modernism in form. Or as Clark remarks of Manet's *Olympia*, as exemplar of the modernist revolution both in content and in form: 'Olympia is not an enigma, not a courtisane, the final factual existence (of the naked woman) on the bed is the key to that of the paint'.[14]

This explanation understands 'realism' and early or proto-modernism not to be diametrically opposed to one another, but as two sides, form and content, of the same modernizing process in the aesthetic sphere. Thus Baudelaire and Flaubert can be seen without contradiction as both realists and early modernists. When Baudelaire wrote to Manet, 'you are only the first in the decrepitude of your art',[15] he meant presumably to italicize the '*your*' and thus confirm that he, Baudelaire, was the first in the 'decrepitude' of his own art. Baudelaire's was a 'decrepitude' in both content and form. In his departure from classical and idealized content, Baudelaire's decrepitude entailed the realist content of the streets of Paris. In his decrepitude in form, i.e. his departure from received poetic norms, Baudelaire was proto-symbolist or modernist. In the novel, Balzac, Stendhal, and especially Zola illustrate a developing modernization in content, in their shift from the classical and idealized to the social and the every-day and finally, in Zola's case, to approximating the fully contingent. Modernization in form as well, though, is not apparent in these authors as it is in the equally realist Flaubert. Only Flaubert of these novelists applied the lessons of contingency in content to contingency in form. For Zola, modernist content, though laced with facticity and contingency, was of the utmost significance. Flaubert's choice of contingent, and arguably naturalist content in *Madame Bovary* was governed by the very trivial and *in*significant character of such content. Of significance for him, on the contrary, were the words of the novel themselves, which he thought, along the lines of the model of music, should float free from narrative content, and gain their aesthetic value through consonant and dissonant relationships with one another. Flaubert was emblematic of a further development in modernization, in which the referent of the work of art, having evolved from the timeless and ideal to the contingent, now had moved from contingency to virtual insignificance. The shift to fully fledged autonomization and *Eigengesetzlichkeit* (self-legislation), the move to full disappearance of the referent, à la Mondrian or Pollock, was now just a step away.

In this section I have attempted a preliminary outline of a definition of modernism, and tried to draw some of the connections in the generic relationship between modernism and the bourgeoisie. The argument proceeded from the social sphere to the aesthetic sphere. Its main thrust was that challenges to the order and stability of bourgeois hegemony in the social sphere are then registered as challenges to order and stability, first as content and then as form, in the aesthetic sphere.

POPULAR VERSUS BAROQUE MODERNISM: PARIS AND VIENNA

The first section of this chapter has been devoted to a set of theses and arguments concerning the description of (aesthetic) modernism. The main body of the chapter will now address the explanation of modernism. In this, I want to turn initially, through the prism of Schorske's and Clark's work, to the cases of Vienna and Paris. Here we shall see that aesthetic modernism in both cities was conditioned by the destabilization of bourgeois identity due to the eruption into the public sphere of the popular, and 'dangerous', classes. In Viennese cultural modernism this was registered more or less *psychologically*, in terms of the threat of the instincts to the rationality of the ego. In Paris, this was registered more directly and, so to speak, *sociologically*, in the subject matter and painting style of modernist and proto-modernist art. In Vienna, the radical challenge of such a raw aesthetic of the instincts was rather quickly recuperated into an unchallenging baroque and decorative aesthetics. This was due largely to the symbolic hegemony of the court aristocracy in defining Viennese bourgeois identity. In Paris, the power of popular counter-hegemonical challenge persisted, and so did the radical challenge of French modernism.

Visual Arts: 'Psychological' versus 'Sociological' Modernism

The political and social hegemony of the Austrian bourgeoisie (Bürgertum) came very late, very suddenly, and lasted only a very short time. After the defeat of liberalism in 1848, a succession of events documented liberalism's subsequent success. Thus 1848 and 1849 were the years of great reform of the Austrian school system; the defeat of the army by France/Piedmont in 1859 was followed by the establishment of constitutional government; and the defeat of the army by Prussia in 1866 brought liberalism to as close as it would ever come to full state power and led to the establishment of the dual monarchy the following year. As early as the 1880s, however, the new order was already being threatened from below by the rise of mass anti-semitic movements on the right and of the working-class movement on the left. The Austrian universities came to experience a pervasive nationalism from 1875–90, anti-semitic artisan societies took form in the

1880s, anti-semitic Karl Lueger was elected as mayor of Vienna in 1897, and parliamentary government was succeeded by Ernest von Koerber's bureaucractic administration in 1900.

Viennese culture, as Schorske suggests, should be understood in terms of two polar opposite ideal-types, the first aristocratic, Catholic, and aestheticist and the second bourgeois, legalist, rationalist, and moral-scientific.[16] The Viennese Bürgertum itself was never nearly as well characterized by the second ideal-type as were their counterparts in most other countries. Even in the liberal halcyon decades of the 1870s and 1880s, the Viennese Bürgertum was pronouncedly Wagnerian, inordinately concerned with style, and possessed with a marked preference for the Baroque. Yet the 1860s–80s were Vienna's bourgeois-liberal decades. Early Viennese modernism at the time and just after the time of the Secession of 1898, parallel to the rise of the mass popular political movements, challenged this habitus of the Bürgertum from 'below'. Secession leader Gustav Klimt's *Pallas Athena*, painted in 1898, symbolized the 'sensual bearer of the mirror of modern man'. Klimt's women more generally represented sexuality, threateningly juxtaposed against the liberal ego of bourgeois man. Klimt's *Jurisprudence*, a ceiling painting for the University of Vienna, showed, not a belief in legality, but portrayed a central figure who was instead a helpless victim of the law. This early Viennese modernist challenge to *bürgerliche* stability breaks with any sort of aesthetics of harmony and order. Jerzy Olbricht's House of the Secession, built in 1898, was consistent with this ethos in its very resemblance to a pagan shrine.[17]

The subsequent evolution, though, of the Vienna Secession and Viennese modernism was in a direction consistent with, and no longer disruptive to, a now partly modified bourgeois habitus. It was a movement away from an aesthetics of 'life' and the instincts and towards the traditional aesthetics of beauty, a move towards an enervated ornamentalism that was perfectly acceptable to ruling elites. Thus the theme of the Secession's 1902 Beethoven exhibition was that of art as a replacement for religion. Klimt's frieze in the exhibition posed no longer a Nietzschean challenge to dominant political and aesthetic values, but instead seemed to advocate salvation in a fantasy world of art.[18] Klimt's shift from opposition to bourgeois values was evidenced in his movement from art nouveau towards art deco. The famous Wiener Werkstatt designers Kolo Moser and Josef Hoffmann underwent a similar evolution. In this, art nouveau's flowing, organic, and sensual lines were superseded by the rectilinear, geometric, metallic, and crystalline forms of deco. The shift from art nouveau to art deco was one of movement to stasis, of depth to superficiality, and betrayed a self-satisfied, Byzantine ornamentalism. This shift was particularly evident in Hoffmann's pavilion designed for the Secession's 1908 Kunstschau.[19] In place of the spartan simplicity of the original House of the Secession was festive, overly decorative, self indulgence.

What had taken place was that the Viennese Bürgertum had rejected large parts of liberal values to accept substantially the Catholic, baroque, and aestheticist tradition of the court aristocracy. The Viennese modernists, Klimt, von Hofmannsthal, Hoffmann, Moser, had only joined them in this acceptance. This complacency was once again disputed towards the end of the decade, through the expressionist paintings of Kokoschka, through Karl Kraus's biting essays, and through the spartan and functionalist design of Adolf Loos.[20] But Kokoschka and Kraus were to be more comfortable in Berlin, and Loos's principles were only to be realized on a major scale by the Bauhaus architects.

Viennese modernism, which had a briefer period of flourishing than the modernism of other great cities, was also the least oppositional, the least social-critical, of modernisms. Even prior to modernism, there was no Austrian equivalent of the French social realist novel, but instead the inner-oriented and individualistic *Bildungsroman*, which ran not counter to, but incorporated, the baroque tradition of fantasy. The Wiener Werkstatt was not social-critical in the sense the British Arts and Crafts movement was. Viennese painting and literature never rendered the sometimes brutal urban landscapes of their French counterparts. The problem was the aristocractic aestheticism that the court nobility had bequeathed to Viennese bourgeois culture. This made it difficult for modernist aesthetics to become oppositional. In Schorske's words, only in Austria was aestheticism 'not a form of protest versus bourgeois civilization' but 'an expression of that civilization, an affirmation of an attitude to life in which neither ethical nor social ideals played a dominant part'.[21]

In Viennese modernism, then, the court aristocracy was, in relation to the Bürgertum, the most salient social class. To a certain extent the eruption of the popular classes (i.e. the petite bourgeoisie and the working class) served to destabilize bourgeois identity in Vienna, and was paralleled by a radical phase in Viennese modernism. The very centrality of the aristocracy and its culture in Vienna, however, made possible the restabilization of *bürgerliche* culture, partly through the integration of a substantial element of aestheticist aristocratic culture into the bourgeois habitus. Viennese modernism thus became in large measure a conservative modernism.

In late nineteenth-century Paris the aristocracy played no such central role. Paris never indeed provided a space for the baroque and its accoutrements in the sense that Vienna did. Instead it was the popular classes themselves, and especially the petite bourgeoisie, that were the most salient social classes in relationship to the Parisian bourgeoisie. These were the very classes whose disruption of bourgeois identity was enabling for a vital, oppositional, and radical modernism. Hence Paris modernism was able to persist as a vital and radical force. To speak of a 'significant other' among social classes in a given national modernism is also to speak of the culture associated with that significant other class. It is not clear, especially to the untrained eye, whether the subjects for Klimt's paintings were drawn from bourgeois or aristocratic culture. It is clear, however, that the subject for the French *décadents*, as well as for the naturalists and impressionists, was the culture of the popular classes. Distinct from the previously existing 'folk culture', it is only in the late-nineteenth-century city that one can speak with any degree of certainty about the existence of a mass and *popular* culture. Popular culture, thus, and high modernism were born in the same places at about the same time.[22] Moreover, popular culture was the subject, and arguably the condition of existence, of high modernist culture.

The undermining of bourgeois identity in Paris came from three directions: from the popular classes, from the instincts, and from the commodity form itself. In 1863, Manet's *Déjeuner sur l'herbe* was rejected at the annual Salon only to be exhibited at the Salon des Refusés. The 1865 Salon did exhibit Manet's *Olympia* but quickly moved it to a place that made viewing almost impossible for the public. The critics, the press, and responsible opinion were outraged by the painting. Why? Critics and the viewing public were quite accustomed to seeing the nude and even courtisanes in pictures. The point is however that Olympia was *not* a classic nude or even a high-class courtisane, but as Clark notes, a 'fille publique', 'a faubourienne'.[23] This forced a threatening combination of sex, class, and the commodity onto the unsuspecting bourgeois viewing public. Seurat's *Dimanche après-midi à l'île de La Grande Jatte* moved towards the abstract and uniform in form as it did in content, thereby making class distinctions between the figures on a Sunday outing that he drew difficult to see. Manet's *Olympia* similarly allowed the features defining the prostitute to lose their clarity. At the same time in portraying a *fille publique* from the lower orders, Manet let the 'difference between the middle and the margin of the social order become blurred'. Previous nudes, even when taking the form of courtisanes, never allowed the odour of money to tarnish their classical form; in *Olympia*, money is clearly at issue, sex becomes a commodity. Manet's break with classicism was threefold. He painted not the general, but the particular; not the nude, but the naked, thus bringing sex back in an especially embarrassing way. He painted, finally, not the beautiful and rich, but the unseemly and chaotic popular classes. *Olympia* provoked such a reaction because it 'altered and played with identities the culture wanted to keep still' and 'because such identities were on the surface in such a brutal and unmediated fashion'.[24]

Paintings such as Degas's *Femmes devant un café* and *Au Café-concert* and Manet's *Un Bar au Folies-Bergère* only reproduced the characterization of contemporaries of the modern Parisian crowd as 'callicots [white-collar clerks] et des filles de joie'. These also were central participants in the famous 'café-concerts'. Some conservative commentators linked the bawdy songs performed at the café-concerts with the uprising of the Paris Commune, and censors were employed to recast the song material in a more harmless mould. The café-concerts were the stuff of the birth of popular culture. The crowds were drawn from the popular classes. The sometimes inattentive audience only betrayed the fact that they were as much participants in the total popular-cultural spectacle as the performers. The singer gave expression to the pulsing life of the popular classes, and the painter gave expression to the whole popular-cultural process.[25] The spectacle of the café-concert was above all the home of disorder, and particularly of the disruption of the orderly bourgeois habitus.

The special salience of a radical French petite bourgeoisie has long been the subject of commentary for historians and political scientists. The popular classes entered on the political scene in France earlier than elsewhere, and the petits bourgeois were long the arbiter of the popular. While surely not proletarian uprisings, 1789, 1830, 1848, and the Commune surely were *popular* uprisings, with considerable petit-bourgeois and artisan participation. The Radical and Radical-Socialist parties were petit-bourgeois parties largely *avant la lettre*. The historically radical, and later red, character of large sections of the French peasantry is both legend and well documented. The mainstream of early French political socialism was for a long time essentially peitit bourgeois, in its absence of *rapprochement* with trade unions, in its party organizational form, and in the social background of its parliamentarians and membership.[26] This leadership of the petite bourgeoisie within the often closely allied popular classes in France couldn't contrast more strongly with the German and Austrian cases, in which the petite bourgeoisie was substantially polarized to the right and the working class to a large degree stood on its own.

Social class and the uses of urban space

Perhaps most important in understanding the nature of modernism in Paris, though, was the very *social* visibility of the popular classes. And for this we have to scrutinize the comparative process of urban development. All cities, in so far as they became modern cities in the last decades of the nineteenth century, underwent the following changes in the organization of public space: (1) The development of separate commercial districts. This connected with the massive extension of the general process of commodification, which for Simmel was responsible for creating the characteristically blasé urban character, bereft of identity and inner meaning. (2) Spatial changes promoting a shift from private sociability to public sociability, or, if one likes, from 'particularized' to 'generalized' forms of sociability. These spatial changes include the building of department stores, railway stations, exposition halls, large factories. (3) A new centrality of the streets and circulation, comprising especially the construction of boulevards, trams, and urban railways. (4) An extension of the checkerboard principle in the layout of city streets.[27] (5) The specific organization of public spaces as 'spectacle' to be consumed by the masses.[28]

These changes are generic for the modern metropolis. The crucial question though for the *comparative* sociology of urban modernity – that is, the question that identifies, not the constants, but the variables – is the following: What social content, and especially what social *class* content, consecrates the new reorganization of public space? And this question can be at least partly reduced to: who used the new public space? In Vienna the aristocracy and its Baroque culture left their imprimatur on this reorganized public space. In Paris, this space, much more than elsewhere, became both popularized and classless. That is, in Paris, Haussmannization, so to speak, let loose the popular classes into the new modern spaces it had created. And this very social visibility to the popular in Paris was registered in the city's characteristic aesthetic modernism.

The new boulevards and open spaces that Baron Haussmann created displaced 350,000 people and some one-fifth of the streets of central Paris. As the centre of Paris moved west, masses of workers were evicted from the city centre, some to move along with the new factories to the banlieue. The movement of the city centre to the grands boulevards and the Bourse left the absolute majority of workers still in their quartier, and most of the quartiers still remained. But the quartier did become much less the frame of reference for work, trade, and consumption for the popular classes. The new *grands magasins*, for example, sent agents into the quartiers for purposes of purchasing craft and other goods.[29]

The eruption of the popular classes into the public realm gave to Haussmann's Paris a sort of 'classless' character; the edges dividing the social classes became blurred; an arena of interclass communications and interactions was opened. In the 1860s before Haussmannization had taken effect, class barriers were strong enough so that the 'public idiom' still was not satisfactorily standardized. In the Paris that Proust describes or that

Manet painted in *La Musique aux Tuileries*, sociability was mainly intraclass, in a plurality of narrowly circumscribed public realms. But by the 1880s the new clientele, of shop assistants and stock-exchange speculators, was found in restaurants, cabarets, and as shoppers in the grands magasins. The popular classes, strolling on the grands boulevards, could observe the dining practices, previously invisible to them, of the bourgeoisie in sidewalk restaurants. This blurring of class identities may have provoked Manet to have been impressed, not so much by Paris's streets, but by the 'queerness' of the people who used them.[30] It is this sort of 'flattening' of identity in the creation of blasé urban character that occasioned Clark's observation that 'the pleasures of seeing' in Haussmann's Paris involved 'some sort of lack', a certain 'brazenness'. The city, he continues, was a 'sign of capital'; it 'took up and eviscerated the varieties of social practice and gave them back with ventriloqual precision'.[31]

The popular character of modern urban Paris finds its counterpart in the baroque character that the court nobility imparted to Viennese urban modernity. First, at this juncture a few points in regard to what might be meant by 'baroque'. The baroque is first of all laden with a set of Counter-Reformation characteristics including a salience of symbolism, monumentality, voluptuousness, and grandeur. Its very opening out of public space, to be seen for example in Munich, Prague, or above all Rome, is strikingly modern in comparison with the traditional and labyrinthine Gothic street plans. Equally modern was the initiation by Baroque city planners of systematic works of right-angle streets. In their opening up of public space, Baroque planners organized vast vistas in order to highlight central monumental features. The idea was to create a spatial framework that would carry the sightline of viewers towards a central focus. It was to magnify the buildings and their symbolism. If the open spaces and checkerboard streets were modern, baroque symbolism, monumentality and voluptuousness were definitely not. Also distinctly non-modern in comparison with, say, Renaissance construction, were the heavy, articulated block-like volumes of baroque buildings.[32]

The Ringstrasse, which took shape in the 1860s and 1870s, was Vienna's counterpart of Haussmann's boulevards. The

Ringstrasse was built on a huge tract of open land surrounding the city which had previously served as a military fortification. The decline of the place of the military and the improvement of the position of the bourgeoisie and liberalism in the Austrian state, consecrated by the beginning of municipal self-government in 1850 and rapid economic growth throughout the 1850s, were pivotal in deciding the development of the Ringstrasse.[33] But the mode in which the Viennese Bürgertum created the Ringstrasse was still heavily coloured by baroque visions. Unlike Paris, in which according to Benjamin, modernity opened up a previously labyrinthine structure, Vienna's traditional inner city was largely already baroque. And this persisted into modern Vienna. In the 'new cities' in European metropolises and in America's great cities a 'functional' ethos predominated. Not so in Vienna, where the import of the new buildings in the Ringstrasse lay in their symbolism. The old baroque inner city was dominated by the symbols of the first and second class estates; the modern Ringstrasse by the symbols of the Third Estate. And unlike in other Western cities the Third Estate was conceived along cultural, rather than economic, lines. The parliament, the Rathaus, the University (interestingly in the new and not the old city), the Burgtheater, each built in a different historicist style symbolizing each building's aims and principles, were conceived on a scale of monumentality rarely seen elsewhere in modern Europe. Not just the scale and grandeur of the Ringstrasse, but the open spaces in front of the buildings and in the buildings and in the vast squares adjoining the street, suggested the persistent power of the Baroque. The Ringstrasse's new bourgeois *Mietpalaste* (apartment houses) also bore the mark of the old court nobility, their lavish stairways and vestibules, taken, as Schorske notes, from the old palace architecture and aimed at rhetorical impact.[34]

What, apart from Third Estate symbolism, was specifically *modern* about the Ringstrasse? Perhaps above all the underscored centrality of the horizontal space of the street. In Haussmann's Paris as well, all had become subordinated to traffic; everything was organized around circulation, in straight lines from railway stations along the boulevards. Rather than the buildings it was the lights and circulation in the new centre of Paris – on the Avenue de l'Opéra, the Boulevard Madeleine, the Boulevard des

Capucines, the Rue Auber, the Boulevard des Italiens – which attracted the foreign visitor and was registered in the cityscapes of Monet and Renoir in the 1970s.[35] In Vienna's Ringstrasse, Schorske observes, the new representative buildings did not face one another; instead each faced the street as if to italicize the circular flow. This modern urban vision of the street was only further extended by Otto Wagner, first as established Ringstrasse architect and speculator, and later as a Secession leader and critic of the Ringstrasse. Wagner's Österreichische Landerbank had no vertical lines at all on the lower portion of the building; instead, horizontal masonry reinforced the trajectory of the street. Wagner's philosophy advocated a 'temporal trajectory', which gave priority to flow movement. In the late 1890s the municipal railway replaced the grand boulevard as the symbol of urban progress. Wagner was a key actor from 1894 to 1901 in the construction of the Vienna system, making pioneering use of iron in station construction as a symbol of technical change.[36]

Wagner's and later especially Adolf Loos's functionalist critique of Ringstrasse symbolic monumentality underlines the elements of Baroque that underpinned Viennese modernity. Camillo Sitte's traditionalist and communitarian critique of the Ringstrasse emphasizes instead the above-indicated *continuity* of the baroque and the modern. Sitte, in opposition to baroque and modern rectilinearity, advocated the Gothic free-form of mediaeval streets. In place of the anonymity of the 'reign of the street' he argued for 'enclosed space'; instead of large impersonal urban squares, space should be internalized to promote the values of community. Instead of the Baroque or modern architect, Sitte promulgated the values of the mediaeval master builder.

Restructured urban space and the visual arts in the modernist city were mirror images of one another. In Vienna, challenge to bourgeois stability came, on the one hand, from the unbridled sexuality of the painting, for example, the young Klimt and Kokoschka. And on the other from a conception of the built environment proffered by Wagner and Loos which was grounded in rejection of classicizing and historicist idealism. It promised the replacement of the latter by spartan cleanness of line and a materialist urbanism of movement, which itself was realized in the new Viennese street plans and urban railways. All of this was, however, compromised and overshadowed as modernism in Vienna was recuperated as a 'cultural resource' which reinforced a now altered bourgeois identity. Thus the decorative sumptuousness of the no longer oppositional, visual arts was matched by monumentalism, baroque self-indulgence, and primacy of symbol over function in Vienna's built environment.

MODERNIST BERLIN: STATE VERSUS CIVIL SOCIETY

The city and statist modernization

If the relationship bourgeoisie is constituted via the popular classes in Paris and via the court aristocracy in Vienna, then it is constituted via the state in Berlin. Above, I defined modernism in terms of disruption of the values of order, repose, stability, authority, and consonance associated with a national (or urban) bourgeoisie. If in Vienna these bourgeois values were partly hegemonized by Catholic aristocratic culture, in Berlin they were strongly pervaded by statism. The Prussian state, as often noted, was not just an external entity, but an entity profoundly incorporated into the consciousness of individual Germans. Hence the famous German *Beamtenbewusstsein*. Hence the very overwhelming number of German Beamten (civil servants). So when modernity in Berlin – in the arts, in the massive new development of the city – took shape, so to speak, against the state, it also took shape in opposition to the identity of the German Bürgertum. The very statist nature of the constitutive elements of German bourgeois identity made German national-ism a substantially different phenomenon than nationalism in other countries.[37] If one is curious about where the modern is in Berlin, the place to look is where the state isn't. That is, in a very important sense the modern in Berlin was the anti-state or at least the non-state. And the Jew and the proletarian were, not without good reason, seen as harbingers of this modern.

A whole list of factors contributed to Berlin's statist character: the relatively weakly developed guild system and mediaeval urban structures more generally; the relative insubstantiality of a Prussian *noblesse de robe*; the relatively powerless position of the mercantile bourgeoisie under absolutism. Perhaps most important was the lateness of development of the absolutist state. This bequeathed to Berlin and Prussia the advantages of what might be called 'political backwardness in perspective', and enabled the creation of an inordinately powerful military and bureacratic apparatus.

In pre-modern Berlin the claims on land of this expanding state machinery had already driven land values famously high. Hence workers in pre-industrial Berlin were crowded into unusually small spaces in what is today's Mitte (centre) and experienced an absence of light and air that made conditions even in contemporaneous London and Paris seem favourable.[38] The second half of the nineteenth century witnessed a repetition of this process. This time in modernizing Berlin, the now much more greatly expanded needs of the state for public space, together with the rapid commercialization of the centre and especially the Friedrichstrasse–Leipziger Strasse axis, largely evicted the working class altogether from the Mitte. The very centre of the Mitte was most fully 'cleaned out' – the population of Alt-Berlin diminished from 32,000 to 9,000 from 1871 to 1913; the population of Alt-Cölln from 16,500 to 6,200. But also the large Friedrichstadt Stadtteil (in today's Mitte) which had 76,350 inhabitants in 1871 had only 33,505 in 1913. These evicted workers joined other newcomers to the now rapidly industrializing Berlin to live in the massively expanding properly urban working class districts outside of the Mitte – thus the population of 'red' Wedding increased ten-fold to 254,000 between 1871 and 1913; the population of the Rosenthaler Vorstadt, much of which is now East Berlin's Prenzlauerberg, increased seven-fold to 319,000 in 1913; and the population of Stralauer Viertel and Königsviertel, much of which now is Friedrichshain, increased taken together between three and four fold to 489,000.[39]

This rate of growth pales, however, in comparison with the expansion of the 'suburbs', which were incorporated into Berlin as administrative districts in 1920. The four large middle-class suburbs grew at especially great rates – Charlottenburg from 20,000 inhabitants in 1871 to 323,000 in 1919, a growth of 1,667 per cent; Schöneberg from 4,500 in 1871 to 262,000 in 1919; Steglitz from 1,900 in 1871 to 83,400 in 1919 and Wilmersdorf from 1,662 to 139,400. Taken together the expansion of the middle-class suburbs was from about 28,000 inhabitants in 1871 to over three-quarters of a million (808,000) just after World War I. The other large suburbs, of mixed population, though with working-class majorities, experienced similar trajectories: Lichtenberg grew from 4,700 in 1871 to 145,000 in 1919, Rixdorf/ Neukolln from 8,145 to 262,000, and Spandau from 20,500 to 95,500.[40] The total population growth of just these large above-mentioned mainly working-class districts was of the order of 1.3 million from 1871 to World War I, a phenomenon which taken together with the revolutionary uprising of 1918 must have been frightening to Berlin's middle classes in a manner hardly imaginable today.

The Berlin equivalent of Paris Haussmannization and Vienna's Ringstrasse was the *Bebauungsplan* of 1862. The plan, largely developed in the late 1850s by Berlin *Baurat* James Holbrecht, was itself taken from a cartographic concept already established by Haussmann. It included the development of suburbs, canalization, the creation of boulevards and a Ringstrasse, the building of living quarters, a new street system, and considerable development in transport. The idea was to plan for an increase in Berlin's population to 1.5 million. But despite the power of the state's repressive, military and administrative, apparatus, Holbrecht could not mobilize sufficient public power (as had been possible in Paris and Vienna) to oppose the interests and manoeuvres of property owners. The interests and power of the railway companies put paid to Holbrecht's ideas for a Ringstrasse and for a north–south through boulevard. His planning powers were also insufficient to enable the breaking through of older residential areas to construct Paris-type boulevards. Success was only achieved in the construction of the two central rail stations, Potsdamer and Anhalter Banhofs; and in the construction of a row of boulevards in the south part of the city bearing (characteristically) the names of illustrious generals such as Yorck, Gneisenau, Bülow, Kleist, and Tauentzien.[41]

Holbrecht's street plans had provided for the planning of living quarters, i.e. the planning of *Baublocke* and of the buildings in these blocks. His idea was that the parcellization of building land would enable the construction of blocks that were 120–150 metres wide and some 75 metres deep. These *'Mietkaserne'* (literally 'rental barracks'), to avoid the slum problem of a London or central Berlin, would be four storeys

high and would open up on an interior square that was green
and ample enough to permit plenty of light and fresh air.
Holbrecht advocated a mix of social classes in the same building;
his outline was for a single apartment to be on the first floor of a
typical building; for two apartments each on the *Erdstock*, the
second storey and the third storey, and for three apartments on
the fourth floor, as well as smaller flats on the ground floor and
in the courtyard. The outcome, due to the power of speculators
and property holders, was that Berlin's *Mietkaserne* became a
symbol throughout the West for substandard housing. Their
population was not mixed, but exclusively working class, including many unskilled workers and unemployed. In place of Holbrecht's large yards, developers built Hinterhöfe (back
courtyards) several deep, and tiny Hinterhöfe at that. Buildings
were five to six storeys high, and this, combined with the tiny
Hinterhöfe, allowed inhabitants virtually no light and minimal
air circulation. Numerous tiny apartments looked out onto these
ever-smaller back courtyards, and (contrary to Holbrecht's prescriptions) filled the cellars of the buildings. In fact during so-
called modernization from 1861–75 there was actually an increase
in the already unfavourable ratio of inhabitants per square metre
of living space.[42]

Thus the state, which largely forced the overflow of working-
class citizens outside of the central part of the city, was unable to
amass sufficient powers decently to house these individuals
outside of the centre. Nor was it powerful enough, outside of a
few streets with Prussian generals' names, to force through a
genuinely modern network of boulevards. The putatively
modern new business district was more or less haphazardly
established along the Leipziger Strasse, just a bit west of the old
city centre. Real boulevard creation, making what is now the
centre of West Berlin, around Kurfurstendamm, had to wait for
its beginnings in the 1920s and its maturity under Allied rule in
the 1960s.

The role of the state was even more pronounced in Berlin in
the cultural sphere. As a military-bureaucratic city, without
either the tradition of a court nobility, an important mediaeval
university, or even an independent mercantile culture such as
existed in Hamburg or Lübeck, Berlin was, in comparative
perspective, so to speak, bereft of culture. Culture in Berlin came

first through state institutions, and developed very late and all at once. The city's Friedrich-Wilhelm Universität was founded only after Baron von Stein's reforms in 1810, yet by 1870 it was setting international standards in history, classics, physics, chemistry, and medicine. Considerable advance came under the Prussian Minister-Director for Higher Education, Friedrich Althoff. He began to move the university (now the Freie Universität) from the city centre to Dahlem. He oversaw the final establishment of the Technische Hochschule (now the Technische Universität) in Charlottenburg through the joining of the Bauakademie with the Arts and Crafts School in 1882. And just after his term of office the Kaiser-Wilhelm Society for the Promotion of Science was grounded (1910), whose eminences included Max Planck and Albert Einstein; the Society became the Max Planck Institut in 1948. Apart from higher education, other cultural developments were retarded. The Royal Opera, anti-Wagnerian for a considerable time, only achieved world class status in the last decade of the nineteenth century. The Music College was founded only in 1869, and the Berlin Philharmonic Orchestra only in 1882. Berlin equally did not have any kind of status until very late in the day in publishing, literature, theatre, and painting.[43]

Aesthetic modernism: the 'Anti-State'

The predominant thrust of the city's rise to world class cultural status came apart from and was often opposed to the state. This is perhaps best instantiated in the Berlin Secession. The Wilhemine state was able to use a number of institutions of art to attempt to prevent the Secession's promotion of an autonomous and modernist painting. These institutions included the following.

(1) The Royal College of Art.

(2) The Royal Academy of Art. This was founded in 1696; separate music and painting academies were established in 1833. The Minister of Culture had strong ties with the Academy and determined its funding. Other German cities had colleges as well as Academies.

(3) The Society of Berlin Artists. This was the local branch of the 1856-founded Federation of German and Berlin Artists, which won royal recognition in 1867; the latter meant royal subsidies for the holding of exhibitions and for magazines, etc. in

exchange for kingly veto powers over organizational rule changes and decisions.[44] These Societies were in opposition to the differentiation and autonomization model of modernity that I am using in this paper. They were largely economic interest groups – that is, their economic function was not yet differentiated from their aesthetic function. Thus they often promoted what their leaders knew was mediocre art in the interests of all their members.

(4) The Berlin Salon. This was an annual exhibition. Other large German cities had bi-annual salons. The model was the Paris Salon established in 1830. A city's Academy typically funded its Salon, chose the pictures which were to be exhibited, and awarded medals to prizewinners. In Berlin, the same man, Anton von Werner, was director of the Royal College and leader of the Society of Artists from 1887. He also was very close to the Kaiser's family. The Society came to receive quite substantial funding from the Kaiser from 1888–1910. The Society thus was able to purchase a new building as well as take over much of the running of the Salon. The Salon, which had mostly only exhibited Berlin and German painters, put on exhibitions with an international character in 1891 and 1892. In 1892 the exhibition of painting by Edvard Munch created a scandal after which state control over the Salon was reinforced. These events provoked secession movements from the official Societies in a number of German cities. In Berlin a splinter group formed within the Society, but it did not secede until 1898. The famous Vienna and Berlin Secessions were two of the very last of these movements. The dominant form of painting that the state supported, and which was also popular among the conservative middle and upper classes, was historical painting. Von Werner was an historical painter, often of very recent historical scenes. Kaiser Wilhelm II had effective veto power over the awarding of prizes at the annual Berlin Salon.[45]

(5) The National Gallery. Liberal Hugo Tschudi, sympathetic to modernist movements, was Director from 1896. He was in charge of the commission to decide on the nature of the German exhibition at the St Louis World Fair of 1904. The commission decided to exhibit a mixture of mainstream and avant-garde German artists. The Kaiser and von Werner disagreed; only mainstream artists were exhibited in St Louis; and von Tschudi

was replaced at the National Gallery by the ubiquitous Von Werner.[46]

Standing opposed to these state institutions was another set of institutions more or less representing modernization and, so to speak, 'civil society'. The first of these was the Secession itself. The Secession was led by Max Liebermann and joined by such dominant figures as Max Slevogt and Louis Corinth. Liebermann was Professor and member of the Academy of the Arts. He was born in 1847 and was hence 40–45 years older than the young Expressionists who, less than a decade after the Secession was founded, gave to German painting its character-istically modernist form. Liebermann, also influenced by seventeenth-century Dutch painting, was an impressionist.[47] He was educated during the 'positivist' era just after German unification and his views always bore the mark of its pronounced rationalism. Liebermann was a self-professed and proud bourgeois. He was a leader of the 1892 splinter group in the Berlin Society. His powerful institutional role was nonetheless confirmed by the award of a gold medal (to which both von Werner and the Kaiser assented) in the Salon of 1897. Liebermann was a leader of the 1898 Secession, to which he was elected president, an office which he held until 1911. In 1899 the Secession held their first (as an alternative to the Salon) exhibi-tion; here no foreign painters were exhibited, but at the same time neither were the didactic and patriotic paintings typical of the Salon. The 1900 Secession exhibition was significantly international, but still included only a minority of avant-garde paintings. These exhibitions received a lot of favourable criticism from the Berlin bourgeois press. Equally, patrons such as Walter Rathenau and banker Carl Fürstenburg advanced sums of money for quarters for a Secession gallery. Anton von Werner, chief Secession opponent, was not an anti-semite. Yet German nationalists tended to see modernists and the Secession as cos-mopolitan, internationalist, French, and Jewish. Liebermann was scurrilously attacked in anti-semitic cartoons.[48]

By 1904 most of the best of non-academic German painters were Secession members, and after the St Louis affair even most establishment figures did not take academic painting seriously. From 1906–10, foreign artists such as Munch and van de Velde became Secession members as well as German representatives of the newer styles such as Beckmann, Nolde, and Lyonel Feininger. Part of the hostility of the academic *Kunstgenossenschaft* against the Secession's *Kunstlerbund* stemmed from the weak market position of the academic painters.[49] It was also the prejudice of the less gifted against the more gifted. Thus can be explained the attack led by the mediocre and unsuccessful ex-Worpswede painter Carl Vinnen against 'Non-German art'. Vinnen, whose offensive smacked of anti-semitism in that it centred on the figure of Paul Cassirer and lambasted the critics for being in the service of speculators and dealers, called for a boycott on the purchase of non-German art. The President of the Akademie der Künste signed Vinnen's manifesto, as did, surprisingly, Käthe Kollwitz. But established Secession figures as well as younger modernists like Beckmann, Pechstein, Kandinsky, Marc, and Macke mobilized against it.[50]

If reaction in Berlin saw the established Secession impressionists as somehow 'French' and 'Jewish', they were even more offended by the work, seen as 'Negroid' and 'primitive', of the younger Expressionists. The Expressionists, and especially the leading Brücke painters Nolde, Erick Heckel, Ernst Kirchener, and Schmidt-Rottluff, were shown in Secession exhibitions, though the critics and public reacted mainly either with hostility or indifference. In 1910, however, the relatively conservative and impressionist-dominated (by Liebermann, Slevogt, Corinth, and others) executive committee of the Secession refused to give space to the Brücke painters at the annual exhibition. This provoked a mass exit and the founding of the Neue Sezession under the leadership of Max Pechstein. In 1913, for not dissimilar reasons, Liebermann and the remaining majority left the Secession, though substantial figures such as Corinth stayed in the organization.[51]

In any event the experience of the Berliner Sezession points to a hostility of the state to modernity that bears comparison with the Viennese case. If, in Berlin, the Secession pitted civil society against the state, in Vienna the battle was fought out within the sphere of civil society itself, while the state acted as arbiter between competing forces. That is, where the Berlin Secession defined itself against the Wilhelmine state, its Viennese counterpart defined itself against the bourgeois values of the Ringstrasse culture of the 1860s and 1870s. This is apparent when one considers the relationship of state and secession in Vienna. In Vienna the Secession *did* win representative status from the Austrian government and was, for example, able to mount exhibitions in foreign expositions. Otto Wagner, along with Klimt major Secession leader, had a professorial appointment from 1894 at Vienna's Academy of Fine Arts; in the late 1890s he was commissioned to build local railway stations. And in 1905 the state built Wagner's daring Post Office Savings Building, perhaps the most modern building financed by a European state since the Eiffel Tower.[52] From 1900 von Koerber's government set out on a programme of economic and cultural modernization. This meant state encouragement of the Secession, especially through the offices of new Minister of Culture Wilhelm von Hartel. Von Hartel operated through the Advisory Arts Council, of which again Wagner was a member. Hartel opened a state-sponsored modern gallery in 1903 and created teaching appointments at the Arts and Crafts School for Kolo Moser and Josef Hoffmann. Even 'theoretical modernist' Sigmund Freud used friends of Hartel to secure his own career promotion.[53] This Viennese phenomenon of the state and modernist culture as bedfellows could not be more foreign to Berlin, which an observer even in the late 1920s described as 'Stadt voll protestantischer Staats und Militärphilosophie'.[54]

New class fractions: champions of civil society

Any discussion of the institutions of art, or, more generally speaking, the institutions of culture, in Berlin is incomplete, or even impossible, without discussion of the role of the Jews. The connection between the Jews and modernity - conceived as economic and cultural modernization - is one long of concern to sociologists, and dates at least back to the work of Werner Sombart. The Jews along with the Huguenots were welcomed with open arms by Friedrich Wilhelm after the Thirty Years War in the hope of achieving rapid economic growth on the cinders of destruction. Not much later, in 1670, the Jews were expelled from Vienna, many to settle in the nearby hinterland.[55] Of import to my argument here, however, is not the role of the Jews in the Early Modern period, but in the modernity, here conceived as modern*ism*, of the late nineteenth and early twentieth centuries.

229

And there is an important difference. The Jews of early modernity were famously, 'not a nationality', but the 'state people' par excellence. In the nineteenth century, however, they had entered civil society on a very important scale. In Vienna, emancipation began with the liberal reforms of 1848, and by the 1860s Jews had obtained full freedom of migration. The Jewish population of Vienna increased exponentially from 1857 to 1880 and peaked at about 12 per cent of the city's population in 1890.[56] In Germany the large shift in Jewish identity came in the eighteenth and especially the nineteenth centuries as no longer Yiddish but German became the first language for most Jews. Legislation which made official Jewish equality of citizenship rights was passed in the Norddeutschen Bund in 1869 and extended to a united Germany in 1871. The Jewish population of Berlin also increased and peaked at about 3–4 per cent at the time of World War I.[57] In multi-ethnic Vienna the Jews, though a different and more often stigmatized nationality, were still only yet another nationality. In the more ethnically uniform Berlin the Jews were rather clearly *the* other nationality. Moreover, as the Jews came to populate and impart, importantly, economic and cultural form to a now modernist civil society, Vienna and Berlin are again at opposite poles. In juxtaposition to the rather comfortable at points virtual 'merging' of state and civil society in Vienna stands the age-old Prussian hostility and incompatibility of the two realms.

Our concern in this context is with the institutions of culture. And, in painting, the Jews were ubiquitous. Secession leader Max Liebermann was a Jew as was Neue Sezession leader Pechstein. Pechstein and Jewish architect Erich Mendelsohn were active later in the *Novembergruppe*. The most important areas of gallery space, again as apart from state institutions, offered to first impressionists and later to expressionists, were provided by Paul Cassirer. Cassirer's gallery exhibited avant-garde art as early as 1895. He organized the original Secession gallery on Kurfürstendamm and then with two Secession painters built a new gallery further west on Kurfürstendamm in 1904. Cassirer was elected chairman of the Secession in 1912 and staged what probably was its most impressive exhibition in 1913. Cassirer's brother Bruno's publishing house served both Secessionists and the new Expressionist poets as did the magazines, *Kunst und Künstler* and *Pan,* that he edited. During the war the Cassirers edited the liberal and patriotic periodicals *Bildermann* and *Kriegzeit.*[58] Cassirer was a friend and sponsor of the young architect Erich Mendelsohn. In sort of a virtuous circle, talented Jewish architects such as Alfred Breslauer or the gifted (designer of Wertheim department store in the Leipziger Strasse) Alfred Messel would build single family houses in the Tiergarten for Jewish art dealers such as Alfred Flechtheim (also editor of *Der Querschnitt*) and Cassirer. The latter's own gallery was in his house in Viktoriastrasse not far from a whole set of galleries and new theatres in Berlin's 'alten Westen' around Lützowplatz and Potsdamer Strasse. Jewish funders of the arts such as Rudolf Mosse and Jules and James Simon, Mycenae for the national Kaiser-Friedrich museum, lived in villas nearby.[59]

Closely connected with expressionism, and hence in opposition to 'conservatives' like Liebermann, as well as with the political left was Herwarth Walden (née Levine). Walden, born in Berlin, a musician who also wrote some plays and poems, was the some time lover of the esteemed (Jewish) expressionist poet Else Lasker-Schüler. Walden, whose nickname 'der Bürgerschreck' seems to have been well earned to judge from Kokoschka's portrait of him, was in his socialism and later communism a forerunner of the much more politicized cultural scene of the Weimar Republic. His own aesthetic was based on Viennese art historian Alois Riegl's idea of an absolute *Kunstwollen*, in which art, based on an inner vision, takes the place of religion. Walden's magazine *Der Sturm* regularly featured Brücke painters and especially Oskar Kokoschka. Under the aegis of *Sturm*, and financed by, among others, Karl Kraus, Walden ran a publishing house, a bookstore, and a series of exhibitions.[60]

In the theatre, Jews provided the institutions that helped Berlin emerge as a world-class cultural city. And again these modernist institutions of culture in civil society were set up distinctly apart from, and largely opposed to, the state. As in painting, the shift to the modern in Berlin theatre took two steps. The first step here, paralleling the Secession, was the constitution of the *Freie Bühne* movement, which was associated with naturalism in the theatre. The second was the break with naturalism, led by Max Reinhardt, which paved the way for expressionist theatre. The state sponsored, bürgerliche, equivalent of historicism in painting and architecture, was the poetic idealism of Goethe and Schiller with its beautification and classicized, non-realist, dialogue.[61] The order and poetic classicism of this conventional theatre was disrupted by a 'scandal' which paralleled that of the exhibition of Munch's painting in the visual arts. This was the uproar caused in official circles and among the public by the performance of a play written by naturalist dramatist Gerhart Hauptmann in the Lessing Theater in 1889. In the same year, four men, all Jews, convened an historic meeting in the Cafe Schiller. The men were Theodor Wolff (later Chief Editor of the *Berliner Tageblatt*), Maximilian Harder (actor and journalist), publisher Samuel Fischer, and director Otto Brahm. The meeting was historic in its establishment of the basic conditions for the creation of the 'Freie Bühne', which itself was the institutional embodiment of modern theatre in Berlin, or, in Zivier's words, 'der Ausgangpunkt aller späteren deutschen Theater-Erneuerungen'. Brahm became Berlin's leading naturalist director. His naturalism was intended to make the audience 'forget the theatre', and featured sparse sets and underplayed gestures. Berlin naturalism, which thrived in the framework of the 'Verein der Freie Bühne', a large proportion of whose sponsorship and membership was Jewish, was called 'Arme-Leute Theater' and 'Juden-Theater' by its opponents.[62]

In 1900 Brahm's pupil, Max Reinhardt, met with a group of other young actors in Berlin's Cafe Monopol. This group had come to oppose what they saw as the 'sterile-naturalistic' style of Brahm's productions. Strindberg had in 1888 called for an 'intimate theatre'. And Reinhardt followed suit and had Peter Behrens rebuild Arnim's Theater (Unter den Linden 44) according to his specifications. The theatre was rebuilt in a heavily ornamental classicist style, complete with doric columns and decorative masks. The stage was small and the auditorium had only 366 seats. Reinhardt's first big public success was an anti-naturalistic production of Gorki's *Nachtasyl*. Working with Jewish theatre architect Oskar Kaufmann, Reinhardt was the first to make wide use of a fully *ausgebauten Bühnenapparates*, of full plasticity of scenery and new adventurous use of lighting. Reinhardt put on, not just modernist, but a great variety of plays. The most highly respected expressionist director, working

232

mostly in the post-war years, was Leopold Jessner, who also was Jewish. Jessner was well known for doing the classics in expressionist form.[63]

One could multiply examples ad infinitum in regard to Jewish presence in Berlin's modernist institutions of culture. In the press Rudolf Mosse and Leopold Ullstein published the two big liberal Berlin dailies, the *Berliner Tageblatt* and *Vossische Zeitung*. Could this liberal press have been a factor in the very high vote among the Berlin bourgeoisie for the left-liberal Freisinnige Volkspartei in the years immediately before World War I? These liberal dailies employed a high proportion of Jewish journalists, a number of whom as critics helped create an audience for the new movements in painting, theatre, literature, and music.[64] Other important institutions were public places in which avant-gardes could meet, like the legendary 'Neopathetisches Cabarett'. The latter was more than anything else a showcase for younger expressionist poets like Georg Heym. Beginning in 1910, it put on performances as often as once a month, at which texts from, for example, Nietzsche, Rilke, Wedekind, and others were read. Younger figures, perhaps above all the exciting young Jewish expressionist poet, Jakob von Hoddis, dominated the organization, the 'Neuen Club', which was responsible for these events. These would draw as many as 250 people, including established names such as Karl Kraus, Heinrich Mann, and Else Lasker-Schüler, and received wide press coverage. Most of the leading active members of the Neuen Club were Jews, several of whom wrote for publications like *Sturm*, *Demokrat*, *Revolution*, and *Aktion*.[65]

CONCLUSIONS

Thus in the two and one-half decades prior to World War I a whole set of modernist institutions of culture were forged in German civil society, often in opposition to the state, and unusually often by Jews. When the fighting broke out, Berlin had come almost from nowhere to become a world-class culture centre. The sharp opposition of state and civil society was fundamentally altered in the years of the Weimar Republic when a much friendlier set of public bodies served partly as framework for the Bauhaus, and for Brecht's and Piscator's theatre. The transmogrified complexion of the state in the Weimar years is well reflected in the membership of the Akademie der Künste. Heinrich Mann was chair of the Literature section, which included Alfred Döblin, Thomas Mann, Franz Werfel, and Jakob Wasserman. The Section for Visual Arts included Kokoschka, Mendelsohn, Pechstein, Bruno Taut, Ernst Barlach, Otto Dix, Ernst Ludwig Kirchner, Kollwitz, Mies van der Rohe, and Schmitt-Rottluff. The Music Section included Arnold Schoenberg. The reassertion of the state/civil society opposition is documented by the fact that all of the above names either quit or were excluded from the Akademie in 1933.

We have come full circle now. In our delineation of different national and urban modernisms in Paris, Vienna, and Berlin, we began with discussion of the Bürgertum or bourgeoisie and have ended with discussion of *bürgerliche Gesellschaft* or civil society. At the very beginning, modernism was defined in terms of the disruption of bourgeois identity. What differentiated national modernisms was (1) where the disruptive force came from and (2) what kind of identity was disrupted. I argue along with T. J. Clark that Parisian modernism is most distinctive in terms of the disruptive force. This force in the French case was the 'popular classes' and especially the petite bourgeoisie. In Vienna, what was most distinctive was the type of bourgeois identity, which I argued was a 'baroque' identity, largely conditioned, as Carl Schorske noted, by the salient presence of a Catholic court nobility. In Berlin, distinctive too was the type of bourgeois identity, in the German case conditioned by the salience of the state. Discussion of the state led then to consideration of the state/civil society relationship.

What however is the implication of all this for the relationship of Bürgertum, or bourgeoisie, and bürgerliche Gesellschaft? I understand bürgerliche Gesellschaft in the Anglo-American sense of 'civil society'. When Anglo-American political analysts use this term 'civil society', they tend often to refer to the example of contemporary Poland. Here Solidarity has represented the flourishing of civil society against the state. Civil society in this context means the whole package promised by an enlightened liberalism including full citizenship rights, free trade unions, representative government, and a culture largely autonomous of state control. This is what I understand 'bürgerliche Gesellschaft' to mean. As a general model, then, it might be fair to say that in early capitalism the bourgeoisie is very often on the side of the development of civil society, and in later capitalism it is often opposed to such development. If the development of civil society in later capitalism means the growth of strong trade unions, socialist parties and a welfare state, then the bourgeoisie might find this disruptive to its material interests. If the development of civil society means in later capitalism, say from the end of the nineteenth century, the flourishing of an independent cultural and aesthetic sphere, then this might, as I argued at length above, be disruptive to the *ideal* interests, indeed to the very identity, of the bourgeoisie. This tension, or, if you will, this contradiction between bourgeois and civil society, seems to be written into the logic of development of Western societies. In the earlier centuries of modernity, modernization entails a partial autonomization of cultural and aesthetic spheres, so that culture is constitutive of bourgeois identity. With further autonomization and the advent of modern*ism*, culture becomes either inaccessible and thus no longer can function positively to construct such a stable identity, or more commonly, as argued above, modernist culture comes to undermine and destabilize bourgeois identity. If the difference of interests of bourgeois and worker is the *social* contradiction of capitalism, then the advent of modernist culture is what Daniel Bell has rightly called the *cultural* contradiction of capitalism. And both of these contradictions of capitalism are built out of a developing incompatibility of bourgeoisie and civil society.

The national bourgeoisie of any country can be divided, following Max Weber's and more recently Pierre Bourdieu's analyses, into two fractions: one which is rooted in 'economic capital' and the other which is rooted in 'cultural capital'. German social historicans refer to the economic-capital fraction as the '*Wirtschaftsbürgertum*' and the cultural-capital fraction as the *Bildungsbürgertum*. Given this context, then how are we to perceive the German case? Two factors, it may be said, separate out the German bourgeoisie from its counterparts in other Western and Eastern nations. The first is the inordinately strong position of the *Bildungsbürgertum* (dependent on 'cultural capital') in comparison with the *Wirtschaftsbürgertum* (based on 'economic capital'). The second is the extraordinary presence, so to speak, of the state as very part and parcel of the Bürgertum. In

England, in France, in Austria, the aristocracy had very much to do with the construction of bourgeois identity. Not so in Germany. The very radical separation of the middle classes and aristocracy in the latter left the state (and the state not conceived as a set of representative institutions along lines of the American model) a large space in the creation of bourgeois identity. Further, in Germany, unlike in the Anglo-Saxon world, the Bildungsbürgertum existed as a major force historically prior to the Wirtschaftsbürgertum. The very strength of the German Bildungsbürgertum meant that it served not only as 'organic intellectual' to the entire Bürgertum, but that it (unlike in other countries) was to be the hegemonic force imparting its own specific type of unity to the whole of the Bürgertum. That is, in Bourdieu's terms, the Bildungsbürgertum dominated the 'habitus' of the German Bürgertum much like the Wirtschaftsbürgertum dominated the habitus of its Anglo-American counterparts. Finally, this Bildungsbürgertum, much more than elsewhere, subscribed to statist values. No other country had such a highly educated corps of civil servants as had Germany. And in no other country did civil servants (Beamten) comprise such a high proportion of the highly educated.

The threefold character of the German Bürgertum – strong state, strong Bildungsbürgertum, statist Bildungsbürgertum – made the situation for cultural modernism and for civil society trebly difficult. What I am trying to argue is that in Germany the contradiction between bourgeoisie and civil society – as exemplified above in the contradiction of state and cultural modernism – was much much sharper than elsewhere. In Poland, 1981 represented the revenge of the state, not just on the organized working class, but on civil society in general. In Germany, 1933 was not just the revenge of the state on the working class, on cultural modernism, and on the Jews. It also was the revenge of the bourgeoisie on civil society.

Chapter Nine

MODERNIZATION AND POSTMODERNIZATION IN THE WORK OF PIERRE BOURDIEU

The number one growth area in sociology at the beginning of this closing decade of the twentieth century – in the USA, in Britain, in Germany, and surely elsewhere too – is the sociology of culture. And the most influential sociologist of culture is, without parallel, Pierre Bourdieu. If 'culture studies', in its broadest sense, is represented paradigmatically by Michel Foucault in philosophy, by Jacques Derrida in modern languages, by Roland Barthes and Umberto Eco in semiotics, by Christian Metz in film theory, Henri Lefebvre in urbanism, and Jacques Lacan in psychoanalysis, then it is represented in sociology by Pierre Bourdieu.

Bourdieu is well known for his work on tribal society in Algeria, for his studies of education, his sociology of art, and his definitive tome, *Distinction*, on the consumer-side of social stratification. He is well known for his theoretical considerations of the 'habitus' and 'cultural capital'.[1] But 'modernization and postmodernization'? Surely no topic would seem to be *less* down the alley of this intellectually peripatetic social scientist. Bourdieu has written on traditional societies and modern society, but does not at all on the face of it seem to have a theory of modernization. Numerous analysts have castigated him, not just for the absence of a theory of modernization, but for the absence of any sort of mechanism and account of social change in his work. And Professor Bourdieu, in response, has claimed that in fact social stasis is a more prevalent phenomenon than social change in empirical reality, and that he has been thus justified in his pronounced concern over his career with the explanation of such social stasis. Pierre Bourdieu has also significantly *not* participated in the debates on modernism and postmodernism. He is sceptical of the existence of any such thing as postmodern culture. He seems to hold the writings of the 'popes' of postmodernism, Baudrillard and Lyotard, in ill-disguised contempt. He has in addition little time for the critical utopianism of Habermas.

This chapter refuses however to take either Bourdieu or his critics at their word. In it I shall argue that there is a theory of modernization *and* postmodernization implicit in Bourdieu's work. And that, whether Professor Bourdieu likes it or not, we can learn a lot about modernism and postmodernism by close analysis of its corpus.

Modernism and postmodernism refer to two sets of phenomena. The first is to a set of phenomena taking place in society. The second is to a set of phenomena that characterize social theory. The aim of this chapter is to address both of these in the work of Bourdieu. Thus we shall look, on the one hand, at analyses of modernization and postmodernization in society. And, on the other, at whether Bourdieu's theory itself can be characterized as modernist or postmodernist. On this count it would seem that his repeated professions of scientificity would place Bourdieu firmly in the modernist camp. I shall argue, however, much the contrary. That is, I shall argue that the power/knowledge assumptions which form the very basis of Bourdieu's conceptual framework place him much closer to Foucault and the postmodernist end of the theoretical spectrum.

This said, the chapter divides into four parts. The first and second parts look at the process of modernization in Bourdieu's work. They do so via his notion of the 'field'. Here I argue that Bourdieu's fields are very much like Weber's economic, aesthetic, political, etc. 'life orders' (*Lebensordnungen*). And that modernization is a process of the progressive differentiation of these fields from an initial unity in traditional societies. Bourdieu speaks of a number of fields: of, for example, an aesthetic field, a legal field, a political field, a cultural field, a field of education, and a religious field. Each of these fields is conceived on the lines of a 'market', with producers and consumers of the symbolic goods produced in the field. For example the field in art consists of painters, purchasers of art works, as well as critics, museum curators, and the like. The point is that the process of modernization and differentiation is also one of the autonomization of fields. That is, in modern societies the various fields have their own autonomous logics of development. In modernization they take on what Weber called a certain *Eigengesetzlichkeit* (self-legislation).

The third section of the chapter takes leave of Bourdieuan modernism to consider his accounts, explicit or implicit, of traditional and of postmodern society. Here we see that in traditional society, power operates according to the principles of a sort of action theory, in which one social actor exercises power over another. While in modern society, power is conceived on the lines of a structuralism, in which it is impersonal structures that exercise power over individuals. If modernization is characterized by the differentiation of Bourdieu's fields, then postmodernization, we shall see, would be characterized by their de-differentiation. And the pervasion of such a principle of de-differentiation presumes a new set of social actors, the new, post-industrial middle classes whose interests are furthered by such a process.

The fourth and final section takes leave of society to look at the realm of theory. It does so via Bourdieu's critique of structuralism and his considerations of reflexivity. Here we see that Bourdieu criticizes structuralism for its assumptions, not of too little, but of too much scientific objectivity. And that his view of reflexivity, unlike that of, say, Habermas, presupposes reflections, not on the content of a scientific proposition or a social norm, but on the position in social power relations of the actors responsible for the creation of that norm or proposition. In both cases Bourdieu's assumptions of the linkages of knowledge to power place him, I shall contend, rather firmly in the camp of, not the structuralists but the poststructuralists, of not the modernists but the postmodernists.

MODERNIZATION: MARKETS AND FIELDS

The notion of a 'cultural economy' informs pretty much the whole of Pierre Bourdieu's sociology of culture. Bourdieu is, as I shall suggest below, importantly a sociologist of modernization. As such he works from a sort of dichotomy of traditional and modern societies, the former based on his anthropological studies in Algeria. An economic heuristic informs his analyses of both traditional and modern societies; traditional societies being understood in the unmediated exchange of gifts, and modern societies in terms of exchanges mediated by markets. Bourdieu's articles on markets preceded by a few years his pieces on 'fields'. The work on markets was very concentrated around the early 1970s, at about the time of appearance of *Outline of a Theory of Practice*. The work on fields, apart from the very early *Temps modernes* piece, is more prevalent from the mid 1970s to the present.[2] The work on fields is of course key in the context of the issue of structure vs. agency because the fields *are* Bourdieu's structures. The markets, while not identical with fields, provide a skeleton framework for the latter. So let us look a bit more closely at the markets before we go on to the fields.

Key to the work on markets are considerations of change in the world religions and in painting. Bourdieu in the early 1970s was much influenced by Weber's sociology of religion. He recast, in a piece published in English only in 1987, Weber's model of religious change in the framework of cultural markets. Thus Weber's (bureaucratic) priests and (charismatic) prophets are producers of 'symbolic goods' competing for consumers among the 'laity'.[3] In this we already have the three elements of the economy of culture: (1) the supply-side or the producers of cultural goods, (2) the symbolic goods or products themselves, and (3) the demand-side, the consumers of cultural goods. The symbolic goods produced here will only have much of a chance of realizing their value if they stand in a relation of 'elective affinity' to the consumers; that is, to their ideal and material interests. Bourdieu's re-working of Weber keeps intact the Weberian conceptualization of social change via the struggle between bureaucratic priests and charismatic prophets for the allegiance of the socially stratified masses.

I think the benchmark statement on the cultural economy was published in 1971, 'Le marché des biens symboliques'. In this article on painting, Bourdieu explicitly follows the Weberian sociology of religion paradigm. The prophets are the modernist and proto-modernist painters in late nineteenth-century France. The priests of course are the academic painters. In this piece Bourdieu also introduces the institutions of culture as a part of symbolic production. The institutions of art here are 'instances of conservation and consecration'.[4] The Academie Française on this count he notes is similar to (Weber's bureaucratic) church. The institutions include museums, newspaper critics, dealers/gallery owners, and the art colleges. Orthodox painters and avant-garde 'heresiarchs' in this are in competition for the consecration of the institutions. Such symbolic markets for artistic goods and their corresponding 'fields' do not exist in traditional, 'un-differentiated' societies, but only come to exist with differentiation in the process of modernization. That is, in major part, modernization for Bourdieu – and again Weber's conception in 'Politics as a Vocation', 'Science as a Vocation', and the methodological articles on the world religions serve as a model – lies in the differentiation and autonomization of fields. It is fair to say that Bourdieu's fields (the scientific field, the political field, intellectual field, and so on) are more autonomous from class interests than Althusser's superstructures (and indeed Althusser is quoted more often in this context by Bourdieu than Weber) but possess less autonomy, i.e. a smaller degree of *Eigengesetzlichkeit* than Weber's '*Lebensordnungen*'.[5]

Now this very autonomization means for Bourdieu that in one given area there are two 'fields of production'. There is on the one hand the 'de-limited (*restreinte*) field of production' and, on the other, the 'large-scale field of production'. The delimited field of production is co-extensive with the specialized field itself, while large-scale production is for the broader 'social field'. In the delimited field, production is for the other 'producers', i.e. the agents and institutions in the field. That is, in the delimited field the supply-side is also, and at the same time, the demand side.[6] In the art field of late nineteenth-century Paris, then, in the delimited field, bohemians of the avant-garde made paintings for other bohemian and avant-garde painters. Others in this delimited market include academic and avant-garde galleries, museums, and magazines, and catalogues, as well as academic painters. The critics, the galleries, the museum catalogues consecrate certain types of art through their powers of 'nomination'.[7] They thus have the power to 'name' schools of art, to impart value to them, and to impose these nominations in an act of 'symbolic violence' on the ordinary consumers in the wider social field. The delimited field thus consists of agents and institutions and involves three types of struggle – those between 'makers' of art (between, say, makers of consecrated art, makers of avant-garde, heretical art, and makers of 'middle brow' art (*'art moyen'*) such as photography, cinema, and jazz, which also is struggling for consecration by the institutions), those between makers and 'marketers' (in essence the institutions), and those between marketers.[8]

What mediates between the de-limited artistic field (and the other properly cultural fields) and the large social field, in other words what mediates between the field of production and consumption, is for Bourdieu the education system. Unlike the institutions of art which help produce cultural objects, the education system produces not cultural objects, but consumers of art to match the cultural products. That is the education system produces a 'habitus', in this case an 'art habitus'.[9]

What is inculcated in education for consumers of art is on the reception side and is a set of classificatory schema which enables the consumer to 'decipher' the work of art. This is a set of codes which deal not only with the formal aspects of a work of art but also with its iconography and iconology. The more developed the art habitus, Bourdieu writes, the more finely one can classify.[10] If modernization entails the differentiation of an autonomous aesthetic field, then the appreciation of the (modern) art that this brings about entails the inculcation of a 'differentiated' habitus. The visitor to an art museum without any such training or differentiated habitus uses the classifications with which he/she perceives every-day reality to perceive the work of art.[11] Thus his/her appreciation of perhaps a landscape, but the dismissal of, say, a Pollock or Mondrian.

The field of artistic production is, like other fields, relatively autonomous from the social field. Note here that Weber's religious field was also only relatively autonomous. Productive interests in the artistic field would find 'homologies' with class interests in the social field. Because the popular classes are in most cases effectively excluded, on account of relatively undifferentiated cultural capital, from even the large-scale social field of artistic production, the interests which pertain here are those of the two main fractions of the dominant class: the bourgeoisie and the intellectuals. The former tend to have homologies, that is be the relevant consumers of (or have an elective affinity with) the productions of 'consecrated artists' (priests), while the intellectuals have homologies with the avant-garde or *'artistes maudits'*.[12] Striking in this context is the recent massive influx of members of both fractions of the dominant class (and even considerable numbers of petits bourgeois) into the delimited field of cultural production itself. Consider the increasing employment in newspaper and magazine journalism, television (especially with de-regulation), the music industry, part- and full-time musicians, video and advert production, commercial and community arts organization, expanding number of museum employees, and the like. The de-limited field is itself now forming a mass market. Hence the success of 'specialist' broadcasts on, for example, Britain's innovative Channel Four.

STRUGGLES FOR MODERNIST AUTONOMIZATION

Just how Bourdieu's fields (and markets) work can be encapsulated in the following statements. (1) The specific and differentiated fields are sites of collective symbolic struggles and individual strategies. (2) The aim of such strategies and struggles is to produce (or be associated with the production of, in the case of institutions and marketers) valuable cultural goods. (3) The value of a symbolic good depends upon the value which is assigned to it by the relevant consumer community. (4) These value judgements are in most fields determined by the amount of symbolic capital that the producer (or producers) has accumulated. (5) Victory in a symbolic struggle means that one's symbolic goods have been judged to possess more value than those of one's competitors. (6) The fruits of such victory is the right to impose one's symbolic goods on the social field; that is, to exercise symbolic violence on – and this entails the complicity of those subject to such violence – the 'consumers' in the social field.

How much 'relative autonomy'?

Let us unpack these propositions in terms of the various fields and then scrutinize their implications. The above paragraph describes what is constant across the whole range of Bourdieuan fields. The central axis of their variation is their degree of autonomy. Bourdieu is not entirely consistent in his assessment of just what this autonomy is from. At points it is from the dominant classes in the 'field of power' (e.g. in *Homo Academicus*). At points it is from the entirety of the social field. The degree of such autonomy is neatly captured by Bourdieu via the economic heuristic. The more autonomous a field is, the greater the extent to which production in that field is only for other producers and not for consumers in the social field (or field of power).[13] Thus the most autonomous of fields is the scientific field. The academic field and artistic field (high culture) occupy rather intermediate positions, autonomy in the former being from the field of power and in the latter from consumers in the social field. Still less autonomous is the legal field. And least autonomous, and the relevant field here is the social field (all classes in the social field), is the political field.

Struggles and strategies in the fields have at stake not just the value of symbolic goods but also the degree of autonomy of a given field. For example as the scientific field emerged historically from the religious field, some agents struggled against others for such autonomization.[14] In general, 'prophets' tend to gain by the autonomization of fields, while 'priests' stand to lose. Thus the various 'secession' movements in the arts (Paris, Berlin, Vienna) struggled for autonomy from the field of power, while those associated with the 'academies' struggled against it. Or in the academic field, the 'priests' associated with the *Ecole nationale d'administration* (ENA), the Sorbonne, the *Foundation nationale des sciences politiques*, the aggrégation, and the teaching and reproduction function have tended to struggle against autonomization from the field of power. In contrast the 'prophets' of *L'Ecole des hautes études en sciences sociales, the doctorat du troisième cycle,* and research and cultural production have struggled for autonomy.[15] The scientific field is the paradigm case of autonomy. The more a field is autonomous from the social field and field of power, the more, Bourdieu notes, the field speaks the language of science. This is the logic of 'true and false' instead of the 'friend/foe' logic of the field of power.[16] Yet the main stake in the scientific field, according to Bourdieu, is not the production of valid statements but the 'socially recognized capacity to speak and act legitimately'. That is at the same time the power of imposition of the definition of science; that is, the power to draw the limits of the field, to decide who is in and who is out. The stake then is the 'monopoly' of 'scientific competence' or 'authority'.[17] If these are the fruits of victory, then what is the path to victorious symbolic struggle? It is not, at least not in the first instance, the formulation of clear, precise, and coherently related propositions backed up by sufficient evidence and argument. It is instead the accumulation of 'scientific capital'. The latter is less a cultural capital of scientific competences than a symbolic capital, based on the prestige of the university one went to, the graduate school, one's references, one's membership on prestigious editorial boards, grant committees, and institutes.[18] The sort of habitus which, it seems, would enable this sort of accumulation is one not primarily structured by scientific competence but one attuned to the accumulation of symbolic capital. Bourdieu argues, however, that such a state of affairs would tend, not to impede, but to promote 'scientific progress'. Why? First, because the competition of 'priests' with 'conservation' strategies, and 'prophets' with 'subversion strategies', for scientific symbolic capital tends to encourage innovation. Second, because of the inculcation of scientific cultural capital, in the form of scientific method, which used in an agent's own selfish interests helps promote cross-control of results.[19] Scientific truth then is relegated to the place of an unintended consequence of the instrumental (and not substantive) rationality of agents in the economy of scientific practice.

Bourdieu scores some penetrating insights into legal practice in his consideration of the forms of autonomy of the juridical field. Its comparative absence of autonomy is underscored by the very absence of 'prophets' in the field. The centrality of hierarchical institutions in this field (and its closeness to the field of power) means that collective struggles will be between classes of 'priests' safely ensconced in institutions.[20] Two of the main protagonists here are the 'professors' and the 'judges'. The professors have an interest in autonomization and the elaboration of a 'pure theory of law' à la Hans Kelsen. The judges are closer to the power field of the 'friend versus foe' relation between litigants. British notions of equity and fair play are evidence not of a modernized, but of a traditional, undifferentiated legal system, in that equity and fair play are the language of the field of power, of friend versus foe. If Britain is the paradigmatic country of the judges, Germany is probably that of the professors.

But the general trend in most countries is that of legal modernization, and hence the 'professorial' transformation of the friend versus foe logic of the power field into the true/false logic of the autonomous scientific field.[21] This displacement imparts to law a certain universality which gives to it symbolic efficacy in removing, or at least concealing, its arbitrariness. At stake in the legal field is 'the right to say the law', which is an 'act of nomination'. Acts of nomination are at the same time acts of 'classification'. And the means by which agents in the legal field can obtain this stake is through the accumulation of symbolic-legal capital, mostly in the form of institutional positions.[22]

Whereas statements in the autonomous scientific field are descriptive statements, legal utterances are performatives in their very effects of power over the social.[23] This power is of course symbolic power. What is then the demand-side (in the social) of the large-scale field of juridical production? It is on the one hand among the *'profanes'* who consume legal services in their litigation struggles. And on the other hand the less litigious masses among the laity who are complicit in their belief in the universality of these legal symbols.

The political field is the least autonomous of fields. This means that it is furthest from the logic of true/false and must speak the friend/foe vernacular. It means most of all for Bourdieu that the value of political products is largely determined outside of the political field.[24] But even the political market tends to increase in autonomy from the social field during the process of modernization – the Michelsian oligarchic mass party was one step in this direction; its recent supersession by politics as presentation through the media is a further step.[25] Yet it is still the least autonomous of fields. The value then of a political product (produced of course by the professionals in the political field) is dependent on two factors: (1) the symbolic capital of the political agent and his/her party (political-symbolic capital includes the holding of party posts and the holding of local and less major national offices; its maximization entails hyperconformity to social norms)[26] and (2) the extent to which these political symbols (Bourdieu likens them to 'signifiers') corresponds to the interests and central meanings ('signifieds') of stratified consumers in the social.[27] Note the similarity of this to 'elective affinities' in the religious field.

246

What are these political products? They are symbolic products or in some sense 'signifiers' and include 'positions, programmes, analyses, commentaries, concepts, and events' produced by the professionals (including journalists and psepholologists, etc.) of the field. These political symbols have three functions *vis-à-vis* their relevant 'reception classes' in the social world. They are (i) instruments of perception, (ii) instruments of expression, and (iii) instruments of mobilization.[28] Instruments of mobilization are crucial for class formation. Though, structurally, classes already exist through 'objective relations' in the social field, what Bourdieu calls 'empirical classes' do not yet exist. They instead have to be 'made', formed into working class parties and trade unions, and this entails the work of professionals from the political field.

TRADITION AND POSTMODERNITY

What Bourdieu means by modernization and modernity is clarified through consideration of his analysis of traditional, tribal societies. His model here comes of course from his early anthropological studies of Kabylia in Algeria. As in modern societies, in traditional societies interaction operates via exchanges, and indeed, as in modern societies, via symbolic exchanges. Only these exchanges are mediated by the 'market' in modernity, while they are unmediated in tribal societies. Four of the most significant exchanges in traditional societies for Bourdieu are: (1) gifts, (2) injury, (3) wives, and (4) land.

The first two of these follow the logic of Marcel Mauss's gift. The most significant gifts in Kabylia were those given for weddings, births, and circumcisions. If the receiver of the gift cannot respond in due time with a 'counter-gift' (counter gifts cannot be given too soon after gifts, because this would imply a logic of calculation which would deplete the symbolic force of the exchange) then the giver is in a position of creditor and the receiver in one of debtor. And the creditor would hold 'symbolic power' over the debtor. The creditor's honour or symbolic capital would have undergone 'expanded reproduction', while the debtor's symbolic capital would have experienced 'disaccumulation'. The exchange of injuries occasions a not dissimilar cycle, but this time one of offence and riposte. When a challenge has not, at a certain point in time, been countered by a riposte, then the person who has suffered injury has come under the symbolic power of the challenger. And the latter stands as a 'creditor' in relation to him.[29]

Both the cycle of gifts and of offence and revenge are aimed at the preservation or accumulation of symbolic capital. Exchange of women and land partly are motivated by economic profit, though symbolic profit is the prime objective. The difference is partly that gifts and the offence–vengeance cycle are routes to intragenerational mobility, while exchanges of women and wives have more to do with intergenerational mobility. Symbolic capital has a much more central place in traditional than in modern societies. In tribal societies lineages commonly subordinate their material to their symbolic interests. For example, if one branch of a lineage puts up some 'core land' (i.e. land of substantial symbolic meaning for the lineage's patrimony) for sale, another branch will buy it instead of some more fertile outlying land in order to maintain intact the honour (or symbolic capital) of the lineage. Or material profits involved in the break-up of the landholdings of a lineage would be sacrificed to the symbolic profits associated with keeping the lineage's patrimony intact.[30]

In much of his treatment of Kabylia Bourdieu is loath to speak of symbolic capital at all. He rather speaks of 'honour'. Bourdieu writes, for example, that the habitus in traditional societies enables the agent to 'produce all the practices and judgments of honour'. That the 'sense of honour' is a 'permanent disposition, embedded in agents' very bodies'. That not the obedience to rules, but the 'sense of honour' enables agents to 'engender all the practices consistent with the logic of challenge and riposte'.[31]

Modernization as process

Consistent with a whole tradition in social theory, modernization according to Bourdieu is a process of differentiation. The first principle of this is that the universe of ideas in traditional societies is characterized by one single undisputed 'doxa', while in modern societies principles of 'heterodoxy' and 'orthodoxy' engage in struggle.[32] The immediate touchstone for this, as we noted above, seems to be Weber's logic of heterodox and charismatic 'prophets' versus orthodox and bureaucratic 'priests'. Only Weber, unlike Durkheim (conscience collective) and Bourdieu, speaks little of an original moment of doxa. The notion of heterodoxy versus orthodoxy as a 'motor' for modernization is integral to a theoretical genealogy which sees change as brought about by the tension of 'ought' versus 'is', whether in Hegel's tension between the universal and the particular, jurisprudence's counterposition of positive law and natural law, or Adorno's well known 'utopian moment'.

What is the significance of this in Bourdieu's systematic sociology? The main principle of collective struggle in modernity (and in the fields), as we saw above, was that concerning heresy and orthodoxy. Hence without the existence of heterodoxy and orthodoxy, collective struggles diminish greatly in importance in traditional societies. The main Bourdieu categories of practice are 'struggles' and 'strategies'. Strategies have as aim the accumulation of (usually symbolic) capital. Struggles aim at power and the imposition of a set of heterodox or orthodox norms and symbols. In the absence of such competition, struggles are less likely to exist. In primitive societies, practice for Bourdieu must then primarily be about strategy. And indeed in much of his discussion of Kabylia (in his methodological writings) it is. Strategies concern usually the lineage, or individuals within the lineage. They are to maximize the lineage's accumulation of symbolic capital, and not primarily over principles of power over a whole society. In modernity, Bourdieu's individuals and families may have strategies, but his social 'classes' and 'groups' wage struggles. In this sense 'groups' are far less important in traditional society. Further, this conceptualization does proffer a mechanism for social change in modernity. It even offers a model for change in the direction of an increase in rationality. Thus traditional society assumes a 'universe of doxa'. But the struggle of heterodoxy and orthodoxy in modernity presumes a 'universe of discourse' and the necessity of 'legitimation'. Heterodoxy or heresy originally arises as opposed to doxa, which takes the shape of 'orthodoxy' to defend itself from the heretical challenge. As orthodoxy, it must systematize its precepts and legitimate them. So, in counterposition, must heterodoxy.[33] This opening for Habermas-like communicative rationality, however, is nipped in the bud by

Bourdieu's above-discussed imperative of the instrumentally rational accumulation of symbolic capital. It does, though, present a genuine model for substantive social change. What Bourdieu has in mind here is clearly not at all primarily the classificatory struggles concerning types of symbolic goods that form so much of the subject matter of *Distinction* (cf. also *Un art moyen*). What he means is fundamental change of the class order of a society. Indeed he says that the principle of 'heresy' enters a social formation either through cultural contact or through its indigenous class divisions.[34]

Bourdieu's theory of heterodoxy/orthodoxy also concerns the representations or habitus of social agents. As Durkheim and Mauss suggested, these 'practical taxonomies' are 'transformed, misrecognizable forms of the real divisions (age, class, gender) of the social order'. They are in traditional societies embodied in 'mythico-religious systems' such as rites of passage (age) and cosmetics and clothing (gender). In turn they 'contribute to the reproduction of order by producing . . . practices adjusted to those divisions'.[35] In the universe of doxa of primitive societies there is 'full correspondence of (such) mental structures' to doxa and thus a relatively undifferentiated habitus. In modernity, to leave space for the production and reception of heterodoxy, this full correspondence must no longer exist and the habitus becomes differentiated.

Postmodernism

I believe that Bourdieu's conceptual framework opens up the social-scientific study of postmodernism in several ways. The key to the analysis is that new entrants into both fractions of the dominant class as well as a number of petits bourgeois would be apposite reception classes for postmodernist culture. These would be mainly among the culture producers of the new middle classes. These groups would be involved in a 'demand-side' classificatory struggle with the more established members of the dominant classes whose aesthetic tastes would be for high modernist art. Mike Featherstone was the first, to my knowledge, to develop this argument. John Urry and I then broadened it and transformed it to make it the cornerstone of our chapter on postmodernism in *The End of Organized Capitalism*, especially by locating it within a framework of a book which is essentially a comparative political economy of advanced capitalist societies. This idea has also been developed by a number of urban sociologists and geographers.[36] The main points of the explanation that I would suggest are the following.

(1) The new entrants to the middle classes who are the audience for postmodernist culture are members of the post-industrial middle classes. The new middle classes of *industrial* capitalism produced symbols which helped realize the value of industrial commodities. The *post*-industrial middle classes produce symbols which help realize the value of other symbols.

(2) The post-modern culture which these social classes consume (e.g. in architecture and painting) is at the same time middle-brow culture (*art moyen*) and an avant-garde challenge to orthodox modernism. So the classificatory struggles involved both on supply and demand side here take a particularly complex form.

(3) These new classes are created on account of, and as conditions of, the accumulation of capital in the contemporary, post-industrial and post-Fordist era. There are several factors which directly connect postmodernism and the new mode of economic regulation. For example, shifts in the work ethic. Or the rise of 'specialized consumption'. Or the shift from 'producer capitalism' to consumer capitalism, in which, for example, the moment of distribution has come to assert itself versus the moment of production. But perhaps the most important element connecting economy and culture are the (new) classes themselves with their material (economic) and ideal (cultural) interests. One side of social class is thus economic, the other side symbolic, rather like the two sides of goods themselves. This sort of framework attributes a much greater importance to the real, existing economy than Bourdieu's own analyses.

(4) This plays itself out in spatial terms in the restructuration of the centre of our great cities and the creation of a large group of central-city dwelling 'yuppies' among the post-industrial middle classes. This arises first from the economic effects of the accumulation of capital. That is, post-industrial growth has brought about a second wave of 'tertiarization' of our cities, in which massive extension of office building has marked the 1980s, often in postmodern architecture. At the same time there has been

the renovation (cf. the also postmodern, 'heritage industry') of living quarters not far from these post-industrial central city districts. All of this is for economic reasons. But the new gentrification (or yuppification) is conditional on the existence of social agents, the 'gentrifiers' themselves, who have to choose to move into these areas.[37] Part of the reason they do so is cultural and has to do with the elective affinity of their habituses with postmodern culture. Hence economic growth and cultural change (post-Fordism and postmodernism) constitutes as it were the two sides of these new post-industrial urban middle classes.

(5) Postmodern culture seems to proclaim itself as an avant-garde at the same time as announcing that avant-gardes no longer exist. A Bourdieuan framework can help make sense of this in several ways:

(a) Reception of modernist culture necessitates a differentiated habitus and a sort of specialized cultural capital. The untrained eye from 'off the street' cannot apply the classification of every-day life to high modernist art. But postmodernist culture is often consumed, though differently (e.g. a film like *Robocop*), by both those (1) who use the categories of every-day life, and (2) those with the specialized classificatory frameworks who then see postmodernism in terms of transgression of modernist conventions.

(b) If modernization means the differentiation of fields, postmodernization means at least the partial collapse of some fields into other fields. For example, as I just indicated, the implosion of the aesthetic field into the social field. Or, with 'commodification', the collapse of the aesthetic field into the economic field.

(c) There has developed in the past decade or two a mass audience for previously specialized cultural forms. Part of this results from the explosion of the student population, which is now a 'morphological factor' in the social field.[38] So are the very large numbers now working in the culture industries. This makes up such a large audience that the de-limited field of cultural production is no longer de-limited. This implies that heterodoxy or avant-gardes are, so to speak, merged into the mass audience. That avant-gardes of culture producers are not necessarily ahead of audiences or the demand-side because the latter itself is now a mass of culture producers.

(d) The avant-garde was always opposed to the 'academy'. Now it seems to have become collapsed back into the academy. Especially with the development of the European new universities and expansion of the human sciences from the 1960s. Much of the 'new academy' has comprised, as Bourdieu maintains, downwardly mobile bourgeois, 'poorly endowed with academic capital', who otherwise would have been excluded from the academy.[39] But these latter in their occupation of positions in the academic field, as university teachers and as students, have provided a sort of *bas-clergé* for the new institutions and subjects, and have been important institutional mediators for the pervasion, previously of Marxism and now of postmodernism, in the intellectual field. Again this is partly 'middle brow', partly sophisticated high-cultural, but surely not avant-garde.

(6) The reception of postmodernist culture is associated not only with a new type of habitus, but with a characteristically 'de-centred' habitus, in which classificatory schema can be loose and boundaries blurred. Hence the social positions of the university's new class that Bourdieu describes in *Homo Academicus* are 'ill defined' and have their 'future surrounded with an aura of indeterminacy and vagueness' which 'allows students to perpetuate as long as possible . . . an indeterminacy of social identity'. Bourdieu likens this to 'the professions of writer or artist', and notes that these agents often find places in the 'new professions' 'on the frontiers of the intellectual or the university field'.[40] The postmodern obsession with 'surfaces' could also link to the more general and growing indeterminacy of the middle classes who need to put on a Goffman-like front in order to impose their 'nominative powers'.[41]

(7) Finally the Bourdieu thesis which views modernization as a shift from the primacy of agency to that of structure is paralleled by the debates within contemporary architecture. In these, for example, Peter Eisenman sees the premodern in terms of (classical) Ancient and not archaic tribal societies. But here, similarly,

Ancient architecture is humanist and modern architecture structuralist.[42] Postmodernism in this context endorses a new humanism.

MODERNISM/POSTMODERNISM AS SOCIAL THEORY

Pierre Bourdieu, perhaps more than anyone, has contributed to making significant inroads on the problem of the relationship of structure and agency. The question that I should like to address is what are the implications of Bourdieu's standpoint on the structure/agency problem for issues of reflexivity, truth, and validity. The answer, we shall see, is that Bourdieu's position on these matters is a far cry from Habermas's universalistic modernism. It is instead much closer to the postmodern-type power/knowledge assumptions of Foucault. In terms of setting up his particular theoretical perspective, Bourdieu's reactions to structuralism have been more crucial than his response to action theories. Let us note at the outset that Bourdieu's anti-structuralism is vastly different from other such critiques. He does not, as does, say, Jon Elster, challenge structuralism for its putative functionalism. Indeed Bourdieu is wont to speak of functions or their functional equivalent. Equally any body of work, such as Bourdieu's, to which the process of reproduction is so central, leaves itself open to attacks as functionalist. But I do not think that Bourdieu's particular type of functionalism is open to Elster's criticisms. Elster's critique of functionalism is largely based on the latter's absence of an 'explanatory mechanism' between the structure at issue and its reproduction-enabling effects.[43] Bourdieu goes a long way to remedying this defect in his treatment of actual practices in his structure (fields). Equally, Bourdieu's complaints about structuralism are not couched in moral arguments about human freedom, which is surely the argument against structuralism that one was most accustomed to in the 1970s.

Bourdieu's critique of structuralism seems to have three central components. The first is against structuralism's putative 'objectivism'. This is not unconnected with Bourdieu's objections to elitism in French higher education. Philosophy and later social-science structuralism à la Lévi-Strauss are seen by Bourdieu to be, in their 'objectivism', somehow *au dessus de la mêlée.* Bourdieu notes that philosophers such as Althusser and Foucault followed Lévi-Strauss (Canguilhem was a model here) in their valuation of objectivist scientificity. For Bourdieu the social scientist is as involved in the mêlée of every-day life as any other social actor. This means 'immediate investment' in the practices of every-day life inside of the university, instead of the elitist adoption of an objectivist and 'presidential' stance. It also means subscription to Foucaultian power/knowledge assumptions that are difficult to square with demands for modernist universalism.[44]

This first critique of structuralism thus concerns the subject and not the object of sociological investigation. It is of enormous importance to Bourdieu, as evidenced in the considerable work involved in *Homo Academicus,* his recent articles on the Grandes Ecoles, and his work in general on the school system and the intellectual field. That is, in his work concerning modern society, the major critique of structuralism is not so much one of the relative weights of structure versus agency in the social world, but regarding the absence of objectivity, free-floatingness, transcendence in scientific and intellectual work. Seen in the perspective of free will versus determinism, this means paradoxically that scientists, intellectuals, and artists have less and not more free will than on the structuralist model. That is, we are only producers in an economy of symbolic goods like any others. And we are thus subject to the constraints of these symbolic markets. Ironically, Bourdieu's action theory means we human scientists are more constrained by structures than in Lévi-Strauss's or Althusser's structuralism.

Bourdieu's second criticism of Lévi-Strauss is that he misses the very specific nature of the exercise of power in traditional societies. In traditional societies, before the differentiation of fields, symbolic power is exercised intersubjectively. This has been noted by sociologists from Weber – in his contrast of traditional and legal-rational domination – through Parsons's pattern variables. Lévi-Strauss misses all this by reading power into structures even in traditional society. Lévi-Strauss reads then a very modernist Kelsenian 'legalism' into pre-modern societies and hence misses their very characteristic form of power relations.[45]

In tribal (and perhaps feudal) societies the exercise of power necessitates the day-to-day work of symbolic violence through obligations and the incurrence of debts created by (a) the fit and (b) the protection that the superordinate offers the subordinate. This includes the complex and continuous 'weaving of affective bonds'. In modern societies, by contrast, direct symbolic violence between subjects declines. Instead, institutions reproduce domination. 'Mechanisms in fields' 'assure their own reproduction by their very functioning'. Power passes from persons to 'titles', to occupational 'places', to 'things'.[46] If *subjects* exercise symbolic violence in traditional societies, fields or *structures* produce symbolic goods and hence exercise symbolic violence in modernity. A number of other social theorists as well have attributed power to structures in modernity. In this sense methodological individualist analyses of power wildly miss the point. For Marx power of course was not in the capitalist but in (the means of production as) capital over the labourer. For Althusser, power lies in all of the structures. For Foucault, in discourse. For Baudrillard, in the 'mediascape'.

But Bourdieu's notion of structure (partly because it *includes* agency) in modernity has a number of advantages over these other analysts. This concept of structure is particularly difficult to grasp because it appears not once but twice. First, there are the structures as objective relations between agents (possessed with the three types of capital) in the fields. Second, the fields themselves function as structures. It is the former, 'objective relations', which give shape to both the habitus and the fields. In so doing, they, so to speak, structure the structures. Thus the objective relations immediately fulfil two roles. They (1) determine the habitus and (2) are the basis of the empirical interactions in the fields. This empirical interaction takes place largely along the lines of the symbolic economy in the de-limited fields of production. The empirical interaction in the fields then produces an outcome, i.e. the symbolic object which will have effects of symbolic power on the social field. It is the entire field which produces this outcome, which is then an effect of the field or structure. Hence it is the *structure* which has effect on the 'laity' in the social field in the symbolic economy of the 'large-scale field of production'. In this the structure constitutes the supply-side and individuals in the social field comprise the demand-side. Bourdieu's critique of Lévi-Strauss is powerful. It shows that pre-modern power takes place via a set of unmediated exchanges between subjects, while modern power stems from a relationship between fields (whose symbolic economy imparts to them their structure) and the 'consumer' who is subject to this power.

Bourdieu's third challenge to structuralism concerns its empirical inadequacy in the investigation of traditional societies. This involved his formative experience as a young anthropologist. Lévi-Strauss, Bourdieu notes, took Mauss's notion of the gift – which concerned an exchange between subjects – and turned this exchange into a structure, into a 'constructed object' which then assumed the status of an 'unconscious principle'. In doing so, Bourdieu continues, Lévi-Strauss skates over the 'temporal nature' and cycle of reciprocity involved in symbolic exchanges and the hard empirical reality of symbolic power that creditor exercises over debtor.[47]

Crucial for Bourdieu's challenge was his observation in Kabylia that Lévi-Strauss's principle of exogenous marriages did not hold. Instead the rule was rather of parallel-cousin marriage (father's brother's daughter). But even this rule was broken under certain conditions. Bourdieu concluded that the point was not to look, as structuralists did, for the rule, but instead for the 'strategy'. On the one hand, exogenous marriages (for example cross-cousin marriage, i.e. mother's brother's daughter) can strengthen alliances – that is, help build a network of affines, and perhaps bring a prestigious maternal uncle into the lineage. On the other, there were a number of different meanings for parallel-cousin marriage. It could, for example, solidify the lineage. It could have the objective of keeping the lineage's property from being divided. It might save the honour of a father's brother who is otherwise unable to marry off his daughter. In the case of a father's brother who has no sons, it keeps the father's brother's descendants in the lineage.[48]

In some cases Bourdieu speaks of individual strategies intended to reinforce one's own position within the lineage. For example, he gives a number of cases of brotherly rivalry in patrilineal, patrilocal, and patriarchal Kabylia. Or of the mother who promotes cross-cousin marriage so that a new member of her own lineage can be brought into her adopted one, so that she will be less of an outsider in the latter. But most of the strategies are those of the lineage itself. It is the lineage which rests on a 'community of dispositions and interests' and has common 'ownership of the material and symbolic patrimony'.[49] The point Bourdieu makes versus structural anthropology is that it is not the marriage rule (or genealogy) that counts, but the economic and political strategies of the lineage. Even where informants invoked the 'rule' of parallel cousin marriage it was mostly as a 'second order strategy'. That is, they were conscious of the rule, and rather than following it out of obligation, they were using it for their own benefit, as a sort of 'officializing' or 'universalizing' strategy in order to 'cloak themselves in legitimation'. Bourdieu wonders how structural anthropologists could be seduced into positing the existence of the rule when informants were just using it as a strategy.[50] And all of these strategies of course were through exchanges to maximize the lineage's accumulation of symbolic and material capital.

Reflexivity and validity

No pure theory of structure or pure theory of agency can have a notion of reflexivity. Reflexivity assumes (1) a subject, (2) an object, and (3) a medium of reflection. Theories of reflexivity differ to the extent that these three parameters vary.

(a) The reflecting subject can be an individual, a social class, an entire society. If an individual it can be *inter alia* an intellectual, an artist, a scientist, a sociologist.
(b) The object can be the norms which structure society, or the norms which structure a part of society. The object can be symbolic. It can be aesthetic or ethical. It can be the products of knowledge of, for example, sociology.
(c) The medium of reflection is usually either consciousness or language.

Hence, for example, in Habermas it is a speech community which reflects through language primarily on social or ethical norms. For Lukács, class subjects reflect through consciousness on the social. In Giddens, reflection is largely on social rules.

One thing that all these writers hold in common is that reflexive action is only possible in modernity. And that in modernity (probably Giddens is clearest in this statement) social actors can take cognizance of, and reflect rationally on, rules that had previously been only implicit for them. This of course opens up possibilities of positive social change. Of Weber's four types of action, only *zweckrational* and *wertrational* were characteristically modern. The implication is that the modern actor is capable of formulating and reflecting on his/her means and ends of action, which was impossible in traditional action, structured by unreflective convention. Weber's 'ethics of responsibility' (and its subsequent neo-Weberian formulations) are also exemplifications of reflective action in which the demands of the different *Lebensordungen* are weighed and assessed.

Reflexivity can also mean the reflection of the subject on the subject itself. This is true in Hegel's *Selbstbewusstsein*. It also is at least implicit in Gouldner's demand for a reflexive sociology heralded in *Coming Crisis*. Bourdieu's sort of reflexivity seems to be rather closer to this type. Hence the stated aim of *Homo Academicus* to 'classify the classifiers'. Reflexivity in this sense looks at the producers of knowledge. On Bourdieu's account these producers are most importantly understood through their habitus, and through their individual strategies and collective struggles. These strategies and struggles (and self-reflexivity) inhere in their structural position in three senses: (1) their position in the objective relations of the academic or sociological field, (2) their position and trajectory in the objective relations of the social field, (3) their position in the struggles between orthodoxy and heterodoxy which determine the output of structure in the academic/sociological field.

What are the implications of this for truth and validity? Bourdieu says in *Homo Academicus* that the idea is, not to render uncertain, but 'to make more secure the foundations of sociological thought'.[51] And that the *modus operandi* here should not be 'transcendental reflection' but through 'classifying the classifiers'. He maintains that the 'self-reflection of sociology' will lead to anti-relativism and to 'scientific profits'. He also says in a recent interview that the way to the 'universal' is not through 'foundations' but through 'reflexive critique'.[52]

How can we make sense of this? Given the assumption of self-interest and instrumental action built into Bourdieu's economics of symbolic practice, there are three routes to truth and universalism: (1) through the innovations of 'heterodoxy', (2) through cross-control by scientific method, (3) through the autonomization of the given field. He uses these elements effectively to speak of validity in the aesthetic field. Here he writes that with the succession of avant-gardes taking the place of established avant-gardes there is a certain *'épuration'* of poetry in which the latter is 'reduced' to its own 'proper materials'.[53] This sounds very much like Adornian 'aesthetic rationality'. Art that is too much tied to the field of power has little to worry about from avant-gardes. This is true also if 'cross-control' is separated from the field of power. Similar prescriptions would hold for sociology's 'self-reflexive critique'. These would be (1) to examine and criticize the openness of sociology to challenging heterodoxies, (2) to try to ensure the autonomization of sociology from the field of power, (3) to sharpen methods of cross-control. Is this what Bourdieu advocates? To what extent is this different from self-reflexivity as the prolonged and systematic reflection on the sociological habitus outlined just above? In one case or the other, these are prescriptions for the examination of the *producer* more than the product. Would not systematic critique of the descriptive utterances of sociology (i.e. of sociology's *products*) be a more promising way to truth and the universal?

Also, Bourdieu's presuppositions make it seem as if a rational way forward is more or less ruled out in the political field. Autonomous fields such as science and to a lesser extent art follow the 'logic of true and false' (valid and not valid). But the political field is inscribed with the logic of friend and foe. Here statements are not descriptive utterances but performatives. Here, unlike the scientific field, it is no great advantage to be 'armed with reason'. How, then, does the Bourdieu view of reflexive critique give any hope for a political future?

SUMMARY AND CONCLUSIONS

Pierre Bourdieu instructs us to 'classify the classifiers'. How, then, I wonder, might we thus, sociologically, classify Bourdieu? He might best, I suspect, be classified as riven by a set of social contradictions. Bourdieu is, on the one hand, the enemy of avant-gardes, the outsider flouting 'tout Paris', the sturdy opponent of aesthetes and trendy left politicos. This Bourdieu is the man of solid roots in the provincial *couches populaires*; the 'hands on' proletarian of research in an almost Anglo-American empirical mode. But Bourdieu is on the other hand very French, very Parisian, and as seductively avant-garde in sociology as Foucault, Lacan, Barthes, Lefebvre, Derrida, and Deleuze are for other academic disciplines. It is this second Bourdieu that this chapter has explored, or, more accurately, used in order better sociologically to understand modernization, modernism, and post-modernism.

What are then the main elements of such a theory present in the work of Bourdieu?:

(1) Tradition versus modernity

(i) In traditional society, power is exercised unmediatedly by one agent over another. Relationships of power are effectively 'exchange relationships', based on the indebtedness of subordinate agent to his/her superordinate. As for Nietzsche and for Mauss, for Bourdieu this relation of debt also determines status and cultural valuations and classifications. In modernity, power is exercised via the mediations of Bourdieu's fields, which are in effect structures. Cultural valuations (e.g. the social value attached to a work of art, a law, a scientific theory, a political policy) and classifications are then structurally determined by the fields.

(ii) Culture in traditional societies is structured by a single 'doxa'; while, in modernity, culture is a stake for which 'orthodoxy' and 'heterodoxy' do battle. In contrast to tradition's 'universe of doxa' stands modernity's 'universe of discourse', which presupposes that ideas must be legitimated in order to achieve hegemony, and hence presumes a certain autonomy of ideas from power relations.

(iii) Thus in Bourdieu's traditional society, like Hegel's Orient, stasis and not change is the rule. In modernity, social/cultural change is introduced through heterodoxy. Change also presupposes, à la Weber, the existence of (often emergent) social classes or class fractions whose ideal interests these heterodox values serve.

(iv) For Bourdieu the distinction between 'strategies' and 'struggles' is crucial. 'Strategies' are held by individuals as familiar. 'Strategies' aim at the accumulation of symbolic capital. Their goal is mobility and attainment of wealth, power, and status. 'Strategies' assume a given and static socio-cultural context. 'Struggles' are between collectivities – as supports of heterodoxy versus orthodoxy – and can lead to socio-cultural change. In traditional society (taken as ideal-type), there are only strategies. In modernity, both strategies and struggles figure importantly.

(2) Modernization

(i) Bourdieu's 'fields' are structures in which these strategies and struggles take place. Modernization is a process of the differentiation and autonomization of the 'de-limited fields' (*champs restreints*) – i.e. the legal, political, intellectual, artistic, academic, cultural, and religious fields – from the more general 'field of power'.

(ii) Modernization can only take place through struggles. The battles of heterodoxy against orthodoxy are not just for changes, but for the autonomization of a given field from the field of power. Thus they are struggles for modernization. In these struggles, Bourdieu generalizes the model from Weber's sociology of religion and speaks of avant-garde 'prophets' supporting heterodoxy and modernist autonomization in struggle versus bureaucratic 'priests' who support orthodoxy. The priests represent tradition and the field of power versus such autonomization. Note the Weberian, and even Nietzschean, notion of a 'charisma of creativity' implicit here, in which artists, scientists, and religious heroes are more or less interchangeable in the role of prophet.

(iii) The field of power operates from a Carl Schmitt-like logic of 'friend versus foe', while the autonomizing de-limited fields operate increasingly, along with modernization, on a logic of 'true versus false'. This true/false logic holds for the whole range of autonomizing fields, in the sense that aesthetic, scientific, normative, and legal statements can be understood as more or less valid. This (modernity) is obviously the (Habermas-like) 'universe of discourse'.

(iv) Modernization is not just a process of change in structure, it is also one of change in agency. Thus the Bourdieuan 'habitus' also undergoes a process of differentiation along with modernization. The cultural capital of such a modernized and differentiated habitus is capable of using differentiated classificatory schema to understand, say, the modernist work of art in terms of its own particular aesthetic conventions. The less differentiated, and more traditional, habitus perceives works of art in terms of the same visual classifications of every-day life.

(3) Modernism and Postmodernism

(i) Full modernity or complete modernism presupposes the absolute autonomy of fields. This never in fact takes place, in that the fields are always sites of struggle for the stake of more or less autonomization.

(ii) Post-modernization would be a process of de-differentiation and a reversal of autonomization. This includes a process of de-differentiation of fields or structures, and de-differentiation of agency, or the habitus. The latter comprises a partial breakdown or de-centring of the grid of classificatory rules which structure the habitus.

(iii) As in modernization, there are two 'motors' of postmodernization. The first lies in the emergence of new social classes as vehicles, both of production and reception, for the new postmodernist cultural forms. Key here is the development of the post-industrial middle classes, the cultural-capital based fraction of the bourgeoisie. In contemporary times, the cultural field of these symbol-producing middle classes undergoes such expansion, such 'mass-ification', that it begins to engulf or implode into the more general social field itself. The cultural field expands thus to such a point that it bursts through the barriers that had previously contained it as only a de-limited field.

(iv) The second motor of postmodernization lies in the development of a new sort of prophet, a new type of avant-garde. This new sort of avant-garde promotes, not heterodoxy and modernist autonomization, but orthodoxy and dis-autonomization. Thus postmodern architects such as Venturi and Denise Scott-Brown reject the experimentation of Corbusier and van der Rohe, and proudly claim that 'we like convention'. In this sense Martin Pawley has described postmodernism as 'an avant-garde leading from the rear'.

A parallel process of postmodernization has taken place in the realm of theory, in which the autonomization (whether relative or absolute) of structures and of theory itself has been under challenge. Hence Derrida's poststructuralism challenged the modernist and autonomous science of autonomous linguistic structures of Saussure and Barthes. And the Nietschean post-structuralism of Foucault's later ('genealogical') work broke with the scientistic study of autonomous structures of knowledge and discourse in his *Order of Things* and *Archaeology of Knowledge*. It is in this social-theoretical context that we can understand Bourdieu's effectively poststructural challenge to Lévi-Strauss's and Althusser's eminently modernist conceptions of scientific objectivity and autonomous structures. Bourdieu's epistemology, like the poststructuralists, grants only minimal autonomy to human-scientific practices from the field of power.

Equally running counter to modernist scientificity is, we have seen, Bourdieu's notion of reflexivity. Social scientists in this are instructed to reflect, not on the validity of statements and propositions, but on the social and power position of the producer of these statements. Attention is drawn thus not to the autonomous 'universe of discourse' and its logic of 'true versus false' but to the field of power and its logic of 'friend versus foe'.

Pierre Bourdieu's work is thus riven with contradiction indeed. He is one of the great proselytizers for the virtues of science; yet he challenges the autonomy and objectivity, and even the possibility of validity of scientific statements. The conditions of his social scientific success have been the denunciation of the Parisian intellectual avant-garde, which he is at the same time quite integrally part and parcel of. The Parisian poststructuralist avant-garde, in their rejection of the modernist autonomization of cultural practices, have functioned effectively as 'priests', though in the guise of prophets. In this the absence of any self-reflexivity on the part of these 'priests in drag' has been remarkable. Bourdieu in his self-conscious rootedness in the provincial popular classes, far away from Paris and avant-gardes, at least seems to know where he stands.

Ironically, Althusser's autonomous structures and optimistic scientific objectivity and Habermas's autonomized cultural realms and rational discourse are, in a significant sense, two halves of the same neo-Marxist and modernist equation. The power/knowledge critique of structuralism from French theoretical *post*modernism, must as it rejects Althusser, also reject Habermas. Professor Bourdieu's work is of great, great value and is one of my main sources of inspiration for the sociology of culture developed through the pages of this book. But the power/knowledge assumptions of his work do place him rather uncomfortably close to his post-structuralist prima-facie opponents. Both Bourdieu and the poststructuralists are somehow 'avant-gardes leading from the rear'. The difference is that the poststructuralists put themselves forth as heterodox prophets and turn out to be priests of convention. While Bourdieu's self-deprecatory claims to priesthood and orthodoxy turn out to be a cover for a very avant-garde sociology of culture. The only casualty along the way, and this is indeed a cause for distress, may be the modernist validity of social-scientific knowledge.

NOTES

CHAPTER ONE: POSTMODERNISM: TOWARDS A SOCIOLOGICAL ACCOUNT

1 T. Parsons, *The Structure of Social Action*, New York: Free Press, 1968, vol. 2, pp. 563 ff.

2 M. Weber, *Ancient Judaism*, New York: Free Press. 1967.

3 See, for example, R. Boyer (ed.), *La flexibilité du travail en Europe*, Paris: Editions de la Découverte, 1986.

4 J. Baudrillard, *In the Shadow of Silent Majorities*, New York: Semiotexte, 1983.

5 M. Weber, 'Religious rejections of the world and their directions', in H. Gerth and C. W. Mills (eds), *From Max Weber*, New York: Oxford University Press, 1946, pp. 323-62; M. S. Whimster and S. Lash, Introduction to id. (eds), *Max Weber, Rationality and Modernity*, London: Allen & Unwin, 1987, pp. 1-33.

6 J. Habermas, *Theorie des kommunikativen Handels*, Frankfurt am Main: Suhrkamp, 1981.

7 G. W. F. Hegel, *On Art, Religion, Philosophy*, New York: Harper & Row, 1970.

8 Stuart Hall (ed.), *Resistance Through Rituals*, London: Hutchinson, 1976.

9 See, e.g., S. Heath, 'Narrative space', in id., *On Cinema*, London: Macmillan, 1981, pp. 19-75, 27-35.

10 D. Bordwell, *Narration in the Fiction Film*, Madison, Wisc.: University of Wisconsin Press, 1985.

11 Richard Rorty, *Philosophy and the Mirror of Nature*, Oxford: Blackwell, 1980.

12 Umberto Eco, *A Theory of Semiotics*, Bloomington, Ind.: Indiana University Press, 1976, pp. 66-72.

13 Clement Greenberg, 'Complaints of an art critic', in C. Harrison and F. Orton (eds), *Modernism, Criticism, Realism*, London: Harper & Row, 1984, pp. 3-8.

14 C. Schorske, *Fin-de-Siècle Vienna, Politics and Culture*, New York: Vintage, 1981; D. Bell, *Cultural Contradictions of Capitalism*, London: Heinemann, 1976; D. Frisby, *Fragments of Modernity*, Cambridge: Polity, 1985; T. Adorno, *Aesthetic Theory*, London: Routledge, 1984.

15 Martin Jay, 'Scopic regimes of modernity', in S. Lash and J. Friedman (eds), *Modernity and Identity*, Oxford: Blackwell, 1990.

16 See S. Heath, 'The cinematic apparatus: technology as historical and cultural form', in T. de Lauretis and S. Heath (eds), *The Cinematic Apparatus*, London: Macmillan, 1980, pp. 1–13.

17 F. Jameson, 'Postmodernism or the cultural logic of late capitalism', *New Left Review* 146, 1984, pp. 53–92.

18 S. Gablik, *Magritte*, London: Thames & Hudson, 1970.

19 N. Abercrombie, S. Lash, and B. Longhurst, 'The crisis of classic realism?', in S. Lash and J. Friedman (eds), *Modernity and Identity*.

20 See Annette Lavers, *Roland Barthes, Structuralism and After*, London: Methuen, 1982, pp. 59–70.

21 S. Lash, *The Militant Worker*, London: Heinemann, 1984, chs 1, 2.

22 M. Berman, *All that is Solid Melts Into Air*, London: Verso, 1983.

23 S. Lash and J. Urry, *The End of Organized Capitalism*, Cambridge: Polity, 1987.

24 J. E. Berendt, *The Jazz Book*, London: Paladin, 1984, pp. 240–3.

25 L. Mulvey, 'Visual pleasure and narrative cinema', in T. Bennett *et al.* (eds), *Popular Television and Film*, London: Open University, 1981, pp. 206–15.

26 See E. Durkheim and M. Mauss, *Primitive Classification*, Chicago: University of Chicago, 1967.

27 P. Bourdieu, *Distinction*, London: Routledge, 1984.

28 M. Tafuri, *The Sphere and the Labyrinth*, Cambridge, Mass.: MIT Press, 1987.

29 M. Featherstone, 'Lifestyle and consumer culture', *Theory, Culture and Society* 4(1), 1987, pp. 55–70.

30 T. De Lauretis, *Alice Doesn't*, London: Macmillan, 1984.

31 P. Bourdieu, *Ce que parler veut dire*, Paris: Fayard, 1982.

32 J. Stacey, 'Desperately seeking difference', *Screen* 28(1), 1987, pp. 48–61.

33 W. H. Walsh, *Kant's Criticism of Metaphysics*, Edinburgh: Edinburgh University Press, 1975.

34 S. Kern, *The Culture of Time and Space, 1880–1918*, London: Weidenfeld & Nicolson, 1983.

35 A. Kroker and D. Cook, *The Postmodern Scene*, New York: St Martin's, 1986.

36 See, F. Jameson, 'Reification and utopia in mass culture', *Social Text* 1, 1979, pp. 130–48.

37 D. Hebdige, *Subcultures*, London: Methuen, 1979.

38 B. Martin, *A Sociology of Contemporary Popular Culture*, Oxford: Blackwell, 1981.

39 S. Hood, 'John Grierson and the documentary film movement', in J.

Curran and V. Porter (eds), *British Cinema History*, London: Weidenfeld & Nicolson, 1983, pp. 99–112.

40 See P. Gourevitch *et al.*, *Unions and Economic Crisis: Britain, West Germany and Sweden*, London: Allen & Unwin, 1984.

41 A. Touraine, *Production de la société*, Paris: Seuil, 1973.

42 S. Beer, *Britain Against Itself*, London: Faber, 1982; K. Middlemas, *Politics in Industrial Society*, London: Andre Deutsch, 1979.

43 S. Huntington, 'The United States', in M. Crozier *et al.* (eds), *The Crisis of Democracy*, New York: New York University Press, 1975.

44 J.-F. Lyotard, *The Post-Modern Condition*, Manchester: Manchester University Press, 1984.

45 Examples of the former are the journals *Economic Geography* and *Environment and Planning D: Society and Space*; of the latter, commentators such as Tafuri, Aldo Rossi, Lewis Mumford, and Leon Krier.

46 See, e.g., D. Harvey, *Social Justice and the City*, London: Edward Arnold, 1973; M. Castells, *City, Class and Power*, London: Macmillan, 1978.

47 Aldo Rossi, *The Architecture of the City*, Cambridge, Mass.: MIT Press, 1982.

48 See, e.g., S. Zukin, *Loft Living*, London: Radius, 1988.

49 This paraphrases L. Mumford's description in *The City in History*, Harmondsworth: Penguin, 1966, pp. 313–23.

50 See E. Panofsky, *Meaning in the Visual Arts*, Chicago: University of Chicago Press, 1983.

51 Mumford, *City in History*, pp. 486 ff.

52 W. Benjamin, *Charles Baudelaire*, London: New Left Books, 1973.

53 See M. Tafuri and F. Dal Co, *Modern Architecture*, vol. 2, New York: Rizzoli, 1987.

54 Lash and Urry, *End of Organized Capitalism*, ch. 1.

55 O. Williamson, *The Economic Institutions of Capitalism*, New York: Free Press, 1985. Schmitter, Streeck, and Rogers Hollingsworth are editing two volumes on the governance of economic sectors, to be published by Sage, London.

56 M. Piore and C. Sabel, *The Second Industrial Divide*, New York: Basic Books, 1984.

57 See C. Offe, *Contradictions of the Welfare State*, London: Hutchinson, 1984.

58 I am indebted on these points to discussions with Martin O'Brien.

59 Baudrillard, *For a Critique of the Political Economy of the Sign*, St Louis, Mo.: Telos Press, 1981.

60 See A. Ellis and K. Kumar (eds), *Dilemmas of Liberal Democracies*, London: Tavistock, 1983.

61 C. Lasch, *The Culture of Narcissism*, London: Sphere, 1980.

62 See, e.g., Gunther Anders, *Die Antiquiertheit des Menschen, 2, über die Zerstörung des Lebens im Zeitalter der dritten industriellen Revolution*, Munich: Beck, 1987.

63 J. Gershuny, *After Industrial Society?*, New York: Humanities Press,

1978.

64 J. Urry, 'Cultural change and contemporary holiday-making', *Theory, Culture and Society* 5(1), 1988, pp. 35–56.

65 C. Offe, 'The future of the labour market', in id., *Disorganized Capitalism*, Cambridge: Polity, 1985, pp. 52–79.

66 See P. Hirst, *Law, Socialism and Democracy*, London: Allen & Unwin, 1986.

67 K. Marx, *Capital*, vol. 1, Harmondsworth: Penguin, 1976, p. 128.

68 Benjamin, 'The work of art in the age of mechanical reproduction', in id., *Illuminations*, London: Fontana/Collins, 1973, pp. 219–54.

69 M. Horkheimer and T. Adorno, *Dialectic of Enlightenment*, New York: Seabury Press, 1972, 120–67.

CHAPTER TWO: GENEALOGY AND THE BODY: FOUCAULT/DELEUZE/NIETZSCHE

1 I should like to thank Roy Boyne, Brian Longhurst, Georg Stauth and Mike Featherstone for their comments on a previous draft of this chapter.

2 This is made clear in Deleuze's contemporaneously delivered (1973) paper, 'Nomad thought', in which, of the 'three moderns', Nietzsche is pitted as a 'dawning of the counter culture' against 'Marxian' and 'Freudian bureaucracies'.

3 I shall draw extensively on *The Will to Power* in the following discussion. *The Will to Power* consists of material from Nietzsche's notebooks which were edited and published posthumously. These notebooks, which date from 1883 to 1889, contain the basis for most of Nietzsche's work after *Thus Spake Zarathustra*; i.e. for *Beyond Good and Evil*, *The Genealogy of Morals*, *The Antichrist*, and *Twilight of the Idols*. Ideas which are presented in a literary form in these latter works, often only through rhetorical hints, are spelt out and argued for in the notebooks. Because it was not Nietzsche himself who edited and published the notebooks, there are some, though arguably not major, problems with their validity. Thus I shall make no claims as to Nietzsche's concept of the body which are inconsistent with the published work of 1883 to 1889; indeed all the points I shall make are at least touched upon in this published work.

4 Deleuze adopts this notion of 'event' in *Logique du sens*; see above.

5 Let me emphasize at this point that I am not maintaining that most of Nietzsche's discussion of slave and noble moralities is carried out in terms of the body. A good deal of his discussion of moralities *is* phrased in such terms, however, and the rest of his treatment of moralities is consistent with such a conceptual framework. Equally, in this chapter I use the term 'body' much more frequently than Nietzsche, who, as I mentioned above, spoke in more general context, in which 'the organic', 'the organism', and 'physiology' play as great

a role as 'the body'. My usage of the body is in this section, nonetheless, consistent with Nietzsche's usage, as well as with his more general notions of 'the organic' and 'physiology'.

CHAPTER THREE: POSTMODERNITY AND DESIRE

1 Jürgen Habermas, 'Modernity versus postmodernity', *New German Critique* (22), 1981, pp. 3-14; J. Habermas, 'The entwinement of myth and enlightenment: re-reading and dialectic of the Enlightenment', *New German Critique* (26), Spring 1982, pp. 13-30. An earlier version of this paper was presented at the annual conference of the Swedish Sociological Association, in Örebro, in February 1984. May I thank Brian Longhurst and John Urry for their comments on and criticisms of this version.
2 J. Habermas, 'Neo-conservative culture criticism in the United States and West Germany: an intellectual movement in two political cultures', *Telos* (56), Summer 1983, pp. 75-89; Daniel Bell, *The Cultural Contradictions of Capitalism*, London: Heinemann, 1976. For criticism of Habermas see Andreas Huyssen, 'The search for tradition: avant garde and postmodernism in the 1970s', *New German Critique* (22), 1981, pp. 23-40; Peter Bürger, 'The significance of the avant-garde for contemporary aesthetics: a reply to Jürgen Habermas', *New German Critique* (22), 1981, pp. 19-22; Anthony Giddens, 'Modernism and postmodernism', *New German Critique* (22), 1981, pp. 15-18.
3 Habermas, 'Modernity versus postmodernity', p. 13; id., 'Neo-conservative cultural criticism', p. 89.
4 For a similar distinction, but with differing criteria, see, for example, Huyssen, 'The search for tradition'.
5 See, e.g. Vincent Descombes, *Modern French Philosophy*, Cambridge: Cambridge University Press, 1980; Sherry Turkle, *Psychoanalytic Politics, Jacques Lacan and Freud's French Revolution*, London: Burnett, 1979.
6 'Structuralism and post-structuralism: an interview with Michel Foucault', by Gerard Raulet, *Telos* (55), Spring 1983, pp. 195-211.
7 Michel Foucault, *Madness and Civilization, A History of Insanity in the Age of Reason*, London: Tavistock, 1967; M. Foucault, *Les mots et les choses, une archéologie des sciences humaines*, Paris: Gallimard, 1966. For the distinction between 'hermeneutics' and 'semiology' see Foucault, 'Nietzsche, Freud, Marx' in Cahiers du Royaumont, *Nietzsche*, Paris, Editions du Minuit, 1967. On non-discursive language and 'transgression' see, for instance, David Carroll, 'Disruptive discourse and critical power: the conditions of archaeology and genealogy', *Humanities in Society* 5(3,4), 1982, pp. 175-200. Also see C. Lemert and G. Gillan, *Michel Foucault: Social Theory as Transgression*, New York: Columbia University Press, 1982.

8 M. Foucault, 'Language to infinity', in id., *Language, Counter-Memory, Practice*, David Bouchard (ed.), Oxford: Blackwell, 1977, p. 54.
9 Ibid., p. 54.
10 Michel Foucault, *Surveillir et punir. Naissance de la prison*, Paris: Gallimard, 1975; M. Foucault, *Moi, Pierre Rivière*, Paris, 1973.
11 'Language to infinity', p. 59.
12 Ibid., pp. 62-3.
13 Ibid, p. 66.
14 Michel Foucault, 'A preface to transgression', in *Language, Counter-Memory, Practice*, pp. 29-52.
15 Ibid., p. 30.
16 Ibid., p. 33.
17 Ibid., pp. 30, 32.
18 Ibid., p. 48.
19 Ibid., pp. 34-5.
20 Ibid., p. 46.
21 Michel Foucault, 'La prose d'Acteon', *Nouvelle Revue Française* 135, 1964, pp. 444-59.
22 Ibid., p. 446.
23 Ibid., p. 448.
24 Ibid., p. 457.
25 Foucault, *Les mots et les choses*, pp. 394-5.
26 Edward Said, 'An ethics of language', *Diacritics* 4(2), 1974, pp. 28-37.
27 See Pamela Major-Poetzl, *Michel Foucault's Archaeology of Western Culture*, Brighton: Harvester, 1983, pp. 28-33.
28 Michel Foucault, *This Is Not a Pipe*, Berkeley: University of California Press, 1983, pp. 32-49.
29 S. Gablik, *Magritte*, Greenwich, Conn.: New York Graphic Society, 1971.
30 'Structuralism and poststructuralism', p. 204.
31 See discussion of e.g. Descombes, *Modern French Philosophy*.
32 M. Foucault, *The History of Sexuality*, New York: Vintage, 1980, pp. 81-4.
33 M. Foucault, 'Structuralism and post-structuralism', pp. 200-2; Letter from M. Foucault to S. Lash, 9 May 1984; A. Sheridan, 'Diary', *London Review of Books*, 19 July to 1 August 1984, p. 21.
34 See, for example, M. Bradbury and J. McFarlane (eds), *Modernism 1890-1930*, Hassocks, Sussex: Harvester, 1978; E. Gombrich, *Art and Illusion*, London: Phaidon, 1977.
35 Foucault, *Les mots et les choses*, pp. 388-93.
36 Sheridan, 'Diary'.
37 Jean-François Lyotard, *La condition postmoderne, rapport sur le savoir*, Paris: Editions de Minuit, 1979; J.-F. Lyotard, *Discours. figure*, Paris: Klincksieck, 1971.
38 See, e.g., J.-F. Lyotard, 'Freud selon Cézanne' in id., *Des dispositifs pulsionnels*, Paris: Christian Bourgois, 1980, pp. 67-88.

39 J.-F. Lyotard, 'La peinture comme dispositif libidinal', in *Des dispositifs*, pp. 227-68.
40 J.-F. Lyotard, 'Adorno comme diavolo', in *Des dispositifs*, p. 120.
41 Ibid., p. 115.
42 Ibid., pp. 116-17.
43 Ibid., pp. 118-20.
44 Lyotard, 'Sur une figure de discours', in *Des dispositifs*, pp. 132-3.
45 Lyotard, 'La peinture', p. 243.
46 Ibid., p. 259.
47 Ibid., p. 265.
48 Ibid., p. 266.
49 Ibid., p. 234.
50 *Condition postmoderne*, pp. 8-9.
51 Ibid., p. 31.
52 Ibid., pp. 37-46.
53 Ibid., pp. 50-1.
54 Ibid., pp. 54-9.
55 Ibid., pp. 24-9, 61.
56 Ibid., pp. 71-7.
57 Ibid., pp. 63, 66-8.
58 Ibid., p. 13.
59 Ibid., p. 76.
60 Ibid., p. 98.
61 Ibid., pp. 105-6.
62 Ibid., p. 8.
63 Ibid., pp. 102-4.
64 J.-F. Lyotard, Jean Loup Thebaud, *Au Juste, Conversations*, Paris: Christian Bourgois, 1979, p. 33.
65 Gilles Deleuze and Felix Guattari, *Anti-Oedipus*, New York: Viking, 1977. Deleuze and Guattari, some years after the 1972 appearance of the French edition of *L'Anti-Oedipe*, characterized their project in terms of a 'micro-politics of desire'; see Gilles Deleuze, Claire Parnet, *Dialogues*, Paris: Flammarion, 1977.
66 Gilles Deleuze, *Francis Bacon, Logique de la sensation*, Paris: Editions de la Différence, 1981, 2 vols: all citations are from vol. 1.
67 Ibid., p. 33.
68 This postmodern aesthetic of sensation is best comprehensible in the context of Deleuze's notion of the body. Deleuze speaks of a 'body without organs', a term that is a bit confusing because his concept of the body does indeed include organs. What Deleuze means is a body that is not *'organized'* in the sense that we conventionally accept our biological bodies to be organized. Deleuze willingly concedes the resemblance between such a non-organismic idea of the body and Merleau-Ponty's concept of 'the lived body'. He differs from Merleau-Ponty in his rejection, which is Artaud's rejection, of a unified body. This means that sensation is 'not a reflex of [the body's] living unity, but instead rather like a

272

transgression of this unity by the forces that overflow it and violently carry away the body to seize possession of it'. This means also a break with Merleau-Ponty's assumptions about intentionality. See Gilles Deleuze and Felix Guattari, *Mille Plateaux*, Paris: Editions de Minuit, 1980, pp. 185-204. For a comparison of Foucault and Merleau-Ponty, see Hubert L. Dreyfus and Paul Rabinow, *Michel Foucault, Beyond Structuralism and Hermeneutics*, Brighton: Harvester, 1982. Also see Patrick Vaudray, 'Ecrit a vue: Deleuze–Bacon', *Critique* 38, 1982, p. 963. If Deleuze's body is possessed with organs, they are not the organs of biology or of common sense. It is sensations that determine a body's organs, and only then provisionally, at the spaces of intersection between forces and waves. Bacon's painting is circumscribed by a logic of sensation in so far as he is *par excellence* the painter of the body without organs. To the extent that he paints forces and their effects of deformation on bodies, he paints sensation (*Francis Bacon*, p. 34). We can understand Bacon, Deleuze maintains, through a 'clinical aesthetic'. The body without organs that Bacon paints is the body of the hysteric. The hysteric feels the body to be, so to speak, *under* the organism; he or she senses transitory organs underneath the fixed organs. Hysteria has always been a matter of more than just functional disturbances of the body; it has also been a matter of such 'excesses of presence'. When Bacon paints Velasquez's *Innocent X* caged in plate glass and crying out in horror, he is painting the hysteric, giving substance to an *art hysterisé* (ibid., pp. 36-7).

69 Lyotard, *Discours, figure*.
70 Deleuze, *Bacon*, p. 39.
71 Ibid., p. 42, ch. 8.
72 Ibid., p. 36.
73 Ibid., pp. 79-80.
74 Ibid., p. 38.
75 Lyotard, 'La dent, la paume', in *Des dispositifs pulsionnels*, pp. 97-8.
76 See, e.g., Huyssen, 'The search for tradition'; Bürger, 'The significance of the avant-garde'; Giddens, 'Modernism and postmodernism'.
77 Jürgen Habermas, *Theorie des kommunikativen Handels, Band 1, Handlungsrationalität und gesellschaftliche Rationalisierung*, Frankfurt am Main: Suhrkamp, 1981, pp. 225-61.
78 J. Habermas, 'A reply to my critics', in J. B. Thompson and D. Held (eds), *Habermas, Critical Debates*, London: Macmillan, 1982, pp. 219-83.
79 Umberto Eco, *A Theory of Semiotics*, Bloomington: Indiana University Press, 1979, pp. 68-72.
80 Thomas McCarthy, *The Critical Theory of Jürgen Habermas*, Cambridge, Mass.: MIT Press, 1981, p. 279; Eco, *Theory of Semiotics*, pp. 48-53.

81 J. Habermas, 'What is universal pragmatics?', in id., *Communication and the Evolution of Society*, London: Heinemann, 1979, pp. 3–20; McCarthy, *Critical Theory*, pp. 272–91.
82 McCarthy, *Critical Theory*, pp. 291–333.
83 R. Dworkin, 'Is law a system of rules?', in id. (ed.), *The Philosophy of Law*, Oxford: Oxford University Press, 1977, pp. 38–65.
84 Max Weber, *Wirtschaft und Gesellschaft*, Tübingen: Mohr, 1980, p. 500. This is distinct from, and partly at odds with, the *Rechtssoziologie*'s discussion of the formal and material rationalization of the law; see *Wirtschaft und Gesellschaft*, pp. 468–82.
85 Agnes Heller, *The Theory of Need in Marx*, London: Allison & Busby, 1976; McCarthy, *Critical Theory*, pp. 314–15. For a discussion of the notion of rights in regard to the work of Marx and Weber, see Scott Lash, *The Militant Worker, Class and Radicalism in France and America*, London: Heinemann, 1984, pp. 10–46.
86 G. A. Cohen, 'Freedom, justice and capitalism', *New Left Review* 126, 1981, pp. 3–16.
87 Immanuel Kant, *The Metaphysical Elements of Justice*, Indianapolis: Bobbs-Merrill, 1965, pp. 51–67, 75–113.
88 Russell Keat, *The Politics of Social Theory*, Oxford: Blackwell, 1981, pp. 191–4; Steven Lukes, 'Of gods and demons: Habermas and practical reason', in *Habermas, Critical Debates*, pp. 138, 143.
89 R. Dworkin, *Taking Rights Seriously*, London: Duckworth, 1977, pp. 82–108.
90 McCarthy, *Critical Theory*, p. 83.
91 I am indebted on this point to discussions with Professor W. Mommsen and Professor E. Böckenförde.
92 Richard Rorty, 'Beyond Nietzsche and Marx', *London Review of Books* 3(3), 19 February to 4 March 1981, pp. 5–6; Foucault, 'On popular justice: a discussion with Maoists', in id., *Power/Knowledge*, Brighton: Harvester, 1980, pp. 1–36.
93 Foucault, 'Truth and power', in *Power/Knowledge*, pp. 121–5.
94 See, e.g., J. Finnis, *Natural Law and Natural Rights*, Oxford: Clarendon, 1980, pp. 199–204.
95 Foucault, 'Power and strategies', in *Power/Knowledge*, pp. 136–44.
96 See Peter Dews, 'Power and subjectivity in Foucault', *New Left Review* 144, 1984, pp. 72–3.
97 For a useful discussion of rights and powers, see G. A. Cohen, *Karl Marx's Theory of History, a Defence*, Oxford: Clarendon, 1978, pp. 35, 216.
98 J.-F. Lyotard, 'Réponse à la question: Qu'est-ce que le postmoderne?', *Critique* 419, 1982, pp. 357–67.
99 See J. B. Thompson, 'Rationality and social rationalization: an assessment of Habermas' theory of communicative action', *Sociology* 17(2), 1983, pp. 278–94, p. 291.
100 See also Keat, *Politics of Social Theory*, pp. 196–7.
101 Lyotard, 'Qu'est-ce que le postmoderne', p. 358; Habermas, 'Reply', p. 249.

102 Lukes, 'Of gods and demons', pp. 146-7.
103 Lyotard, 'Qu'est-ce que le postmoderne', p. 359.
104 Ibid., p. 367.
105 Habermas, 'Reply', pp. 235-6.
106 Lyotard, 'Qu'est-ce que le postmoderne', p. 365.
107 Ibid., pp. 363-4.
108 Habermas, 'Reply', p. 229.
109 Quine has maintained that it is not incoherent to speak of rights in the absence of philosophic foundations. See discussion in R. Rorty, *Philosophy and the Mirror of Nature*, Oxford: Blackwell, 1980.
110 See M. Bakhtin, *The Dialogic Imagination*, Austin: Texas University Press, 1981, in which the notion of dialogic underpins the relation and mutual influence between the Dionysian and the Apollonian. The relationship of ego and unconscious is understood in a similar manner by Jacques Lacan in, e.g., *Les complexes familiaux dans la formation de l'individu*, Paris: Navarin/Seuil, 1984.
111 Habermas, 'Reply', p. 232.
112 Lyotard, 'Qu'est-ce que le postmoderne', pp. 359-62.
113 This theme is central, for example, to E. P. Thompson, *The Making of the English Working Class*, Harmondsworth: Penguin, 1968 and H. G. Gutman, *Work, Culture and Society in Industrializing America*, New York: Vintage, 1977.
114 This seems to be the view, not only of the *désirants*, but is a central theme around, and against, which much of the 'cultural conservatism' literature is organized. See, e.g., Daniel Bell, *Cultural Contradictions*; C. Lasch, *The Culture of Narcissism*, New York: Warner Books, 1983.
115 Two of the foremost examples here of how anthropological notions of symbol have been used in conjunction with the formation of collective identity in historical studies are Eric Wolf, *Europe and the People without History*, Berkeley: University of California Press, 1982; Eric Hobsbawm and Terence Ranger (eds), *The Invention of Tradition*, Cambridge: Cambridge University Press, 1983. For a similar use of how symbol helps constitute resistance in the popular culture literature, see, of course, the literature from the Centre for Contemporary Cultural Studies: for example, Birmingham University, Centre for Contemporary Cultural Studies, *Culture, Media, Language*, London: Hutchinson, 1980; CCCS, *Unpopular Education*, London: Hutchinson, 1980. Lyotard, with his significant departures from a problematics of desire in the past half-decade, seems to be coming to a position that shows some understanding of this. Despite, however, his recent usage of language-games and the play of language to interpret resistance to power, he has signally neglected to apply these notions to popular culture and popular resistance.

CHAPTER FOUR: COMMUNICATIVE RATIONALITY AND DESIRE

1 Manfred Frank, 'The world as will and representation: Deleuze and Guattari's critique of capitalism as schizo-analysis and schizo-discourse', *Telos* 57, Autumn 1983, pp. 166–76.

2 Anthony Wilden, 'Lacan and the discourse of the other', in Jacques Lacan, *The Language of the Self*, New York, 1975; see also Vincent Descombes, *Modern French Philosophy*, Cambridge: Cambridge University Press, 1980, especially ch. 5.

3 This point is reinforced upon consideration of the notion of subjectivity developed in Deleuze and Guattari's critique of Lacanian structuralism. Frank misses this critique which is so central to *Anti-Oedipus*. This is evident from his understanding of desire in terms of 'wish'. Lacan's rendering of desire as wish and hence as *lack* is strongly challenged by Deleuze and Guattari (and by Lyotard) who want to reconceive desire as 'libido'. Deleuze and Guattari's overall claim is that desire becomes constituted as lack (as wish) *because* of the Oedipus. They see the Oedipus complex as creating a situation in which the investment of sexual energy in partial objects, or in significant other persons, becomes the *symbolic* investment of libido in the 'mummy-daddy-me'. This, then, is the cathexis of absent objects; it is desire as wish or lack. The Oedipus as phallic signifier, product of Lacan's mastery, structures the unconscious as the symbolic, like a language. These types of ideas, in which the symbolic investment of sexual energy imparts form to the unconscious, are prominent in Freud and Lacan, and it is precisely the accompanying negativity of desire that Deleuze and Guattari wish to oppose. They want to see the cathexis of significant others as *real* investment of libido, and not as symbolic investment in the mother, father, or phallus. Their view of subjectivity and desire is cast as a critique of Lacan's structuralism of the symbolic.

4 See the various articles in *Le Monde* during July 1983.

5 G. A. Cohen, 'Freedom, justice and capitalism', *New Left Review* (126), March–April 1981.

6 Jean-François Lyotard, *Des dispositifs pulsionnels*, Paris, 1980.

7 Jürgen Habermas, 'Psychic thermidor and the rebirth of rebellious subjectivity', *Berkeley Journal of Sociology* (25), 1980.

8 Jürgen Habermas, 'New social movements', *Telos* (49), Fall 1981.

9 Jürgen Habermas, 'Modernity versus postmodernity', *New German Critique* (22), Winter 1981, p. 13.

10 The 'back-to-nature' component of this culture is not, however, consonant with poststructuralist thinking: Frank is incorrect to see Deleuze and Guattari in Spenglerian terms, because capitalism, with its 'decodification' of desire, represents an advance over earlier social forms that were 'over-coded'.

CHAPTER FIVE: MODERNITY OR MODERNISM? WEBER AND CONTEMPORARY SOCIAL THEORY

I should like to thank Sam Whimster for his helpful criticisms.

1 Foucault's description of the Modern sciences in *The Order of Things* also parallels aesthetic modernism in its assumption of constant change. In contrast to the relative stability of Classical knowledge, the chronology of the Modern human sciences which Foucault narrates is one in which each succeeding discourse cuts away the foundations of its predecessors. Thus Foucault more or less idiosyncratically presents a vision in which a sociology of action is replaced by a sociology of structure; the latter is then undermined by semiotics, itself only to be subject to critique and undercutting by psychoanalysis (Foucault 1970, pp. 356-79).

2 Thus for Foucault the Modern asylum 'would guarantee bourgeois morality a universality of fact and permit it to be imposed as a law on all forms of insanity' (1967, p. 259). In the Modern no longer 'is unreason set outside of judgement, but it is recognized, classified and made innocent forever . . . in a perpetual judgement . . . an operation which takes place through the intermediary of the internalization by man of the juridical instance' (pp. 268-9). Modern discipline through the creation of a moral and rational consciousness in the madman, while underpinned by therapeutic legitimations, is carried out on the model of the family. Here in the asylum madness becomes childhood, where the madman is 'subject to the authority and prestige of the man of reason, who assumes for him the concrete figure of an adult'. This process becomes only worsened in psychoanalysis, in which 'the powers of the asylum become abolished and concentrated in the person of the doctor'. The moral and rational consciousness now becomes super-ego; the doctor more literally becomes parent through the transference (Foucault 1967, p. 278). Further, 'thrusts of the instincts' are no longer just against a rational-moral consciousness, but . . . 'against the solidity of the family institution itself and against its most archaic symbols' (1967, p. 254).

3 Equally, for Weber, consistent with Rickert's neo-Kantian views, Western knowledge has greater validity because it operates through rationalized modern Western values. This does not entail, however, a realist epistemology, in which knowledge somehow corresponds to reality (Bürger 1976, pp. 49-56; Schluchter 1981, p. 144; Habermas 1984, p. 186).

4 On the juxtaposition of different elements within English law, see the instructive analysis recently put forward by David Sugarman: *Weber, Modernity and 'The Peculiarities of the English': The Rationality and Irrationality of Law, State and Society in Modern Britain*, 1986.

5 The very focus on enactment and the destruction of meta-juristic principles in Weber's legal-positivist jurisprudence are also resonant with the destabilizing and continually disruptive ethos of modernism.

6 Full rationalization of the law comes about only in modern formal rationality, in which the process of intellectualization begins to question and then undercut the very rational foundations of natural law itself. Thus modern formally rational law is characterized by a separation of law and ethics, a focus on enactment in the absence of meta-juristic principles, the clear and consistent separation of general legal rules from particular legal events that can be subsumed by those rules, and an enhanced importance for the intentions of legal actors. Weber's formally rational legal positivism assumed a 'logically clear, internally consistent . . . gapless system of rules, under which . . . all conceivable fact situations must be capable of being logically subsumed' (Weber 1978, p. 656).

7 What Weber himself desired, it has been argued, was a system of civil law that favoured the interests of the bourgeoisie as a class, and a constitutional law based on a norm that promoted national interests (see Mommsen 1984, pp. 406, 450–1).

8 The rise of sociological jurisprudence which features an instrumentally rational (i.e. interest-linked) notion of law was roughly contemporaneous with the rise of aesthetic modernism (see Dicey 1962).

9 I am indebted for this point to Professor E. Böckenförde.

CHAPTER SIX: CRITICAL THEORY AND POSTMODERNIST CULTURE: THE ECLIPSE OF AURA

1 This chapter has benefited from the comments of Brian Longhurst, John Urry, and John Wilson.

2 There is surely a significant thematic of Benjaminian allegory in surrealist painting, in the poeticizing of petrified figures by De Chirico and Ernst, not to mention Dali, or even in De Chirico's later more kitsch method of juxtaposing scenes from antiquity with the banal present. De Chirico himself, upon arriving in New York, compared its architecture to his metaphysical paintings in a very Benjaminian vein as a 'homogeneity and harmonic monumentality formed by disparate and heterogeneous elements'. Such surrealist allegory mirrors the processes of displacement and condensation in dreams and in the primary process more generally. See Dell'Arco (1984).

CHAPTER SEVEN: DISCOURSE OR FIGURE? POSTMODERNISM AS A 'REGIME OF SIGNIFICATION'

1 I am grateful to Celia Lury, Nick Abercrombie, Norman Fairclough, Doug Kellner, John Urry, Brian Longhurst, and Mark Poster for comments on previous drafts of this chapter.

2 I am indebted on this point to a conversation with Richard Rorty, Berlin, July 1987.
3 The idea that, if I was going to understand the modern in terms of differentiation (*Ausdifferenzierung*) I should understand postmodernity in terms of de-differentiation (*Entdifferenzierung*) was driven home to me in a conversation with Professor Jürgen Kocka, Bielefeld, December 1986.

CHAPTER EIGHT: MODERNISM AND BOURGEOIS IDENTITY: PARIS/VIENNA/BERLIN

1 See, e.g., J. Habermas, 'Modernity verus postmodernity', *New German Critique* (22), 1981, pp. 3–14.
2 Daniel Bell, *The Cultural Contradictions of Capitalism*, London: Heinemann, 1976.
3 J. Habermas, *Theorie des kommunikativen Handels, Band I, Handlungsrationalität und gesellschaftliche Rationalisierung*, Frankfurt am Main: Suhrkamp, 1981, pp. 225–61.
4 Talcott Parsons, *The Structure of Social Action*, London: Free Press, 1968.
5 Sam Whimster and Scott Lash, Introduction to id. (eds), *Max Weber, Rationality and Modernity*, London: Allen & Unwin, 1987.
6 Richard Rorty, *Philosophy and the Mirror of Nature*, Oxford: Blackwell, 1980.
7 Whimster and Lash, op. cit.
8 Carl Schorske, *Fin-de-siècle Vienna, Politics and Culture*, New York: Vintage, 1981, pp. 344–64.
9 Ibid., p. 360.
10 Marshall Berman, *All that is Solid Melts into Air*, London: Verso, 1983; T. J. Clark, *The Painting of Modern Life*, London: Thames & Hudson, 1985.
11 Scott Lash and John Urry, *The End of Organized Capitalism*, Cambridge: Polity, 1987.
12 Clement Greenberg, 'Master Leger', in F. Frascina and C. Harrison (eds), *Modern Art and Modernism*, London: Harper & Row, 1983, pp. 109–14.
13 Clark, *Painting*, p. 21.
14 Ibid., p. 138.
15 Cited in ibid., p. 82.
16 Schorske, *Vienna*, p. xxvi.
17 Ibid., pp. 214–24.
18 Ibid., p. 254.
19 Ibid., pp. 266–9.
20 Karl Kraus, *Literatur und Lüge*, Frankfurt am Main: Suhrkamp, 1987; Aldo Rossi, *The Architecture of the City*, Cambridge, Mass.: MIT Press, 1982, pp. 169–70.

21 C. Schorske, *Fin-de-Siècle Vienna, Politics and Culture*, New York: Vintage, 1981.
22 F. Jameson, 'Reification and Utopia in Mass Culture', *Social Text* 1, 1979.
23 Clark, *Painting*, p. 88.
24 Ibid., pp. 79, 100.
25 Ibid., pp. 213–16.
26 See S. Lash, *The Militant Worker, Class and Radicalism in France and America*, London: Heinemann, 1984.
27 Lewis Mumford, *The City in History*, Harmondsworth: Penguin, 1966, pp. 480 ff.
28 Clark, *Painting*, pp. 15 ff.
29 Ibid., pp. 49–54.
30 Ibid., p. 78.
31 Ibid., p. 69.
32 Mumford, *City*, pp. 396–400.
33 Schorske, *Vienna*, pp. 85–9, 97.
34 Ibid., p. 69.
35 Berman, *All That Is Solid*, pp. 134 ff.
36 Schorske, *Vienna*, pp. 85–9, 97.
37 Scott Lash, 'Coercion as ideology: the German case', in N. Abercrombie, S. Hill, and B. Turner (eds), *Discourses in Dominance*, London: Allen and Unwin, 1990.
38 Gunter Richter, 'Zwischen Revolution und Reichsgründung (1848–1870)', in Wolfgang Ribbe (ed.), *Geschichte Berlins, Zweiter Band, Von der Marzrevolution bis zur Gegenwart*, München: Beck, 1987, pp. 660–1.
39 Michael Erbe, 'Berlin im Kaiserreich (1871–1918)', in Ribbe (ed.), Ibid., p. 697. On Berlin as a 'cleaned out' city, see D. Frisby, *Fragments of Modernity*, Cambridge: Polity, 1985.
40 Erbe, ibid., p. 694.
41 Richter, 'Revolution and Reichsgründung', pp. 663–4.
42 Ibid., pp. 665–7.
43 Erbe, 'Kaiserreich', pp. 778–81.
44 Peter Paret, *Die Berliner Secession, Moderne Kunst und ihre Feinde im Kaiserlichen Deutschland*, Frankfurt am Main: Ullstein, 1983, pp. 17–40.
45 Ibid., pp. 93 ff.
46 Ibid., pp. 137 ff.
47 Peter Gay, 'Begegnung mit der Modern, Deutsche Juden in der deutschen Kultur', in Werner Mosse (ed.), *Juden im- Wilhelminischen Deutschland 1890–1914*, Tübingen: Mohr, 1976, pp. 241–311, pp. 249–52.
48 Paret, *Secession*, pp. 47 ff.
49 Ibid., pp. 229–35.
50 Ibid., pp. 266–85.
51 Ibid., pp. 298–300.
52 Schorske, *Vienna*, pp. 90–1, 227.

53 Ibid., pp. 237–45.
54 Franz Hessel, *Ein Flaneur in Berlin* (Neuausgabe von *Spazieren in Berlin*), Berlin: Das Arsenal, 1984, p. 146.
55 Ivar Oxaal, 'The Jews of Pre-1914 Vienna', Department of Sociology, University of Hull, 1981, pp. 55–6.
56 Ibid., p. 66.
57 Gay, 'Begegnung', pp. 255–6.
58 Irmgard Wirth, 'Juden als Kunstler und Kunstförderer in Berlin', *Emuna* 9(1), 1974, pp. 31–8, p. 35.
59 Ibid., pp. 37–8; Julius Posener, 'Jüdische Architekten in Berlin', in *Leistung und Schicksal 300 Jahre Judische Gemeinde zu Berlin*, Berliner Museum: Ausstellungskatalog, 1971, pp. 61–4.
60 Gay, 'Begegnung', pp. 276–9; Kathe Brodnitz, 'Die Futuristische Geistesrichtung in Deutschland. 1914', in Paul Raabe (ed.), *Expressionismus, Der Kampf um eine literarische Bewegung*, 2nd edn, Zurich: Arche, 1987.
61 Georg Zivier, 'Die Verdienste der Juden um das Theater in Berlin', in *Leistung und Schicksal*, p. 56.
62 Ibid., pp. 59–60.
63 Heinrich Huesmann, 'Max Reinhardts Berliner Theaterbau', *Emuna* 9(1), 1974, pp. 46–54.
64 Hans Wallenberg, 'Jüdische Leistungen in der Berliner Presse', in *Leistung und Schicksal*, pp. 49–54.
65 Thomas B. Schumann, 'Geschichte des "Nueun Clubs" in Berlin als wichtigster Anreger des literarischen Expressionismus, Eine Dokumentation', *Emuna* 9(1), 1974, pp. 55–70.

CHAPTER NINE: MODERNIZATION AND POSTMODERNIZATION IN THE WORK OF PIERRE BOURDIEU

1 Pierre Bourdieu, *Outline of a Theory of Practice*, Cambridge: Cambridge University Press, 1977.
2 Bourdieu, 'Champ intellectuel et projet créateur', *Les temps modernes*, Nov. 1966, pp. 865–906.
3 Bourdieu, 'Legitimation and structured interests in Weber's sociology of religion', in S. Whimster and S. Lash (eds), *Max Weber, Rationality and Modernity*, London: Allen & Unwin, 1987, pp. 119–36.
4 'Le marché des biens symboliques', *Année sociologique* 22, 1971, pp. 49–126.
5 S. Whimster and S. Lash, Introduction to *Max Weber, Rationality and Modernity*, pp. 1–34.
6 'Marché des biens symboliques', pp. 54–5.
7 Ibid., p. 58.
8 Bourdieu, 'The production of belief: contribution to an economy of

symbolic goods', *Media, Culture & Society* 2(3), 1980, pp. 261-94, p. 264.

9 'Marché des biens symboliques', p. 114.

10 'Outline of a sociological theory of art perception', *International Journal of Social Science Research* 20, 1968, pp. 589-612, pp. 592-3.

11 Ibid., p. 598.

12 Ibid., pp. 600-1.

13 'The specificity of the scientific field and the social conditions of the progress of reason', *Social Science Information* 14, pp. 19-47, p. 21.

14 Ibid., pp. 32-3.

15 *Homo Academicus*, Cambridge: Polity, 1988, ch. 3.

16 'La force du droit, éléments pour une sociologie du champ juridique', *Actes de la recherche en sciences sociales* 198, pp. 3-19, p. 10.

17 'Scientific field', pp. 26 f.

18 Ibid., p. 25.

19 Ibid., pp. 32-4.

20 'Force du droit', p. 4.

21 Ibid., p. 6.

22 Ibid., pp. 8, 12.

23 Ibid., p. 13.

24 'La représentation politique, éléments pour une théorie du champ politique', *Actes de la recherche en sciences sociales* 198, pp. 3-24, p. 13.

25 Ibid., p. 6.

26 Ibid., p. 18.

27 Ibid., p. 8.

28 Ibid., pp. 5-6.

29 *Outline of a Theory of Practice*, pp. 6, 11-12.

30 Ibid., pp. 67-8.

31 Ibid., pp. 14-15.

32 *Outline*, p. 164.

33 Ibid., p. 168.

34 *Distinction*, London: Routledge, 1984; with L. Boltanski *et al.*, *Un Art moyen, Essai sur les usages sociaux de la photographie*, Paris: Minuit, 1965; *Outline*, pp. 168-9.

35 *Outline*, p. 164.

36 M. Featherstone, 'Lifestyle and consumer culture', paper delivered to conference on Everyday Life, Leisure and Culture, Catholic University of Tilbury, Holland, December 1985; S. Lash and J. Urry, *The End of Organized Capitalism*, Cambridge: Polity, 1987, pp. 292-6.

37 S. Zukin, *Loft Living*, London: Radius, 1988.

38 *Homo Academicus*, p. 130.

39 Ibid., pp. 170-1.

40 Ibid., pp. 167-8.

41 P. Bourdieu, 'Espace sociale et pouvoir symbolique', *Choses dites*, Paris: Minuit, 1987, p. 159.

42 S. Lash, 'Postmodernism as humanism: architecture and social

theory', unpublished paper, Annual Convention of American Sociological Association, San Francisco, August 1989.

43 S. Lash and J. Urry, 'The New Marxism of collective action: a critical analysis', *Sociology* 18, 1984, pp. 33–50.

44 P. Bourdieu, ' "Fieldwork in philosophy" ', in *Choses dites*, pp. 13–46, pp. 26–7.

45 *Outline*, p. 17.

46 Ibid., p. 184.

47 Ibid., pp. 5–8.

48 Ibid., pp. 66–7.

49 Ibid., p. 35.

50 Ibid., pp. 39–40.

51 *Homo Academicus*, preface to English edition.

52 ' "Fieldwork in philosophy" ', p. 45.

53 P. Bourdieu, 'Le champ intellectuel: un monde à part', *Choses dites*, pp. 167–77, p. 170.

BIBLIOGRAPHY

Abercrombie, N., Hill, S., and Turner, B. (eds) (1990) *Discourses in Dominance*, London: Allen & Unwin.

Alexander, J. C. (1987) 'The dialectic of individuation and domination: Weber's rationalization theory and beyond', in S. Whimster and S. Lash (eds) *Max Weber, Rationality and Modernity*, London: Allen & Unwin.

Althusser, L. (1972) *Lénine et la philosophie*, Paris: Maspero.

Anderson, P. (1984) 'Modernity and revolution', *New Left Review* (144): 96–113.

Barthes, R. (1975) *The Pleasure of the Text*, New York: Hill & Wang.

—— (1979) *A Lover's Discourse, Fragments*, London: Cape.

Bell, D. (1976) *Cultural Contradictions of Capitalism*, London: Heinemann.

Benjamin, W. (1975a) 'The storyteller', in *Illuminations*, London: Fontana.

—— (1975b) 'The work of art in the age of mechanical reproduction', in *Illuminations*, London: Fontana.

—— (1979a) 'A small history of photography', in *One Way Street and Other Writings*, London: New Left Books.

—— (1979b) 'Surrealism - the last snapshot of the European intelligentsia', in *One Way Street and Other Writings*, London: New Left Books.

Berman, M. (1983) *All that is Solid Melts into Air*, London: Verso.

Bouchard, D. (1977) Introduction to D. Bouchard (ed.) *Michel Foucault: Language, Counter-Memory, Practice*, Oxford: Blackwell.

Bourdieu, P. (1987) 'Legitimation and structured interests in Weber's sociology of religion', in S. Whimster and S. Lash (eds) *Max Weber, Rationality and Modernity*, London: Allen & Unwin.

Brubaker, R. (1984). *The Limits of Rationality: An Essay on the Social and Moral Thought of Max Weber*, London: Allen & Unwin.

Bürger, P. (1984) *Theory of the Avant-Garde*, Manchester: Manchester University Press.

—— (1984-5) 'Decline of the modern age', *Telos* (62): 117-30.

Callinicos, A. (1985) 'Poststructuralism, postmodernism, post-marxism?', *Theory, Culture & Society* 2(3): 85-102.

Coates, P. (1985) *The Story of the Lost Reflection*, London: Verso.

Cook, P. (1985) 'Authorship and cinema', in P. Cook (ed.) *The Cinema Book*, London: British Film Institute.

De Lauretis, T. (1984) *Alice Doesn't*, London: Macmillan.

Deleuze, G. (1969a) *Différence et répétition*, Paris: PUF.

—— (1969b) *Logique du sens*, Paris: Editions du Minuit.

—— (1978) 'Nomad thought', *Semiotexte* 3(1): 12-20; trans. of 'Pensée nomade', *Nietzsche aujourd'hui*, Paris: UGE 10/18, 1973.

—— (1981) *Francis Bacon, logique de la sensation*, Paris: Editions de la Différence.

—— (1983) *Nietzsche and Philosophy*, London: Athlone Press; trans. of *Nietzsche et la philosophie*, Paris: PUF, 1962.

Deleuze, G. and Foucault, M. (1967) Foreword to F. Nietzsche, *Oeuvres philosophiques complètes: Le gai savoir*, trans. Pierre Klossowski, Paris.

—— (1977) 'Intellectuals and power', in D. Bouchard (ed.) *Language, Counter-Memory, Practice*, Oxford: Blackwell; trans. of 1972 interview.

Deleuze, G. and Guattari, F. (1977) *Anti-Oedipus, Capitalism and Schizophrenia*, New York: Viking Press; trans. R. Hurley *et al.* from *L'Anti-Oedipe*, Paris, 1972.

—— (1980) *Mille plateaux, capitalisme et schizophrénie*, Paris: Editions du Minuit.

—— (1984) *Anti-Oedipus*, London: Athlone.

Dell'Arco, M. F. (1984) 'De Chirico in America: his metaphysics of fashion', *Artforum*, September: 78-83.

Derrida, J. (1978a) 'Cogito and the history of madness', in *Writing and Difference*, London: Routledge.

—— (1978b) 'The theatre of cruelty and the closure of representation', in *Writing and Difference*, London: Routledge.

Descombes, V. (1980) *Modern French Philosophy*, Cambridge: Cambridge University Press.

Dews, P. (1984) 'The letter and the line', *Diacritics* 14(3): 40-9.

Dicey, A. V. (1962) *Lectures on the Relation between Law and Public Opinion during the Nineteenth Century*, London: Macmillan.

Dreyfus, H. L. and Rabinow, P. (1982) *Michel Foucault, Beyond Structuralism and Hermeneutics*, Brighton: Harvester.

Dworkin, R. (1977) *Taking Rights Seriously*, London: Duckworth.

Eco, U. (1976) *A Theory of Semiotics*, Bloomington: University of Indiana.

Ellis, J. (1982) *Visible Fictions*, London: Routledge.

Esslin, M. (1976) *Artaud*, London: Fontana.

Foucault, M. (1964) 'La prose d'Actéon', *Nouvelle Revue Française* (135): 444-59.

—— (1965) *Madness and Civilization*, New York; trans. of abridged version of *Folie et déraison, Histoire de la folie à l'âge classique*, 1961.

—— (1967) 'Nietzsche, Freud, Marx', in Cahiers du Royaumont, *Nietzsche*, Paris: Editions du Minuit.
—— (1967a) *Madness and Civilization*, London: Tavistock.
—— (1970) *The Order of Things*, London: Tavistock; trans. of *Les mots et les choses*, Paris: Gallimard, 1966.
—— (1971) *L'ordre du discours*, Paris: Gallimard.
—— (1972) *The Archaeology of Knowledge*, London: Tavistock; trans. of *L'archéologie du savoir*, Paris: Gallimard, 1969.
—— (1973a) *Birth of the Clinic*, London: Tavistock; trans. of *Naissance de la clinique. Une archéologie du regard médical*, 1963.
—— (1973b) Présentation, in *Moi, Pierre Rivière*, Paris.
—— (1975) *Discipline and Punish: The Birth of the Prison*, London; Allen Lane.
—— (1977a) *Discipline and Punish*, Harmondsworth: Penguin; trans. of *Surveillir et punir, Naissance de la prison*, Paris: Gallimard, 1975.
—— (1977b) Preface to G. Deleuze and F. Guattari, *Anti-Oedipus*, New York.
—— (1977c) 'Nietzsche, genealogy and history', in D. Bouchard (ed.) *Language, Counter-Memory and Practice*, Oxford: Blackwell; trans. from an essay which appeared in *Hommage à Jean Hippolyte*, Paris, 1971.
—— (1977d) 'Theatrum philosophicum', in D. Bouchard (ed.) *Language, Counter-Memory, Practice*, Oxford: Blackwell; trans. of an essay which appeared in *Critique* (282), 1970.
—— (1980a) *The History of Sexuality*, vol. 1, New York: Vintage; trans. of *La volonté de savoir, Histoire de la sexualité*, Paris: Gallimard, 1976.
—— (1980b) 'Truth and power', interview published in C. Gordon (ed.) *Michel Foucault, Power/Knowledge*, Brighton: Harvester.
—— (1983) 'Structuralism and poststructuralism: an interview', *Telos* (55), Spring: 195–211.
Frayling, C. (1981) *Spaghetti Westerns*, London: Routledge.
Freud, S. (1958) *Psycho-analytic Notes on an Autobiographical Account of a Case of Paranoia (Dementia Paranoides)*, Standard edn, vol. 12, London: Hogarth Press.
Frisby, D. (1985) *Fragments of Modernity*, Cambridge, Mass.: MIT Press.
Frith, S. and Horne, H. (1987) *Art into Pop*, London: Methuen.
Giddens, A. (1981) 'Modernism and post-modernism', *New German Critique* 22: 15–18.
Greenberg, C. (1983) 'Master ledger', pp. 109–14 in F. Frascina and C. Harrison (eds) *Modern Art and Modernism*, London: Harper & Row.
Habermas, J. (1981) 'Modernity versus postmodernity', *New German Critique* (22): 3–14.
—— (1981a) *Theorie des Kommunikativen Handels*, Frankfurt am Main: Suhrkamp.
—— (1981b) 'Modernity vs. postmodernity', *New German Critique* (22): 3–14.
—— (1983) 'Neo-conservative culture criticism in the United States and

West Germany: an intellectual movement in two political cultures', *Telos* 56: 75–89.

—— (1984) *The Theory of Communicative Action, Vol. One,* London: Heinemann.

—— (1985) 'Questions and counter-questions', in R. Bernstein (ed.) *Habermas and Modernity,* Cambridge: Polity.

Heath, S. (1981) *Questions of Cinema,* London: Macmillan.

Hunt, A. (1978) *The Sociological Movement in Law,* London: Macmillan.

Huyssen, A. (1984) 'Mapping the postmodern', *New German Critique* (33).

Jameson, F. (1984) 'Postmodernism or the cultural logic of late capitalism', *New Left Review* (146): 53–92.

Jay, M. (1985) 'Habermas and modernism', in R. Bernstein (ed.) *Habermas and Modernity,* Cambridge: Polity.

Kàtz, B. (1982) *Herbert Marcuse and the Art of Liberation,* London: Verso.

Klein, M. (1932) *The Psycho-analysis of Children,* London: Hogarth Press.

Kocka, J. (1974) 'Organisierter kapitalismus oder staatsmonopolisticher kapitalismus', in H. Winkler (ed.) *Organisierter Kapitalismus,* Göttingen: Vandenhoeck & Ruprecht.

Krauss, R. (1981) 'The originality of the avant-garde: a post-modernist repetition', *October* 18: 47–66.

—— (1985a) Introduction to *The Originality of the Avant-Garde and Other Modernist Myths,* Cambridge, Mass.: MIT Press.

—— (1985b) 'The photographic conditions of surrealism', in *The Originality of the Avant-Garde and Other Modernist Myths,* Cambridge, Mass.: MIT Press.

Kronman, A. (1983) *Max Weber* (Jurists: Profiles in Legal Theory), London: Edward Arnold.

Kuspit, D. (1983) 'Dispensable friends, indispensable ideologies: André Breton's surrealism', *Artforum,* December: 56–63.

Lacan, J. (1958a) 'Les formations de l'inconscient', *Bulletin de Psychologie* 12(4): 250–6.

—— (1985b) 'D'une question préliminaire à tout traitement possible de la psychose', *La Psychoanalyse* IV: 1–50.

Lash, S. (1990) 'Coercion as ideology: the German case', in N. Abercrombie, S. Hill, and B. Turner (eds) *Discourses in Dominance,* London: Allen & Unwin.

Lash, S. and Urry, J. (1984) 'The new Marxism of collective action: a critical analysis', *Sociology* 18(1), February.

Lavers, A. (1982) *Roland Barthes, Structuralism and After,* London: Methuen.

Leigh, J. (1978) 'Free Nietzsche', *Semiotexte* 3(1): 1–6.

Leiss, W. (1983) 'The icons of the marketplace', *Theory, Culture & Society* 1(3): 10–21.

Lury, C. (1987) 'Women's writings groups: an aesthetics of experience', unpublished paper, Sociology Department, University of Lancaster.

Lyotard, J.-F. (1971) *Discours, figure,* Paris: Klincksieck.

—— (1973) *Dérive à partir de Marx et Freud,* Paris: UGE.

—— (1979) *La condition postmoderne,* Paris: Minuit.

—— (1980) 'La peinture comme dispositif libidinal', in *Des dispositifs pulsionnels,* Paris: Christian Bourgois.

—— (1984) *Driftworks,* New York: Semiotext(e).

MacCabe, C. (1980) *Godard,* London: BFI/Macmillan.

MacIntyre, A. (1981) *After Virtue,* London: Duckworth.

Major-Poetzl, P. (1983) *Michel Foucault's Archaeology of Western Culture,* Brighton: Harvester.

Marcuse, H. (1968) 'The affirmative character of culture', in *Negations,* Boston: Beacon.

Metz, C. (1982) *Psychoanalysis and Cinema,* London: Macmillan.

Mommsen, W. J. (1984) *Max Weber and German Politics,* Chicago: University of Chicago Press.

Mulvey, L. (1981) 'Visual pleasure and narrative cinema', pp. 206–15 in T. Bennett *et al.* (eds) *Popular Television and Film,* London: BFI/Macmillan.

Mulvey, L. and MacCabe, C. (1980) 'Images of woman, images of sexuality', in C. MacCabe, *Godard,* London: BFI/Macmillan.

Nietzsche, F. (1956a) *The Birth of Tragedy,* trans. F. Golffing, New York: Anchor; orig. German edn 1872.

—— (1956b) *The Geneaology of Morals,* trans. F. Golffing, New York: Anchor.

—— (1961) *Thus Spake Zarathustra,* trans. R. Hollingdale, Harmondsworth: Penguin; orig. German edn 1883–92.

—— (1966) *Werke in drei Banden,* Munich: Carl Hauser Verlag.

—— (1968) *The Will to Power,* New York: Vintage.

—— (1968) *Twilight of the Idols, The Antichrist,* trans. R. Hollingdale, Harmondsworth: Penguin; orig. German edn of *Twilight and Antichrist* 1888.

—— (1973) *Beyond Good and Evil,* trans. R. Hollingdale, Harmondsworth: Penguin; orig. German edn 1886.

—— (1974) *The Gay Science,* trans. W. Kaufmann, New York; orig. German edn 1882.

—— (1982) *Daybreak,* trans. R. Hollingdale, Cambridge: Cambridge University Press.

Racevskis, K. (1983) *Michel Foucault and the Subversion of the Intellect,* Ithaca: Cornell University Press.

Ratcliff, C. (1985) 'Andy Warhol: inflation artist', *Artforum,* March: 68–75.

Rawls, J. (1972) *A Theory of Justice,* Cambridge, MA: Harvard University Press.

Rickey, C. (1983) 'Unpopular culture (travels in Kienholzland)', *Artforum,* Summer: 47–53.

Rose, G. (1978) *The Melancholy Science, An Introduction to the Thought of Theodor W. Adorno,* London: Macmillan.

Rycroft, C. (1972) *A Critical Dictionary of Psychoanalysis*, Harmondsworth: Penguin.

Schluchter, W. (1981) *The Rise of Western Rationalism: Max Weber's Developmental History*, Berkeley: University of California Press.

Schulte-Sasse, J. (1984) 'Theory of modernism versus theory of the avant-garde', foreword to Bürger, *Theory of the Avant-Garde*, Manchester: Manchester University Press.

Seem, M. (1977) Introduction to Deleuze and Guattari, *Anti-Oedipus*, New York.

Sellin, E. (1968) *The Dramatic Concepts of Antonin Artaud*, Chicago: University of Chicago Press.

Sheridan, A. (1980) *Michel Foucault: The Will to Truth*, London: Tavistock.

Slater, P. (1977) *Origin and Significance of the Frankfurt School*, London: Routledge.

Sontag, S. (1967) *Against Interpretation*, London: Eyre & Spottiswoode.

—— (1979) Introduction to W. Benjamin, *One-Way Street*, London: Verso.

Stone, J. (1966) *Social Dimensions of Law and Jurisprudence*, London: Stevens.

Strauss, L. (1953) *The Political Philosophy of Hobbes: its Basis and Genesis*, trans. E. M. Sinclair, Chicago: University of Chicago Press.

Sugarman, D. (1986) 'Weber, modernity and "The Peculiarities of the English" ', Working Paper Series, Madison: University of Wisconsin Institute of the Legal Studies.

Taylor, C. (1975) *Hegel*, Oxford: Oxford University Press.

Turkle, S. (1979) *Psychoanalytic Politics*, London: Burnett.

Turner, S. P. and Factor, R. A. (1984) *Max Weber and the Dispute over Reason and Value*, London: Routledge & Kegan Paul.

—— (1987) 'Decisionism as politics: Weber as constitutional theorist', in S. Whimster and S. Lash (eds) *Max Weber, Rationality and Modernity*, London: Allen & Unwin.

Weber, M. (1946) 'Religious rejections of the world and their directions', in W. W. Garth and C. Wright Mills (eds) *From Max Weber*, New York: Oxford University Press.

—— (1978) *Economy and Society*, Vol. 2, Berkeley, CA: University of California Press.

Wellmer, A. (1984–5) 'Truth, semblance and reconciliation: Adorno's aesthetic redemption of modernity', *Telos* (62): 89–116.

Whimster, S. (1987) 'The secular ethic and the culture of modernism', in S. Whimster and S. Lash (eds) *Max Weber, Rationality and Modernity*, London: Allen & Unwin.

Whimster, S. and Lash, S. (1987) Introduction to S. Whimster and S. Lash (eds) *Max Weber, Rationality and Modernity*, London: Allen & Unwin.

Wilden, A. (1968) Commentary in J. Lacan, *Speech and Language in Psychoanalysis*, Baltimore: Johns Hopkins University Press.

Willett, J. (1978) *The New Sobriety, Art and Politics in the Weimar*

Period, 1917–1933, London: Thames & Hudson.

Williamson, J. (1988) 'Nightmare on Madison Avenue', *New Statesman*, 15 January: 28–9.

Wolin, R. (1984–5) 'Modernism vs postmodernism', *Telos* (62): 9–30.

Wollen, P. (1982) 'The two avant-gardes', in *Readings and Writings*, London: Verso.

Wollheim, R. (1980) *Art and its Objects*, Cambridge: Cambridge University Press, 2nd edn.

NAME
INDEX

Mies van der Rohe, Ludwig 234, 263
Milhaud, Darius 165
Moholy-Nagy, Laszlo 163
Mommsen, W. J. 144, 147
Mondrian, Piet 161, 210, 242
Monet, Claude 220
Moore, G. E. 95, 173
Morris, William 111
Moser, Kolo 213, 229
Mosse, Rudolf 231, 233
Mulvey, Laura 187, 189, 191, 192
Mumford, Lewis 33
Munch, Edvard 226, 227
Musil, Robert 207

Naville, Pierre 168, 181
Newman, Barnet 193
Nietzsche, Friedrich Wilhelm 55–77;
    Foucault on 86–8; influence 78, 81,
    115, 116, 233; Lukács on 17;
    Lyotard on 94; modern period 82;
    on foundationalisms 172, 205; on
    power 261; sociologistic
    epistemology 10, 118; surrealism
    167; will to power 207
Nolde, Emil 228

Offe, Claus 46
Olbricht, Jerzy 212

Pabst, G. W. 163
Parker, Charlie 18
Parsons, Talcott 4, 75, 95, 149, 204,
    255
Pawley, Martin 263
Pechstein, Max 228, 230, 234
Piaget, Jean 6, 135, 138
Picasso, Pablo 13, 108, 134, 157, 159,
    160
Piore, Michael 41
Piscator, Erwin 162–3, 233
Planck, Max 225
Plath, Sylvia 77, 80
Poincaré, Jules Henri 3
Pollock, Jackson 210, 242
Pound, Ezra 176
Proust, Marcel 108, 128, 207, 218

Rabinow, Paul 55, 59, 65
Racevskis, K. 55
Rahner, Karl 75
Ratcliff, Carter 166–7
Rathenau, Walter 227

Rauschenberg, Robert 162, 166
Rawls, John 105, 119, 143
Ray, Nicholas 192
Reinhardt, Max 161, 231–2
Renoir, Pierre Auguste 220
Rickey, Carrie 166
Riegl, Alois 231
Rilke, Rainer Maria 233
Rimbaud, Arthur 167
Rivière, Jacques 183
Rodin, Auguste 161
Rorty, Richard 80, 106, 117
Rose, Gillian 156
Rossi, Aldo 33
Rousseau, Jean-Jacques 8, 189
Roussel, Raymond 87
Rycroft, Charles 67

Sabel, Charles 41
Sade, Marquis de 56, 82, 84
Said, Edward 86
Sartre, Jean-Paul 75, 129
Saussure, Ferdinand de 8, 22, 81, 102,
    264
Schiller, Johann Christoph Friedrich
    von 232
Schleiermacher, Friedrich Daniel
    Ernst 95
Schlemmer, Oskar 163
Schluchter, W. 125, 142
Schmidt-Rottluff, Karl 228, 234
Schmitt, Carl 96, 119, 147–8, 262
Schmitter, Philippe 38
Schoenberg, Arnold 91–2, 134, 156,
    160, 179, 205–6, 234
Schorske, Carl 10, 202–3, 206, 211–13,
    219, 234
Schulte-Sasse, J. 164
Schwarzenegger, Arnold 188, 191
Scorsese, Martin 188
Scott-Brown, Denise 263
Searle, John 102, 105
Sellin, Eric 184
Seurat, Georges 209, 215
Sheridan, A. 55
Simmel, Georg 11, 148, 155, 170, 216
Simon, Jules and James 231
Sitte, Camillo 220
Slater, P. 154
Slevogt, Max 227, 228
Sombart, Werner 229
Sontag, Susan 167, 168, 175–80, 182,
    193

SUBJECT
INDEX